The Options Trading Primer

The Options Trading Primer

Using Rules-Based Option Trades to Earn a Steady Income

Russell A. Stultz

BEP BUSINESS EXPERT PRESS

The Options Trading Primer: Using Rules-Based Option Trades to Earn a Steady Income
Copyright © Business Expert Press, LLC, 2020.

First published in 2020 by
Business Expert Press, LLC
222 East 46th Street, New York, NY 10017
www.businessexpertpress.com

ISBN-13: 978-1-94999-166-6 (paperback)
ISBN-13: 978-1-94999-167-3 (e-book)

Business Expert Press Economics and Public Policy Collection

Collection ISSN: 2163-761X (print)
Collection ISSN: 2163-7682 (electronic)

Cover and interior design by S4Carlisle Publishing Services Private Ltd., Chennai, India
Cover image by autsawin uttisin/shutterstock.com

First edition: 2020

10 9 8 7 6 5 4 3 2 1

Printed in the United States of America.

Abstract

Buying and selling options is the fastest growing investment strategy when compared with other trading venues such as buying and selling stocks, futures, and foreign exchange currencies. Millions of investors who understand the financial leverage offered by options are earning impressive, steady incomes by buying and selling *call* and *put* options.

The successful investors learn how options work. They develop *watch lists* of trade candidates and study price charts to find prospective trades. And they apply *rules-based* option trading strategies that succeed much more often than they fail. Even when they lose, their rules limit their losses to acceptable levels.

This book was written by a successful option trader. He introduces options and how they work to those who are ready to learn how they work. The book emphasizes the application of time-tested option trading rules. These rules use price charts, market volatility, key option values, and risk graphs to achieve high-probability option trading outcomes. The book also details ten option trade examples that include trade setups, entries, trade management techniques, and supporting illustrations.

Keywords

finance; options; trading; investing; market; trade management; profit and loss; price charts; risk management; risk graph; option greeks; premium; income; technical analysis

Contents

Preface

Several years ago, I read an online article that offered a "secret trading method" that earned a weekly income each and every week without fail. The article stated that this secret method had been discovered by a Russian programmer who had been working for Wall Street financial institutions for twenty years. His name was Boris Kosilov, and the website included a narrated presentation conducted by Boris. He had been contacted by a wealth investment company to send fail-safe weekly trades each Monday morning. The trade setups, based on his secret method, would be revealed to company subscribers. As part of this trading program, Boris would send alerts to subscribers in case the market moved against a working trade that needed to be closed to prevent losses. Boris also recommended the use of a discount financial brokerage to minimize trading commissions.

The subscription cost was $750 per year. This fee would be refunded within 60 days if a subscriber was not completely satisfied. This seemed reasonable for a trading system that would take only a matter of minutes each week to use, especially if it produced a nice weekly income. And they would refund the subscription fees if the subscriber was not completely satisfied with the outcome. However, the termination refund required subscribers to provide their trading records.

I opened an account with a discount brokerage, paid my subscription, and anxiously awaited my first e-mail from Boris. It arrived on the following Monday morning about 30 minutes after the market opened. It included three option trades on three different financial indexes: the S&P 500, the Nasdaq 100, and the Russell 2000, symbols SPX, NDX, and RUT, respectively. The recommended trades sold 100-share call and put option contracts that were far above and below the current prices of these indexes. And all three indexes were unlikely to ever reach the recommended option prices, called *strike prices*. (You'll learn all about option strike prices in Chapter 2 of this book.) The option contract values, called *premium*, ranged from 10 cents to 30 cents per share, or $10 to $30 for each 100-share option contract.

I received step-by-step instructions from Boris that showed me how to trade one or more options on my new trading platform. This entailed opening what is called an *option chain*. One by one, I entered the index symbols at the top of the option chain, clicked on the Bid columns at the recommended option prices, entered a quantity of one, for one contract, and clicked Send. My order filled within a matter of seconds. I repeated this process for the other two indexes—all filled quickly, and as I sold each option, referred to as calls and puts, money was received by my brokerage account. By the end of the first week, all option contracts expired worthless, and I kept the premiums I had collected for all three of my trades. This was too easy! And, as promised, it worked.

When selling one call and one put on the same index, I received about $40 in premium. Trading two or even three contracts on each returned $80 or $120 per week. Not bad, I thought. I could sell multiple contracts on these financial indexes and recover my $750 subscription fee in 4 or 5 weeks.

The investment company held online webinars for its subscribers on Tuesday mornings. The presenter, named Phil, discussed the trading system and answered questions from the members of his audience of novice option traders. Phil's voice sounded exactly like Boris's voice, but without the accent. Phil told us we were trading what option traders call *strangles*— selling a put and a call option above and below the current price of the underlying financial index (the S&P 500, Nasdaq, and Russell 2000).

I began exploring the option chain and discovered several more columns with names like Mark, Delta, Theta, Vega, Gamma, Rho, Open Interest, Last, Extrinsic Value, Intrinsic Value, Probability ITM%, and several more. I already figured out that the Mark was the premium paid to sellers and received from buyers less the brokerage commissions paid when trades were filled. Boris told us in one of his webinars that Open Interest was the number of working trades at each option price (called *strike price*). I didn't have a clue about the meaning of the other column values. But I was making a modest weekly income, so I continued to enter Boris's trade setups for about four more weeks.

I decided to google a few of those column names and found a website called Investopedia. It contained a goldmine of information about options, and I also discovered that there was nothing secret about strangles.

Investopedia also described dozens of other option trading strategies. And since I had found a whole new, low-cost, and high-return trading system, I wanted to learn a lot more.

I also decided to look at how Boris's trade setups would work if I sold them a week earlier. Wow! Giving the trade several more days increased those 15- to 40-cent premiums to the $1.00 to $5.00 range. But it was also obvious that adding time added risk, because it gave the price of those index options more time to move against the trade by moving either higher or lower. Those moves, especially on the Nasdaq and S&P 500, could be as much as a few hundred dollars in a day. I learned from my research how a large, unwanted price move could potentially result in a massive loss—even "blow out" my entire trading account.

I decided it was time to learn more about options on my own. I contacted the financial investment company to cancel my subscription, sent them my weekly trading records, and they credited my bank card for the original $750.

I enrolled in a series of market trading courses from the Online Trading Academy and TD Ameritrade's educational unit that included studies on the use of price charts (technical analysis), options, advanced options, and futures. I also researched the foreign exchange market, called the Forex. I spent five figures in tuition—some of the best money I ever spent, because I was able to make it all back within a matter of weeks. Within just a few years, learning how options work and how to trade them earned several hundred thousand dollars.

Options math gives option traders an edge; they can quickly determine the mathematical probabilities of success for each and every trade they make. Of course, the market can be quite random. Although properly examined option trades usually succeed, the market can turn on a dime. The key is to succeed most of the time.

I also found that there's no substitute for education. Every trade involves a buyer and a seller. Educated traders consistently take money from uneducated traders on the other side of their trades. Thanks for playing!

Seasoned investors who buy and sell stocks and exchange-traded funds (ETFs), options, futures contracts, or foreign exchange currency pairs study the way each of these four trading venues work. Once they understand the dynamics of their chosen investment venue, they develop a set of time-tested *trading rules*. And they follow these rules to enhance the probability of achieving successful trade outcomes. And this works—*most of the time*.

These rules include the analysis of price charts. Every seasoned trader uses them. This *always* includes examining both historical and current price charts. A series of price charts reveal typical price levels, patterns, and common trends durations, where trends can be upward, downward, or sideways. (As one of my instructors used to say, "The trend is your friend—till the end of the trend.")

Today, after several years of high-volume trading, I know exactly what he meant and why. Price charts also reveal both historical and current trading volumes. They display the highs (resistance) and lows (support) price points for a selected security. Each security has a unique ticker symbol such as AAPL, AMZN, GOOG, and SPX for Apple, Amazon, and Google stock and the S&P 500 index, respectively. Traders also determine the average price range (or price movement) and current and historical trading volumes. The measurement of volatility and its use is discussed in detail in Chapters 4 and 5.

This information, and more, is used by all seasoned investors and market *traders*, where a trader is defined as a high-frequency investor. The typical trader enters and exits multiple trades each day or week. And they use much of the same information as long-term investors in order to develop a *trading bias*. Trader biases, sometimes called *market sentiment*, are usually "bullish" when expecting a price increase, or "rally," and "bearish" when expecting a price decrease, or "drop." They are "neutral" when the price is expected to remain within a narrow range. While this book provides readers with the essentials of options trading, it also examines the use of price charts to help develop a fact-based trading bias. This is important to every trading venue.

Disclaimer

Trading and investing always involve risk. Any money traded or invested can be lost. You alone are responsible for any trading or investing activity that you undertake. Neither the author nor the publisher is licensed, qualified, or authorized to provide trading or investing advice, nor will they assume any responsibilities for your actions. Hence, by reading this disclaimer and the information within this book, you understand that there is always risk involved in trading stocks, exchange-traded funds, financial indices, bonds, option contracts, futures, and the foreign exchange currency market. The author and publisher make no representations or warranties for your trading success, nor will they be held liable for your actions.

The Illustrations within This Book

Most of the illustrations within this book are screen captures from the popular thinkorswim trading application and used with permission, courtesy of TD Ameritrade.

Acknowledgments

My thanks to the many members of the North Texas Investment Strategies Club who regularly attend and critique option, futures, and forex strategies that are described in the club's monthly investment and trading strategy presentations. In particular, I wish to thank long-time, professional option traders and instructors Mo Fatemi and Mark Armstrong. And special thanks to my old friend and former classmate Dr. Donald Pearson, MD, who became an active, successful options trader after reading the first draft of my first options book.

CHAPTER 1

Introduction

A Brief History of Options

Options date all the way back to ancient Greece, when olive oil options were traded. And options were also extremely popular during the "tulip bulb mania" of seventeenth century Holland. During that time, tulip wholesalers sold call options to hedge their risks against a poor harvest, while tulip growers hedged their investments in bulbs, fertilizer, and fuel by buying put options.

The price of tulip bulbs continued to rise, leading to a secondary unregulated options market that was available to the general public. And the Dutch investors were ecstatic while the party lasted. But, as often happens, the Dutch economy suffered a major decline in 1638. Thousands of Dutchmen who had invested all of their financial holdings in tulip options suffered massive financial losses. They lost everything, because they were unable to meet their financial obligations. That event gave options trading a bad reputation.

The use of options to hedge (minimize) losses still prevails today among financial institutions and individual investors alike, because put options increase in value when the price of the underlying stock drops in value. So you have read about two kinds of options: call options and put options. Either type of option can be bought or sold, providing, as you will soon learn, tremendous flexibility to those who buy and sell options on a regular basis.

Today options are much safer, because they are heavily regulated. Government-enforced brokerage rules limit investment levels to prevent the possibility of colossal investor losses. And books like this one explain the dos and don'ts of option trading. Of course, uneducated option traders who do not understand how options work enter trades that experienced option traders avoid. This is also true of stock, futures, and foreign exchange traders. There simply isn't any investment vehicle that doesn't carry risk. Even the most experienced and successful market traders have bad days.

Unregulated options trading in the United States began in the 1890s. The volume of option trading in the United States had increased substantially by the 1920s. But the options market was essentially unregulated and attracted some unscrupulous individuals. Some compared options trading to the "wild west," because the lack of regulatory oversight and the practices of unscrupulous characters added substantial risk to options trading. Uneducated option traders made risky investments and lost fortunes. But some options traders became highly successful, while others fell victim to both their limited understanding of how options work and the unscrupulous practices by some *market makers* (those who match buy and sell orders) who were suspected of skimming the option transactions that passed through their shops.

In 1973, the Chicago Board of Options Exchange (CBOE) was formed to create and oversee the options market. Today there are nearly 7,000 optionable stocks, exchange-traded funds (ETFs), financial indexes, and futures. And options are highly regulated by the U.S. Securities and Exchange Commission (SEC). The Options Clearing Corporation (OCC) also contributes to the stability and security of options trading by closing, or *clearing*, all expired options contracts that are subject to assignment by fulfilling the obligations that exist between options buyers and sellers. In addition, there are strict SEC rules that govern options trading. These rules ensure that options traders have sufficient financial equity in their trading (or brokerage margin) accounts to settle their options trades. Furthermore, only those option traders who can demonstrate their options knowledge through either several years of trading experience or by satisfactorily passing an options test are permitted to trade high-risk option strategies such as selling "uncovered calls," which is described in some detail in this book.

The dynamics of buying and selling calls and puts are described throughout this book. Chapter 5 includes a series of essential option trading rules. Follow these rules and you will increase your probability of achieving more successful trade outcomes than losses. These trading rules are also included in substantial detail in each of the option trade examples included in the Hands-On Option Trading Activities contained in Chapter 6.

Once you finish that chapter, you should be ready to try out several rules-based option trades. Trade them in simulation first. Manage them in simulation. And check your win–loss ratio. If you're not batting at least 700, don't risk your money until you are. Some traders will even exceed 800. But what about the few losses? If you never lose a trade, you're probably not trading. The market is a random universe. You're never going to be right 100 percent of the time.

Why We Trade Options

There are many reasons for new and experienced investors alike to be drawn to options trading, several of which are provided here. These reasons are responsible for the increasing popularity and explosive growth in the volume of options trading.

Options Trading Growth

Option trading volume increased by 22 percent in the year 2018—faster than all other trading venues combined. Once you finish this book, you should understand why options trading has become so popular and why people just like you want to learn how to earn steady incomes by becoming competent, high-frequency options traders.

Financial Leverage

Done properly, options can provide much larger financial returns than buying the underlying equity, that is, the stock, ETF, financial index, etc. Investing a few hundred dollars trading options can control stock worth several thousand dollars. This is financial leverage! For example, the synthetic long stock strategy detailed in Chapter 6 cost $275 when filled and can return tens of thousands of dollars in profit. This is also true of other option strategies. Several examples of the financial leverage available in options trades are detailed within this book.

Option Strategies for Every Market Condition

There are options strategies that fit nearly every market condition. Traders can buy or sell a call or a put depending on the trader's bullish or bearish bias. And there are strategies that combine two or more puts or calls. Traders buy one or more calls when buying volume (or current volatility) is relatively low and the market is rallying, because call options increase in value as the price of the underlying increases. They buy puts when buying volume (or current volatility) is relatively low and when the market is dropping. Hence, puts increase in value when the market is dropping. When the market is dropping, option traders sell calls and sell puts when the market is rallying. This book explains both how this works and how it is done.

Traders combine bought and sold options in a variety of ways. Combining bought (long) and sold (short) options are frequently used to limit the maximum amount of money that can be lost. Strategies that combine long and short (bought and sold) options are referred to as "defined risk" trades.

These generalizations show the flexibility of put and call options. And we choose the options based on our bullish, neutral, or bearish bias that is based on what we see on our price charts. (More about price charts in Chapter 3.)

Statistically Predictable Trade Outcomes

Options include mathematically calculated values, including statistical probabilities for success. Success corresponds to knowing the odds of where the price of the underlying equity, such as a stock, is likely to be upon the expiration of the *option contract*. (Every option is a contractual agreement between an option buyer and seller. Every option contract *expires* at market close on a specific date. More about this later.) Option traders study probability statistics to determine the likely outcomes of their trades. This is how so many educated option traders earn steady incomes. It's also why option trading volumes are increasing throughout the world.

We use these statistical probabilities in our option trading. The options math makes this reasonably easy. Even with this information based on probabilities, it's always possible to encounter a loss. In fact, if you become an active options trader, you will lose from time to time, even when you follow all of your rules that are statistically valid.

Consider the blackjack card game for a moment. A score of 21 always wins. You are at the gaming table and are dealt 18. Your personal rules tell you 18 is likely to be a winning hand based on statistical probabilities. The dealer gives 3 to the player to your right. That's the card you need to hit 21! But no worries, the odds are still in your favor because you're holding 18. The dealer draws a 10 off the stack, turns his cards face up, and shows a 20—a Queen and a 10. He taps his cards and picks up your chips. You lost! But your process was right and statistically sound. The dealer got lucky. This happens even when your rules are valid.

So even though we follow statistically valid rules and succeed eight out of ten times, random events happen, just as in a blackjack hand. Stick to your rules! Using them will return many more wins than losses, in spite of the randomness of the market.

CHAPTER 2

Understanding Call and Put Options

Calls and Puts

Call and put options are financial derivatives of other financial instruments, including stocks, exchange-traded funds (ETFs), financial indexes (such as the Dow, NASDAQ 100, S&P 500, and Russell 2000), and even futures contracts. Options can be bought and sold in the same way that shares of stock are bought and sold. Each full-service financial brokerage as well as numerous discount brokerages provide investors with trading applications that support both stock and options trading. Many also support futures and foreign exchange transactions. Some of the full-service brokerages like TD Ameritrade, Charles Schwab, Fidelity, E*Trade, and Vanguard have applications that work on a variety of platforms, such as Windows PCs, Macs, iOS, and Android smartphones and even a variety of tablet computers. Even the discount brokerages like Interactive Brokers, tastytrade, and Robinhood Financial have multiple trading platforms.

Options are bought and sold for a fraction of the cost of the corresponding stock, ETF, index, or future, reducing the money put at risk. When an option is bought, it is referred to as a *long* option. When sold, it's called a *short* option. The long and short terminology is similar to long (bought) or short (sold) stock.

Each standard option contract represents 100 shares of the underlying stock. (We'll often use the word "stock" to represent the other types of securities.) There are also three mini-options that can be bought or sold on the three major financial indexes: the S&P 500; the Dow Jones Industrials of 30 stocks; the Nasdaq 100; symbols XSP, DJX, and MNX. The XSP and MNX is 1/10th of the cost of their indexes, while the DJX is 1/100th the price of the expensive Dow Jones index. Trading volumes for these mini-options is quite low, so they may not last.

The Options Clearing Corporation (OCC) is responsible for option contract expiration schedules. There are weekly, monthly, and quarterly expiration schedules. When this book was written, more than 500 weekly options existed in addition to nearly 6,900 monthlies and quarterlies. The monthly and quarterly options expire on the third Friday of their expiration months.

The primary function of the OCC is to clear all option contracts that expire in the money by one penny. (In, at, and out of the money options are defined later in this chapter.) Hence, the main work performed by the OCC is to exercise every option contract that expires in the money according to the standard terms of option contracts.

The Option Contract: Buyer and Seller Obligations

Each option is a contract between a buyer and a seller with a fixed expiration date that can range from hours to days, weeks, months, or even a few years. Like insurance policies, option *premiums* decrease as they approach expiration from a loss in time value. As you will see in Table 2.1, the value of the option "Greek" *Theta* shows the daily reductions in premium value. Note that Greek letters, like *Vega, Delta,* and *Rho,* are used in mathematical equations that compute the premium values of options. For example, a Theta's value of .05 for a $50 call option tells traders that the $50 call option is losing 5 cents per share per day. Therefore, the day's loss for a 100-share option contract is $5.00. All savvy option traders look at Theta to determine the daily losses in option premium values.

Just like insurance policies that suffer daily losses in value, option values also suffer in the same way. For example, a 365-day insurance policy loses 1/365th of its value each day, while a 365-day option contract responds to several other factors besides just time decay. Price changes in the underlying stock and buying and selling volume, or volatility (referred to as *Vega*), also influence premium values. Several long-standing mathematical formulas constantly calculate and update option premium values. If you watch the option chain of a heavily traded stock, such as Amazon, ticker symbol AMZN, you can watch the Greek and premium values fluctuate up and down throughout the trading day.

Like buying stocks, call options are typically bought on stocks trending upward and later sold for more than the original purchase price for a profit. But the stock's price rally must outpace the reduction in premium value caused by the passage of time. Therefore, option buyers choose long-term option expiration dates when the daily value of Theta (the time value) is still relatively small. Similarly, put options are bought on stocks trending downward so they can be sold for more than the original purchase price. So both long calls and long puts are bought and then sold for less premium than was originally paid when purchased. The decision to buy a call or a put relies on the trader's bullish or bearish bias.

When calls and puts are bought, there must be sellers on the opposite side of these trades who expect to keep the premiums they receive from the buyers on the other side of their trades. Their goal is to keep the credit in premium they receive when their trades are filled. For example, an option trader can sell either a put or call option for perhaps a dollar per share on a $50 per share stock. If the underlying stock price stays within a narrow price range, the passage of time reduces premium value. Even better, if these short options move farther out of the money, the option premiums decline in value even faster. Buying puts is similar to shorting a stock, which is sold at a high price and then closed at a lower price. In shorting a stock jargon, this is called *sell to cover*. Both transactions permit traders to sell high and buy low and keep the difference as profit.

The passage of time is the option seller's ally and the option buyer's enemy. When the trader's bearish or bullish bias is valid, the reward can be substantial. The trader can sell an option for a dollar and buy to close the option contract within a week or two for perhaps 10 cents—a profit of 90 cents per share, or $90 less brokerage commissions. Of course, they can also permit the option contract to expire worthless for 100 percent profit and to avoid trading commissions, but only if these sold options remain out of the money through expiration. Out of the money, at the money, and in the money are labeled in Figure 2.1 and described in some detail in Table 2.1. Sounds easy, right? Buy high, sell low or sell high, buy back low. But before deciding to buy or sell options there are several issues that every option trader considers to enhance his or her probability of achieving a profitable outcome. This includes the use of time-tested option trading rules, described in Chapter 5.

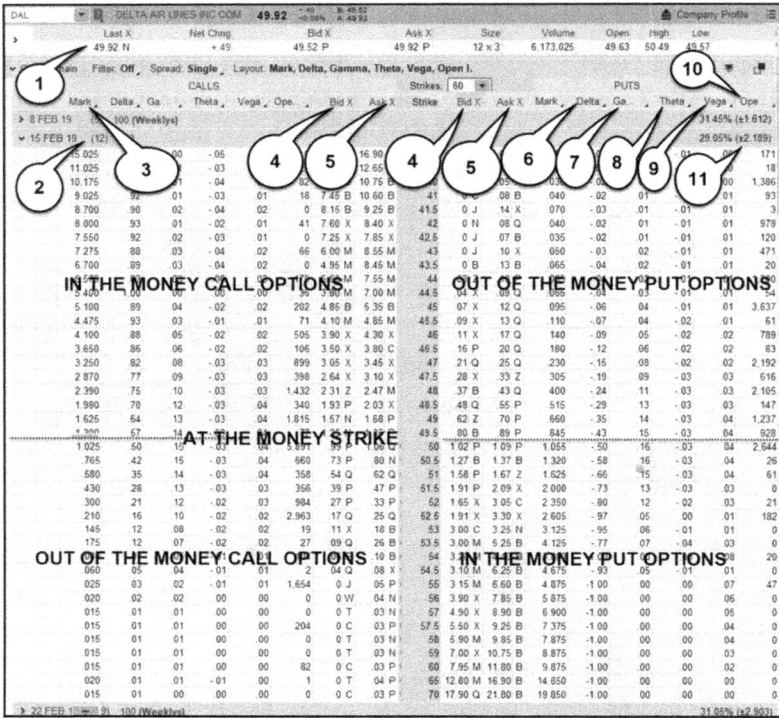

Figure 2.1 A typical option chain

©2019 TD Ameritrade IP Company, Inc. For illustrative purposes only.

Table 2.1 The contents of a typical option chain

Legend	Description
Ticker	The stock symbol (DAL for Delta Airlines), and current price shown in the top row.
1	Stock price, net price change, and the stock's Bid and Ask prices; also shown is the Bid-to-Ask stock trading ratio (12 x 3 indicates a 1200 to 300 ratio), trading volume (6,173,025 shares), and the day's opening, high, and low prices.
2	Option contract expiration date and the number of days remaining until the selected option contracts expire at the close of the trading day on Feb 15, 2019.
3	**Mark:** The Mark (or "market") columns include the option buy and sell values, referred to as *premium*, for each strike price. The Mark is a value that is near the midpoint of the Bid and Ask prices.
4	**Bid:** When an option is sold, traders use a mouse to hover over and click the Bid value on the desired strike price row. Clicking Bid in the call section sells calls; clicking Bid in the put section sells puts.

Legend	Description
5	**Ask:** When an option is bought, traders use a mouse to hover over and click the Ask value on the desired strike price row. Clicking Ask in the call section buys calls; clicking Ask in the put section buys puts. **NOTE** When simultaneously buying and/or selling multiple options, press and hold the Ctrl key, and click the desired Bid and/or Call values. This permits the entry of two to four different options at different strikes. For example, a trader may buy an at the money (ATM) $50 call and sell an out of the money (OTM) call at the $58 strike. This is a "vertical spread," commonly called a bull call vertical spread.
6	**Delta:** Delta is a constant that is used within the mathematical formula that computes option values. This is a constant process, as each option value is continuously updated on the basis of trading volume (volatility) and changes in the underlying stock price. Delta computes the change in option prices (the *premium*) for each one-dollar change in price of the underlying. Delta is commonly used by option traders to estimate each strike price's probability of becoming in the money upon contract expiration. For example, if strike price displays a Delta value of 0.25, the trader considers the corresponding strike to have a 25% probability of becoming in the money at expiration. Experienced traders use Delta values to calculate a trade's probability of expiring in the money. Notice that call Delta values are positive and Put Delta values are negative. In contrast, sold calls have negative Delta values, and sold puts have positive Delta values (more about this later).
7	**Gamma:** Another constant used to compute Delta values. Gamma values are highest at the money. This causes incremental Delta values to be highest at strikes that are closest to the money. Premium value increments between strike prices decline in value as strike prices move farther OTM or deeper ITM.
8	**Theta:** Theta is a Greek letter that represents *time* value. Option premium declines in value as the option contract nears expiration. Hence, when only a few days remain, Theta values begin to reduce premium almost exponentially. A Theta value of -.50 tells traders that the premium value will drop by 50 cents per share. There are 100 shares in each standard option. This tells traders that the day's underlying premium for the option will lose $50.00 (from .50 x 100). The value of Theta will become even higher on the following day.
9	**Vega:** Vega is the volatility constant, although Vega is not an actual Greek letter. Volatility (buying and selling volumes) has the greatest effect on premium values. If a strike's Vega value is .05, a 5% increase in the underlying's volatility changes the corresponding strike's premium value by 5%. If the strike's Mark (premium) value is currently $1.00, the 5% increase in volatility and a .05 Vega increases the premium value by $0.25, resulting in the Mark value moving from $1.00 to $1.25.

(continued)

Table 2.1 The contents of a typical option chain (Continued)

Legend	Description
10	**Open Interest:** Open Interest represents the number of option contracts that are currently working at each strike price. This is referred to as *liquidity*. Option traders avoid those strikes in which Open Interest values are small. They also avoid entire option chains where trading volume is small. Most seasoned option traders look for a few hundred working contracts at each strike price of interest. High Open Interest values indicate strong interest, which leads to faster order execution. Trading strikes with small Open Interest values may never fill. Even worse, it may be difficult to exit a losing trade when Open Interest is small.
11	This is the option's calculated *implied volatility* (IV%) percentage (the current volatility as a percentage of *historical volatility*). Historical volatility represents the underlying's average trading volume over the past 12-month period. The ±2.189 to the right of the IV% is the calculated price movement of the underlying for the time remaining until the option's contract expiration date.
ATM Strike	The at the money strike price is the strike that is closest to the current price of the underlying, in this case the Delta Airlines stock as shown at the top of Figure 2.1.
ITM Calls	In the money calls have strike prices that are less than the at the money strike. ITM call premiums increase in value as they move deeper (downward) ITM.
OTM Calls	Out of the money calls have strike prices that are higher than the at the money strike. OTM call premiums decrease in value as they move farther (upward) OTM.
OTM Puts	Out of the money puts have strike prices that are less than the at the money strike. OTM call premiums decrease in value as they move farther (downward) OTM.
ITM Puts	In the money puts have strike prices that are higher than the at the money strike. ITM put premiums increase in value as they move deeper (upward) ITM.
Next Option Chain	The expiration date and number of days remaining till expiration of the next series of option contracts and its option chain appears in the bottom frame. Simply scroll down to view the data in the option chain below (the next expiration date).

If a trader permits his or her option strike price to remain in force without closing it prior to expiration, which occurs at the end of the trading day when the option expires, the OCC will *auto-exercise* all in the money option contracts. This involves transferring (or *assigning*) stock from put buyer accounts to put seller accounts. The put seller is required to pay for the stock at the option's strike price. The OCC transfers stock from in the money call seller accounts to the call buyer accounts. The OCC transfers cash from call option buyers' accounts to the call option sellers' accounts at the call option's strike price. (See strikes on Figure 2.1.) Finally, the underlying stock is transferred from each call seller's account to the call buyer's account.

As you can guess, most option traders avoid being in the money, which makes them vulnerable to being exercised. There are exceptions. The trader of a short call may permit the stock price to expire a few pennies in the money, especially when the option premium that was originally received is a few dollars more than the few pennies that the seller must pay when assigned.

Options are bought and sold using what are called *Option Chains*. An annotated option chain is shown in Figure 2.1. It is a financial table that option traders use to examine option prices, risks, trading volumes, and the daily reduction in premium values as the option contract approaches expiration. Also included is the effect of buying and selling volumes, called *implied volatility* or *current volatility*, which reflects current buying and selling volumes and how option premium values respond to volatility. An increase in trading volume boosts option premiums, while a decrease in trading volume reduces premium values.

There is much more information on how option traders use option chains. And option chains are customizable to fit a trader's personal preferences. For example, you can add more columns to your option chains until it becomes so cluttered it's difficult to view everything on a computer screen. A trader may add a Last column so that he or she can see the amount paid for the most recent option trade. But the columns shown in the example in Figure 2.1 are usually quite sufficient.

Notice how the illustration of a typical option chain displays call options on the left-hand side and put options on the right-hand side of the table. Option *strike prices* are included in a central vertical column. Also see how these strike prices range from low prices at the top of the table to high prices at the bottom. The central column of strike prices (the option prices traders select when trading) is labeled Strike at the top of the column. Strike price increments (or *strike widths*) vary according to the price of the underlying. Strike widths may range from 5 cents to $100 per strike based on the price of the underlying stock, ETF, or financial index.

Most option chains permit users to specify the number of strike price rows displayed from top to bottom. The number is either increased or reduced according to where the trader plans to trade, that is, at a strike price that is close to the current price of the underlying equity, called the *at the money* strike price, or perhaps a far out of the money strike price. The number of columns on an option chain can also be altered. Figure 2.1 shows a total of eight columns on the call side, a central Strike column, and eight columns on the put side. A few other columns that traders often check are *Extrinsic value* and *Probability ITM%*, and we shall discuss them in more detail later.

The Bid (sell) and Ask (buy) price values that correspond to each strike price are also displayed in vertical columns. These are permanent. Notice the other columns that exist in the option chain in Figure 2.1. These are used by option traders to calculate the risk and reward when they buy and sell call and/or put options. Each of the columns is described in Table 2.1. And more information about calls and puts is also provided in this chapter.

NOTE: Check the option chain in Figure 2.1 to see how price increases and decreases (*rallies* and *drops*) move option strikes either deeper in the money (ITM) or farther OTM. Also notice how the Bid, Ask, and Mark values of both calls and puts change from one strike to the next. These values increase as calls and puts move deeper ITM and decrease as calls and puts move farther OTM. If our trading bias is correct, we take advantage of knowing how call and put premiums at different strike prices respond to price changes in the underlying.

Buying Calls

When bullish on an underlying equity, that is, a stock, ETF, financial index, or a futures contract, option traders consider buying call options because their premium values increase as the price of the underlying equity increases. The upward price increase of the underlying equity causes the premium (or the Mark) of the option's selected strike price to increase in value as its strike moves deeper ITM (farther below the ATM strike). For example, we buy a $50 call option on a stock selling for $50 per share.

The price of the stock rallies to $55. Our $50 long call is now $5 ITM. Once the trader is satisfied with the price rally in the underlying stock and the increase in the option's Mark value, the call option can be sold for profit in much the same way that a stock is sold for a profit by buying low and selling high.

NOTE: The terms long and short, introduced earlier, are used to describe buying and selling throughout this book. A long call is a bought call; a short call is a sold call. The terms long and short calls and puts are common jargon used by most option traders.

Buying Puts

When bearish on an underlying equity, option traders consider buying put options. Put premiums increase in value as the underlying equity drops in value. As the long put's strike price moves deeper in the money (farther above the ATM price of the underlying stock), the long put's option premium rises in value. Once satisfied with the amount of profit, the trader sells the long put options for profit.

Selling Calls

When bearish on the underlying, option trader's sell call options at a strike price that is safely OTM. The goal is to collect a credit in premium when the call is sold. Then the trader can buy to close the short call options for substantially less than the initial credit received. If the short call remains safely OTM, the short call options can be kept until they expire out of the money and worthless. This returns a 100% profit.

When selling options, traders choose near-term expiration dates to limit the amount of time the price of the underlying equity—the stock, ETF, or financial index—has to reverse direction and rally sufficiently to breach the strike price of a short call option. This causes the call to become in the money and vulnerable. In the money calls permit call buyers on the other side of a trade to *exercise* the call options. When this happens, call sellers can suffer a substantial loss because they are required to deliver the "called away" stock to the call buyer who pays for the stock at the agreed upon strike price. The buyer profits and the seller loses by the amount the stock price has risen above the sold call's strike price.

This is why option sellers carefully select strike prices that are sufficiently far enough OTM to prevent a price move in the underlying from breaching the selected strike price. Therefore, option sellers *never* want their options, whether calls or puts, to become vulnerable to a substantial loss by becoming in the money. Fortunately, both call and put option sellers have some protective moves they can take to either prevent the amount of money put at risk or reduce a large loss.

Only traders who understand the vulnerability of a short call option position are permitted by their brokerage to sell calls without either owning the underlying stock at 100 shares per option contract or buying an equal number of call options for "protection," that is, to limit their risk. Ownership of the stock or buying an equal number of calls at a nearby strike "covers" the sold call options.

Some popular option strategies are summarized later in this chapter in the paragraphs entitled buying and selling vertical call spreads and buying and selling vertical put spreads. The popular covered call strategy is also described. As you will see, the covered call strategy involves selling an OTM call option for each 100 shares of the underlying stock owned by the trader. Sold options can also be "covered" (or protected) by buying an equal number of call contracts at a strike price below or above the short calls. Buying options on the same underlying limits the risk. This is called "covering" the short call with a long call. These are called vertical spreads and are extremely popular and heavily used in dozens of option trading strategies. Some option strategies that include vertical spreads are briefly described later in this chapter, while the hands-on trading activities in Chapter 6 provide additional examples of covered calls and *vertical spreads* in substantially more detail.

Selling Puts

When the trader's bias is bullish or neutral, they often sell OTM short-term "cash-covered" puts to collect premium.

Selling OTM puts is an extremely popular strategy that is used daily by millions of option traders. Covering puts with "cash" means a trader has sufficient equity in his or her margin account to pay (or "cover") the cost of the short put options if they become in the money. An in the money put option is when the price of the underlying drops to or below the strike price of the sold put options. For example, a $50 put option is in the money by $10 if the underlying stock drops to $40. If the put option becomes in the money, the underlying stock can be *assigned* (delivered) to the put option's seller by the buyer. The seller pays the buyer $50 per share for stock that is now worth $40. The buyer earns $10 per share, while the seller loses $10 per share. Of course, both must pay brokerage and exchange fees. When the put is in the money by several dollars, the stock price can be worth much less than the strike price.

However, as with the sold calls described in the preceding Selling Calls paragraph, put option sellers can also take protective measures to either prevent or reduce the amount of money put at risk. The buyer profits by the difference between the stock price and the put's strike price. An example of how this works is explained in this chapter and again in chapter 4.

Buying and Selling Call Spreads

A *call spread* refers to an option strategy that includes a long call and a short call at different strikes. These are also referred to as vertical call spreads, because one trade is directly above the other. The bull call spread buys a call and sells a call at one or more strikes above. The short call is usually at a strike that is safely OTM. Because the long call is either at or quite close to the ATM strike, the premium paid for the long call is more than the premium received for the OTM short call. Having to pay to open a bull call makes it a *debit spread*, which means the trader must pay the difference in premium values to enter this trade. The bear call is a *credit spread* because it includes a short call below a farther OTM long call. The short call returns more premium than is paid for the long call. This is an example of a *credit spread.*

When an option buyer exercises a seller's ITM short call(s), the seller is required to deliver 100 shares of stock to the buyer for each 100-share option contract. The seller must pay for the stock at the agreed upon strike price. If the strike of the short call is $10.00 in the money, the option contract permits the buyer to buy the stock shares for $10 below the current market price. The buyer can either keep the stock or sell it for a profit of $10 per share less transaction fees, which include commissions and Chicago Board of Exchange (CBOE) exchange fees (typically $1.00 per option contract). High-frequency option traders can often negotiate lower commission and exchange fee rates.

Buying and Selling Put and Call Spreads

There are dozens of option strategies that buy and sell both put and call options. There are 78 strategies described in *The Option Strategy Desk Reference* from Business Expert Press.

Risk profiles, also called "risk graphs," are described in Chapter 5. Option traders refer to these graphs to determine how the value of their option trades respond to changes in the underlying stock prices. All option traders are encouraged to examine a risk graph before they send their trade to the market.

Every seasoned option trader buys and sells *vertical spreads*. When the trader is bullish and expects the price of the underlying stock or ETF to rally for the next few weeks, the trader is likely to consider trading what is called a bull put spread. This sells one or more OTM put options and buys the same number of put options one or more strikes below the strike of the short puts. Because the strike of the short put options are closer to the money than the strike of the long puts, the bull put spread returns a credit. It is also considered a "limited risk" strategy because the long put serves as "insurance" in case the trader's bullish bias is wrong and the price of the underlying drops below the long put's strike. If both the short and long strikes expire in the money, the maximum loss is the difference between the strike prices. If the short put is $5.00 above the long put, the trader's loss is limited to $5.00 per share or $500 per contract.

Similarly, the bull call spread is a bullish strategy, but unlike the bull put spread, it requires a debit when filled. It typically includes a long call option at or slightly above the ATM strike price and a short call option several strikes farther OTM. The placement of the short call should be sufficient to return a profit if the strike price of the long call rallies to the strike price of the short call. But if the price of the underlying drops unexpectedly, the long call should be closed. If the trader's brokerage permits the use of uncovered short calls, the short calls may be retained to offset the loss. Otherwise, both *legs* of this trade are simultaneously closed.

The bear put spread sells a long put above a short put. This is a bearish strategy because the trader believes the price of the underlying stock is going to drop. If the stock price drops in accordance with the trader's bearish bias and the strikes of the long and short puts move in the money, the trader may close both the long and short put options for a profit.

The short put at the lower strike of this trade can be closed with a buy-to-close order. The long put can either be held for a bit longer or closed to collect the long put's increase in premium value.

Option traders who regularly sell puts and calls are often referred to as "premium collectors." For example, many sell short-term OTM puts and collect premium from the put buyers on the other side of their trades. If the short put remains OTM until the put option contracts expire, the put seller keeps the premium as profit. We refer to this as letting the short options expire worthless.

Credit Spreads (Strategies That Earn a Premium Credit When Traded)

Short Strangles (neutral bias): Sell a short-term OTM call and an OTM put, same expiration. (This is the *secret trade* referred to in the preface. This trade has never been a secret and is used extensively by many option traders.) Experienced traders choose Delta values of the strikes used with short strangles that are typically .25 or less. Their goal is for the strikes they choose to remain safely OTM throughout the duration of the trade. A strike having a .25 Delta value is thought to have a 25% probability of becoming ITM or a 75% probability of remaining OTM through option expiration. Therefore, Delta values are used to calculate *probability*. A 25 percent probability of success is substantially better odds than those of a typical Las Vegas casino. They thrive on 54.5 percent odds, which leaves gamblers with 45.5 percent winning odds. Therefore, a trader that has a 75 percent probability of winning "succeeds" far more often than casinos.

Covered Call (neutral to bullish bias): Sell an OTM short-term call contract for each 100 shares of stock held within the trader's brokerage account. When sufficient premium value exists, traders can sell call options at a strike having a Delta value between $-.30$ and $-.25$. Recall from Table 2.1 that sold calls have negative Delta values, while sold (or short) puts have positive Delta values. The relevance of positive and negative Delta values is described in Chapter 4.

The covered call collects option premium from the sale of the call options. If the underlying stock rallies to or above the short call contract's strike price and is exercised by the call option's buyer, the brokerage is required to deliver the seller's stock to the buyer, who must pay for the stock at the short call option's strike price. This returns a profit to the call's seller from the sale of the stock. If the price of the stock remains below the strike of the short call through expiration, the call seller keeps the original premium received as profit and can continue to sell covered calls for more incremental income.

Some bullish traders who are confident in a price rally also sell cash-covered puts with their covered calls to increase their premium income. But if they are wrong, they risk losing money owing to a drop in the price of the stock and the potential of having their short put options assigned by the buyers of their short puts. This is a "double whammy" and adds a substantial amount of risk to the very popular covered call strategy that is most often used with stocks that are trending upward.

Iron Condor (neutral bias): Trade a short-term OTM bull put spread at or below Delta .25 and a short-term bear call spread at or above Delta .20. This is a credit collection strategy on options that typically expire within a matter of days to a few weeks.

Trade Setup

Sell a Put at Delta .25
Buy a Put 2 strikes below
Sell a Call at Delta .20
Buy a call 2 strikes above

Balanced Long Call Butterfly (bullish bias): The butterfly option strategy is quite popular among option traders. In fact, some specialize in the use of butterfly spreads. Butterfly spreads are constructed using either call or put options. The typical long butterfly includes a central strike, called the *body*, and a strike above and below, called the *wings*. To qualify as a butterfly, the total number of long call options used in the wings must be equal to the number of short call options used in the body.

For example, a long call butterfly could include two long call options in each wing and four short call options in the central body, that is, +2 calls, -4 calls, +2 calls. It is a long call butterfly because the wings are bought (long). This is a balanced butterfly because the wings include an identical number of options.

Notice the incremental strike width in Figure 2.2 is only 50 cents. All options have identical expirations and typically expire between 2 and 3 weeks, although the time till expiration may vary slightly depending on the *average true range* of the stock's price that traders often examine using the ATR(14) chart study.

Trade Setup:

Buy +3 OTM call at Delta .50 (strike price = $50)
Sell −6 OTM calls two strikes above (strike price = $51)
Buy +3 OTM call two strikes above (strike price = $52)

This example of a butterfly option strategy shows a debit of $0.495 per share when the premiums (Mark values in the left-hand column) of all three options are summed, which include:

+3 long options for $1.025 per share at the $50 strike
−6 short options for $0.58 per share at the $51 strike
+3 long options for $0.30 per share.

If the price of DAL stock rallies to $51, the butterfly begins to return a profit, especially as Theta reduces the premium values of all three strikes. Theta (exiting time value) benefits the six $51 short options the most. You can see this on the risk profile, illustrated and described in Chapter 5. Time value (Theta) reduces the premium of all three options, which benefits the six-contract body options the most. The butterfly strategy is usually closed when 25 percent of the time remains till expiration. When closed, the trader receives the premium that remains in each of the six long calls (the wings) less the premium paid for the six short calls (the body).

A properly structured butterfly is usually closed for a profit of between 15 and 30 percent. Because butterfly strategies are set up to expire within a matter of 1 or 2 weeks, the same butterfly option strategy can be traded

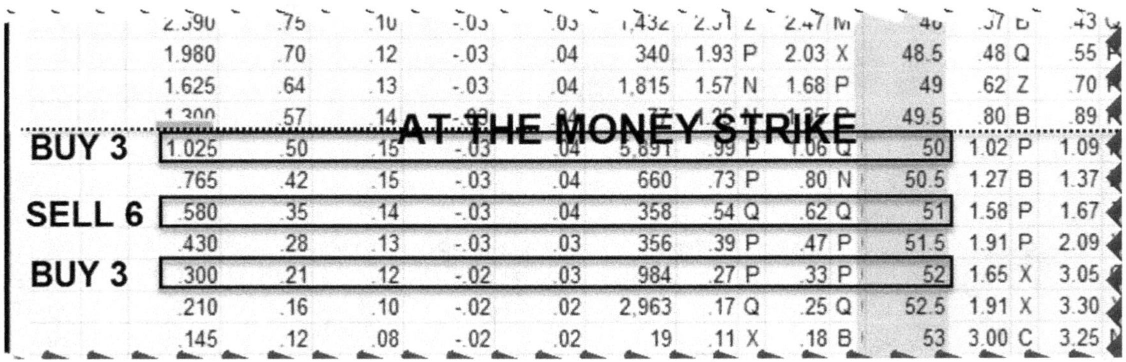

									STRIKE		
	2.590	.75	.7u	-.0s	.0s	1,43z	2.5J z	2.+7 m	4u	.37 b	.43 P
	1.980	.70	.12	-.03	.04	340	1.93 P	2.03 X	48.5	48 Q	.55 P
	1.625	.64	.13	-.03	.04	1,815	1.57 N	1.68 P	49	62 Z	.70 P
	1.300	.57	.14	-.03	.04				49.5	80 B	.89 P
BUY 3	1.025	.50	.15	-.03	.04	5,897	.99 P	.80 N	50	1.02 P	1.09 P
	.765	.42	.15	-.03	.04	660	.73 P	.80 N	50.5	1.27 B	1.37
SELL 6	.580	.35	.14	-.03	.04	358	.54 Q	.62 Q	51	1.58 P	1.67
	.430	.28	.13	-.03	.03	356	.39 P	.47 P	51.5	1.91 P	2.09
BUY 3	.300	.21	.12	-.02	.03	984	.27 P	.33 P	52	1.65 X	3.05
	.210	.16	.10	-.02	.02	2,963	.17 Q	.25 Q	52.5	1.91 X	3.30
	.145	.12	.08	-.02	.02	19	.11 X	.18 B	53	3.00 C	3.25

AT THE MONEY

Figure 2.2 A balanced butterfly example

up to 26 times per year. Some traders stagger their trades by trading every Monday morning. This results in 52 trades (or more) per year, which fits the popular option trader's axiom: *trade small, trade often.*

There are more than sixteen different butterfly strategies. These include the:

Long call butterfly

Long put butterfly

Unbalanced long call butterfly (a different number of strikes in the wings)

Unbalanced long put butterfly

Broken wing long call butterfly (different *strike widths*; also referred to as "skip strike")

Broken wing long put butterfly

Unbalanced broken wing long call butterfly

Unbalanced broken wing long put butterfly (different number of strikes in the wings and different widths)

Another eight short call and short put butterfly strategies that have the same names as the above eight can also be traded, such as a short put butterfly, unbalanced short put butterfly, etc. However, short put and short call butterflies in which the wings are sold and the bodies are bought result in debit spreads. Short butterflies carry much more risk than long butterflies and rarely return a profit without an exceptionally large price rally or drop in the underlying stock.

The butterfly strategies are considered *defined risk strategies* because, regardless of where and how much the underlying's price moves, the trade cannot lose more than a predetermined amount of money. While two legs may lose value, the third leg gains value to offset the loss. This can be seen on the butterfly's *risk profile*, described and illustrated in Chapter 5.

There are other butterfly variations like the double butterfly and the Delta neutral 20-40-60 put butterfly to name two. For even more information about option strategies, examples of 78 different option strategies are included in *The Option Strategy Desk Reference* from Business Expert Press.

Long Call Broken Wing Unbalanced Butterfly (neutral bias): An unbalanced butterfly might be +1 calls, −4 calls, and +3 calls. Notice that there are still four long calls in the wing and four short calls in the central body. A "broken wing" butterfly uses different strike widths between the body and the wings. For example, there could be two strikes below the body and three strikes above. These adjustments are often made to change the opening premium from a debit to a credit. But these changes can also increase the level of risk.

Now consider an unbalanced long call butterfly. This strategy setup returns a credit, but it also increases risk. A similar trade is included in Chapter 6. There, you can see why traders would choose this strategy, which typically expires within two or three weeks.

Trade Setup

> Buy +1 OTM call at Delta .30 (the bottom wing)
> Sell −3 OTM calls one strike above (the body)
> Buy +2 OTM call two strikes above (the top wing)

This long call broken wing unbalanced butterfly is most likely a credit spread that can either be closed if the underlying rallies and achieves a profit of 15 to 20 percent or left to expire OTM, which lets the trader keep the original credit when the butterfly trade filled. Of course, the option trader must have a trading bias based on his or her chart analysis. The Mark values of each strike must also be examined to determine the cost, the risk, and other factors that influence the trade's value and probable outcome. (An example of this option strategy is described in substantial detail in Chapter 6.) Another common setup for this trade places the bottom long call *wing* three or four strikes ITM near a Delta .75, the short call body ATM strike (≈ .50 Delta), and the long call upper *wing* one or two strikes above and OTM.

Debit Spreads (Strategies That Cost Money When Traded)

Long Straddle (neutral bias expecting a large price move): This trade requires option traders to pay a substantial debit when filled because it is placed ATM, where a relatively high Mark value exists. Contract expiration is typically between 90 days and 24 months, and the trader expects a substantial movement in the price of the underlying.

Trade Setup

>Buy a long-term ATM call
>Buy a long-term ATM put

A strong directional price move requires the trader to close the losing put or call option and retain the profitable option. Close the remaining options when sufficient profit is achieved or if the price unexpectedly reverses direction.

Long Strangle (neutral bias expecting a strong price move): This trade requires the trader to pay a substantial debit when filled, although the premium paid is slightly less than the Long Straddle because the strikes are typically two to five strikes OTM.

Contract expiration is typically between 90 days and 24 months.

Trade Setup

>Buy a long-term OTM call at a strike with a Delta value ≤ .35
>Buy a long-term OTM put at a strike with a Delta value ≥ −.35

A strong directional price move requires the trader to close the losing put or call option and retain the profitable option. Close the remaining option when sufficient profit is achieved or if the price unexpectedly reverses direction and the premium begins declining in value.

Synthetic Long Stock (extremely strong bullish bias): This trade uses options to simulate buying a stock that is trending upward; hence the term *synthetic*. It usually requires a small debit when filled, but it can also return a small credit, depending on the current Bid-to-Ask spreads and the premium values of the ATM calls and puts. Contract expiration is typically between 90 days and 24 months.

Trade Setup

>Buy a long-term ATM call
>Sell a long-term ATM put

If the underlying rallies according to the trader's bullish bias, this strategy can return an exceptional amount in profit. Most traders wait for the price of the underlying to rally, which moves the long call deeper ITM and the short put farther OTM. When the call options reach a strike price having a Delta value of 0.75 to 0.80, the trade is closed. In Chapter 4 you see how the value of the Gamma *Greek* declines in value as it moves away from the ATM strike. The strikes reach a point where incremental premium values diminish. This encourages the trader to close the trade for the profits produced by both the ITM long calls and the OTM short puts.

When the trade is closed, the puts are closed by paying a fraction of the premium originally paid when the puts were opened. The synthetic long stock is among the most profitable option trades in use today. However, reward goes hand in hand with risk. If the price of the underlying drops instead of rallying, this trade can empty your brokerage account.

Option Premium Collectors

Many option traders who regularly sell puts and calls are considered *premium collectors*. These option traders regularly sell short-term OTM puts and collect premium from put buyers on the other side of their trades. If the short put remains OTM throughout option contract expiration, the put seller keeps the premium as profit less transaction fees. Transaction fees are trading overhead expenses that include brokerage commissions and option exchange fees collected by your brokerage and paid to the Chicago Board of Options Exchange. Many option traders who are qualified by their brokerage regularly sell both calls and puts (strangles) for premium income. If either short put or short call options become in the money, they can be exercised by the buyers on the other side of their short positions.

Risk Management

To survive, every trader, regardless of his or her trading venue of choice, must know how to manage risk. One or two bad trades could jeopardize their financial survival. Risk management includes trade size; the use of limit entries, protective stops and profit targets (bracketed trades); and the ability to convert a working trade by:

- Rolling up
- Rolling down
- Rolling out

- Legging an option strategy into a different strategy by restructuring a working trade
- Knowing when to stop trading and waiting for the market to settle down

Also included is the ability to develop a sound trading bias based on price chart analysis rather than unreliable sources, such as the talking heads on TV.

Although stock traders have some flexibility, option traders have many more risk management tools at their disposal.

Trade Size

Stock, options, and futures traders can limit the amount of money they put at risk. Some limit the size of each trade to a small fraction of their total brokerage account value. For example, some traders never put more than 2 percent of their account value at risk on a trade. A trader who has $30,000 in his or her account would never risk more than $600 on a single trade. This might be disappointing when buying shares of a $50 stock, because the investor can buy only twelve shares of stock. But an option bought on the same stock might cost $2.00 per share or $200 per contract. The same trader can buy three call options to leverage 300 shares of stock for the same $600 dollars. And if the stock rallies by several dollars in value over the following few weeks, the long options move in the money and the $600 may double in value to $1,200 or even more. This illustrates both the power and the financial leverage available to option traders.

Stop Orders and Bracketed Trades

Just like buy and hold stock traders who place a stop limit order on their long stock holdings, option traders can also use stops. Market stops execute immediately when the price of the underlying reaches the price of the stop order. If a market stop order is placed at $48.50 and the $50 stock drops to $48.50, the trader loses $1.50 per share. The option trader can also use stops in much the same way, although he or she can afford to place the stop even lower. This permits the stock price to drop several dollars more to give the stock price more time to recover and to prevent a premature exit from the trade.

Bracketed orders are used extensively by day traders, but they can also be used by swing traders (including option traders) and long-term buy and hold, dollar-cost-averaging investors. Note that swing traders usually enter a few trades every day to every few weeks in anticipation of a price swing in the underlying stock or ETF.

Example of a Bracketed Order

1. A limit entry order triggers when the stock price reaches the limit entry price. If the limit entry price is $50 and the stock price reaches $50, the trade executes at or below the limit price. If the stock is oscillating up and down, each time it touches $50 more shares are acquired.
2. A protective market stop order fills when the stock price touches the price of the market stop order. Note that market orders buy or sell every share of stock when the protective stop price is reached. If the stock drops to a protective market stop order placed at $48.50, all shares are sold immediately. Some may be sold below the $48.50 stop price.
3. A limit stop order above is used as a profit target. Perhaps the trader wants a $3.00 return in profit. This requires the trader to include a limit stop order at $53.00. If the stock price rallies to $53, the stock is sold. This limit stop order will sell the stock only when it is at or above $53.00.

The bracketed trade, as described, is used by day traders to *scalp* stocks and other financial instruments. The term scalp describes taking small profits when the price of the underlying rises by a few dollars. Note that the same structure is used in reverse when shorting stocks.

Conditional Orders

Another trade management technique is to set a conditional order. Conditional orders send trades to the market when a specified condition occurs. If the specified condition occurs, a working trade order might be triggered either for profit or to prevent a loss. This trade structure includes a market stop order described in the preceding bracketed trade description. Triggers can be based on either a stock price or an option value. Other trigger choices include a Bid, Ask, Delta, or volatility value. Some advanced systems permit conditional orders to be triggered by a price chart study, such as simple moving average or exponential moving average crossover. Traders can also choose the following symbols as part of their conditional order triggers: greater than, less than, equal to, less than or equal to, and greater than or equal to. Be sure to learn how to set up a conditional order by talking to your brokerage's technical support staff.

When an option value is used to send a conditional order, a unique option code must be used in place of the underlying stock's ticker symbol. Each option code is specific to a symbol, expiration date, the option type (put or call), and a strike price. See the option code for a $95 put on Microsoft stock that expires on October 25, 2019, in what follows:

MSFT191025P95

- MSFT = Ticker symbol
- 191025 = Expiration date
- P or C = Put or call
- 95 = Strike price

Alerts

Most full-service brokerages provide full-featured trading applications that are compatible with personal computers, smartphones, and tablets. Traders first use a "Notifications" dialogue where a valid e-mail address and cell phone number are entered. Next, the trader can choose a working trade and use the Alert dialogue to enter one or more values based on either the price of the stock or a Bid, Ask, or Mark value. If the specified value is reached, an e-mail and/or text message is sent to the trader. The trader can respond by opening his or her trading application and taking the appropriate action and close the working order either for a profit or for a loss. The trader may also roll or reconfigure the trade to prevent assignment. (See rolling up, down, and/or out next.)

Rolling Up, Down, and/or Out

Option traders can roll a working trade into a new one. Rolling involves two simultaneous transactions: closing a working trade and opening a new one at the same time on the same underlying that expires at a later date. Simply stated, rolling replaces one open trade with a new one. Working option trades can be rolled out to a later expiration date, rolled up to a higher strike price, or rolled down to a lower strike price. Option trades can also be simultaneously rolled out to a later expiration and up or down and a different strike price. Choosing a higher strike is referred to as rolling up; choosing a lower strike is called rolling down. The ability to roll trades is unique to options. It involves simultaneously closing a working trade and opening another. Stock traders cannot roll. But they can buy or sell one stock and then buy or sell a different one, which is typically done in separate transactions.

Options also provide ways to modify the structure of working trades. One example would be to convert a vertical spread into a butterfly, both of which have been discussed earlier. This is called *legging in*. An example might be to convert a bull call spread consisting of a long call and a short call three strikes above to a long butterfly. The conversion would sell a second short call at the same strike as the existing short call and then add a long call perhaps three strikes above the short call. Hence, we have converted a bull call vertical spread that included +1 call and −1 call into a long call butterfly with a structure of +1 call, −2 calls, and +1 calls above. Regardless of what we call this transformation, manipulations like this give option traders enormous flexibility that is either unavailable or rarely used within other trading venues.

Market Makers and Electronic Communications Networks

Option contract orders are negotiated and ultimately matched by *market makers*, who have contracts with the stock exchanges (like the NYSE, AMEX, etc.). Options have Bid prices from Sellers and Ask prices from buyers. Day traders who buy and sell stocks on trading ladders click in the Bid column to buy and the Ask column to sell—the opposite of options.

This can be confusing to stock traders. Just remember to select the Bid to sell and the Ask to buy option contracts on your option chains, where the *option chain* was introduced in Figure 2.1.

Market makers work behind the scenes to match working buy (Ask) and sell (Bid) orders received from traders over electronic communications networks (ECNs). These ECNs connect brokerages to exchanges. When Bid and Ask orders match, the market maker executes the trade. They make their money from the overlap of the Bid-to-Ask *spread*s, which are either the same or perhaps a few pennies apart. When reasonable, the market makers may take a position in a trade to fill it, and then use their positions to fill new orders.

CHAPTER 3

The Option Trading Process

Developing Watch Lists

Most traders develop a list of stocks, exchange-traded funds (ETFs), and financial indexes that fit the size of their brokerage accounts. There are nearly 7,000 optionable equities out of some 65,000 ticker symbols. However, there are only a few hundred symbols in this "haystack" of equities that are within affordable price ranges and that have sufficient trading volumes to qualify as trade candidates.

These can typically be found on stock search engines such as the "stock hacker" provided in TD Ameritrade's thinkorswim, TradeStation Group's TradeStation application, Tasty Trade's tastyworks, and many others. There are other lists like the ones provided by *Investor's Business Daily*, the *Wall Street Journal*, and other services and publications.

So your personal watch lists should include only those stocks, ETFs, financial indexes, and options symbols that are affordable, have enough trading volume, and that you are willing to own in case of option assignment. And to make scanning your watch list easier, you may want to separate your symbols by market sector, that is, tech stocks, pharmaceuticals, energy, public utilities, manufacturing, automotive, transportation, semiconductor companies, and so on. The stocks within each market sector often move in unison, which is easily seen when organizing your watch lists by market sector.

Avoid stagnant management support companies that exist to pay a salary to their officers. Options on these companies have limited trading volumes and price ranges with miniscule option premiums. You can also check balance sheets, income statements, and insider trading on websites like finance.yahoo.com. Other sites are examined by hedge fund analysts who try to determine employee satisfaction through turnover rates and hiring trends. For example, glassdoor.com is a recruiting website that some financial institutions use.

Although much of the foregoing research, called *fundamental analysis*, is essential to long-term buy-and-hold investors, option traders would rarely spend the time at this level of detail. By the time the trader has done this extensive level of research, the trading opportunity could be lost.

Option traders can typically learn everything they need to know about the underlying equity by examining the price charts and a few chart studies, as described in the paragraphs that follow. So spending the extra research time on a variety of sources is often a waste of time on a short-term option trade that lasts for a matter of a few weeks. However, when investing in an expensive long-term option, such as a long call LEAPS option that expires in a year or more, it can be prudent to conduct some additional research.

NOTE: The acronym LEAPS stands for long-term equity anticipation security. LEAPS options exist on approximately 2,500 equities and 20 financial indexes. Option traders look for stocks and ETFs with prices they expect to trend upward during the life of a LEAPS option, such as the synthetic long stock strategy summarized in Chapter 2 and described in more detail in Chapter 6. Recall how the at the money long call LEAPS combined with an equal number of at the money short put LEAPS can double in value when the trader's bullish bias is right. But the same trade can be punishing if the trader's bullish bias is wrong.

Scanning the Underlying

When you find an affordable equity of interest with plenty of trading volume, you can quickly check several other metrics. Begin by examining the price charts. Other things to examine are listed next. For additional information, read Chapters 7 and 8 of the second edition of *The Only Options Trading Book You'll Ever Need* available from Amazon, which was released in early 2019.

Examining Price Charts

Look at the price charts in order to develop a trading bias (bullish, bearish, or neutral), before you look at the option chain to find a suitable option trade. Most traders learn to examine price charts over different time frames in order to understand how prices respond to market conditions, company earnings, new product releases, dividends, and events within the market sector to which the equity belongs.

- Check the price charts across three to four time intervals (weekly, daily, hourly, and 1 to 5 minutes).
- Look at the price formations across time (a series of smooth upward or downward trends, long periods of sideways movement, choppiness with large price swings, several price gaps between market close and the next day's market open, and so on). Knowing the "personality" of an equity's price levels encourages either a deeper analysis or looking elsewhere.
- Check for typical price support and resistance levels over time, with emphasis on the past few weeks. Support and resistance levels represent the low and high prices over a specified time period. Prices often reverse direction at historical lows and highs. Some refer to these levels as *demand zones* at support (the bottom) and *supply zones* at resistance (the top). Relatively low prices near a demand zone encourage a change from selling to buying. The increase in buying creates a price rally. High prices within a supply zone increase selling, which reduces the stock's price.
- In addition to looking at price rallies and drops over time, look at both the price trend and the price range over the past 2 weeks using the ATR(14) chart study on a daily chart. ATR stands for *average true range*, which displays the average price range over the past 14 days, regardless of the direction.

NOTE: When viewing one or more price charts, most full-featured trading platforms include a list of popular chart studies that can be viewed either as lines on displayed chart or as data strips at the bottom of the chart. Simply choose one or more studies from the list of studies to view. One of the earliest chart studies used by traders was the simple moving average, or SMA(). The number of days included is shown within parentheses, for example SMA(9), which displays a line that intersects the 9-day SMA price across the most recent nine-day period.

The number of days can be adjusted by typing a different value in place of 9. There are also EMA() studies that display the *exponential* moving average. The underlying math for the EMA() study places emphasis on the most recent price levels. Many traders use this study today, looking for SMA or EMA crossovers as buy and sell signals. For example, when an SMA(20) plotline crosses above an SMA(50) plotline, some traders see this as a buy signal as this shows a rally in the price value. Crossing below is considered a sell signal as the price drops. (See Figure 3.1.)

- Some see a trading *alert* when an SMA(10) plot crosses the SMA(20) plot. Alerts encourage traders to be prepared to enter a trade if and when the SMA(20)–SMA(50) crossover occurs.
- In addition to looking at a few price charts, also look at the current price relative to recent highs and lows. Check the price charts over four different ranges, that is, long term to short term in order to understand price highs and lows, typical support and resistance levels, the current price trends, buying or selling momentum, and volatility levels.
- There are many other chart studies in use by traders. It's important to read a description of the studies to understand their meanings. Here are a few more studies that are often used by experienced traders.
  - Momentum studies: RSI (relative strength index); CCI (commodity channel index), MACD (moving average convergence-divergence), and a stochastic oscillator, of which there are nine.
  - Bollinger Bands: This study has been around for many years. It is a measure of volatility above and below a central SMA(20) plotline. The volatility plots are two standard deviations above and below the central plotline.
  - Keltner Channel: The Keltner Channel also uses a central SMA(20) plotline with a central SMA(20) plotline and above and below plotlines that are offset by 1.5 × the ATR(14) value.
  - The Bollinger Bands and Keltner Channel are used together to show a price *break out*, that is, a rapid price change and possible trading opportunity. The following illustration shows the Bollinger Bands with the Keltner Channel. Look at the *crossovers*,

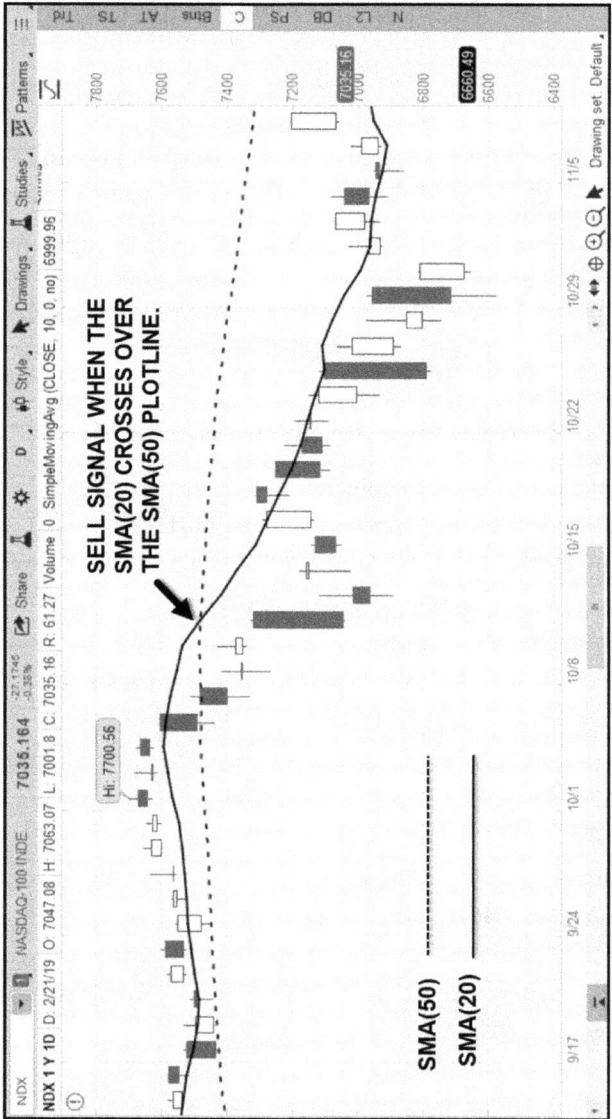

Figure 3.1 Crossover of two simple moving average plotlines

where the Bollinger Bands move outside the ATR(14) plotlines. This is where current volatility (or trading volume) becomes unusually high (Figure 3.2).

○ One long-time market trader, instructor, and chart study developer, named John Carter, developed what he calls the *trade-the-market squeeze*, abbreviated TTM_Squeeze. Carter's study combines additional indicators, such as the Market Forecaster study and scripted code, to forecast an upward or downward direction of the anticipated price breakout. Mr. Carter conducts training webinars and live training courses to teach traders how to configure and use his chart studies. Users of these studies rely on them to catch price moves and increase their odds of achieving successful trading outcomes.

Determining Supply and Demand

Short- to intermediate-term price increases and decreases of stocks and other investment-quality equities are more sensitive to buying and selling volumes of a company's stock or a market sector's ETFs than to company operations and long-term business outlook. However, over the long haul, growth in quarterly earnings and the long-term business outlook are more important for sustained growth in its stock value. This separates the short-term investors from the buy-and-hold, dollar-cost-averaging investors.

Both day traders, who *scalp* small, incremental rallies and drops, and option traders who buy and sell short-lived option contracts that last for days or weeks, thrive on stock supply and demand. Just as in oil or wheat, surpluses drive prices down. And when demand outpaces supply, prices rise.

Many market traders examine price charts in search of breakout opportunities. In addition to SMA() and EMA() crossovers, a TTM_Squeeze, an "engulfed candle," and a host of chart patterns such as some of the following:

- Double tops (bearish) (See Figure 3.3 for an example of a double top.)
- Double bottoms (bullish) (See Figure 3.4 for an example of a double bottom.)
- Bull flag or bear flag (bullish or bearish)
- Cup and handle (bullish)

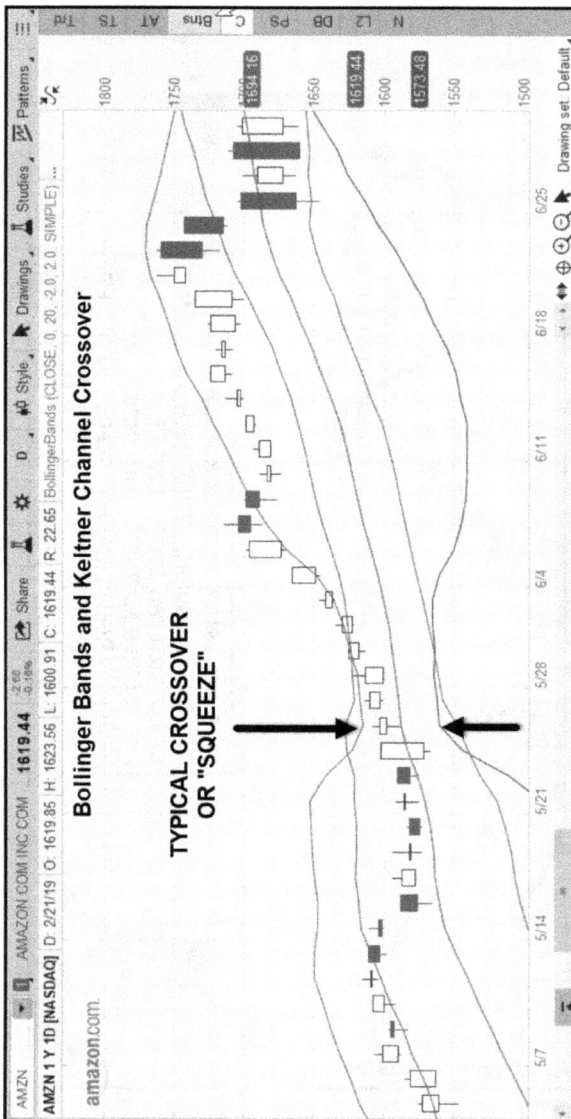

Figure 3.2 The Bollinger Bands and Keltner Channel crossover

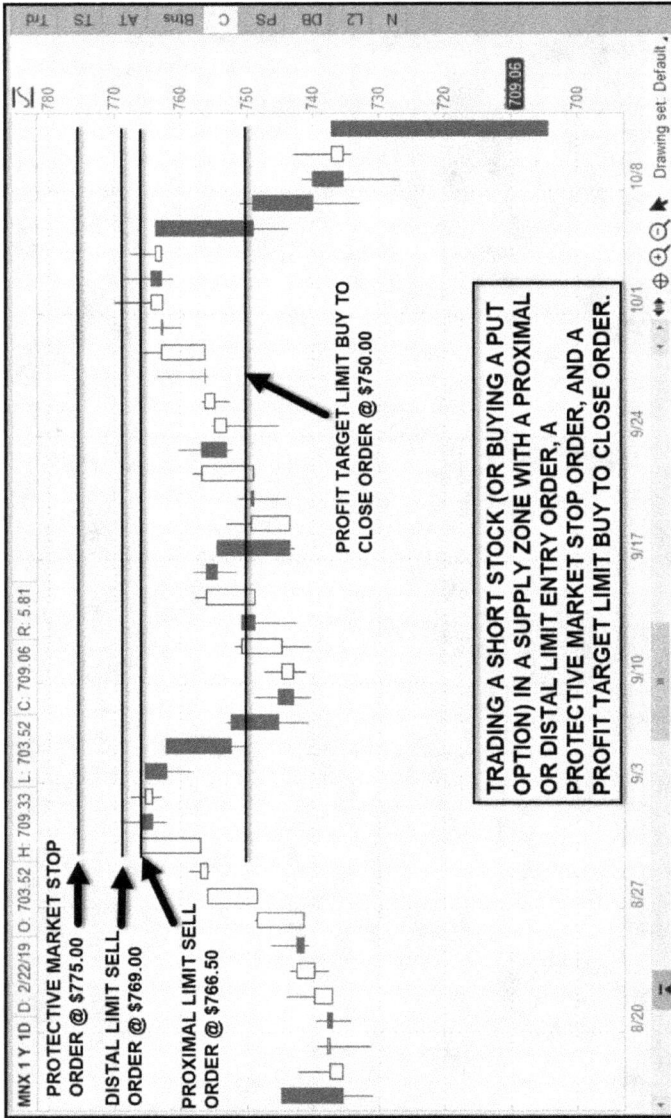

Figure 3.3 Increased supply in an overbought stock (bearish)

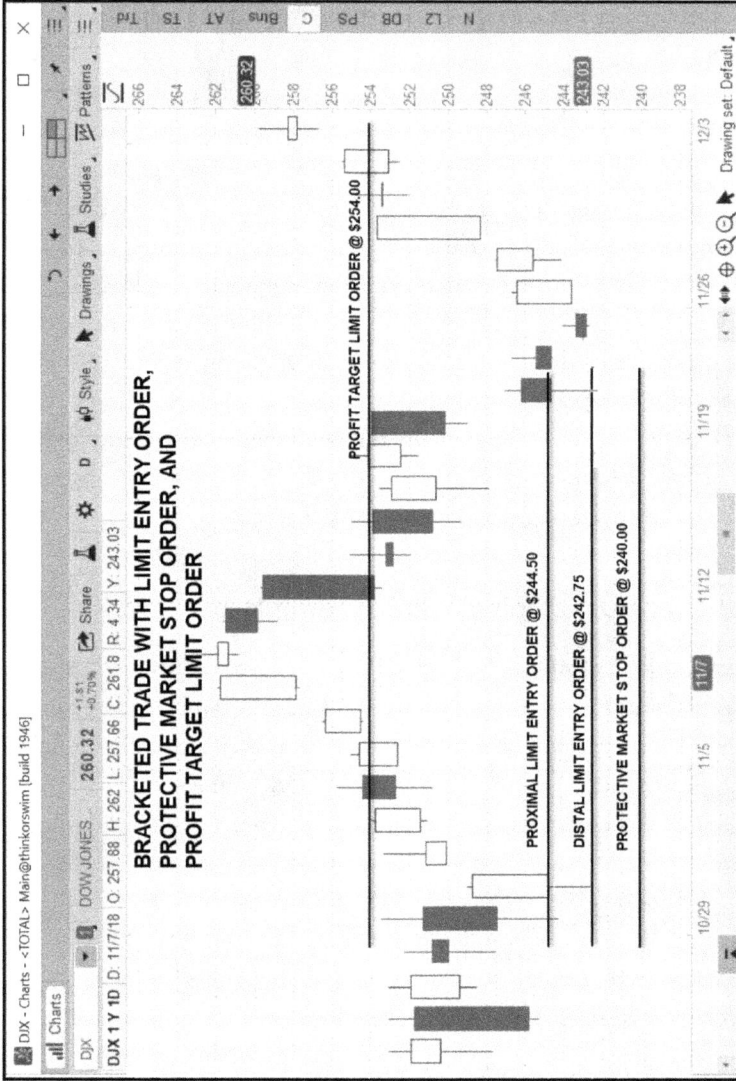

Figure 3.4 Increased demand in an oversold stock (bullish)

There are dozens of chart patterns that traders use, although supply and demand (the current overbought or oversold condition) is considered more reliable.

There are dozens of chart patterns shown and described on the stock-charts.com website. But chart patterns are rarely reliable, as the market is a "random beast." However, buying and selling volumes create oversold and overbought conditions. When oversold, prices are relatively cheap, attracting buyers. This happens in a *demand zone*, which attracts buyers, causing a price rally. Stock traders buy and sell stock while option traders buy calls and sell puts. Both are bullish in anticipation of a price rally.

When overbought, prices that have been driven up through excessive buying, especially by novice traders who follow rather than lead, savvy traders have already begun to sell for profits. Selling at resistance near the top of a price chart or at a historical turning point, typically results in a drop. This attracts bearish traders who short stocks, sell calls, or buy puts—all bearish trades. Many traders thrive on these oversold and over-bought signals, because they understand the dynamics of supply and de-mand caused by overbought and oversold price levels.

Developing Your Trading Bias

Select a trading bias (bullish, bearish, or neutral) based on historical price levels. Verify your bias by using a few readily available, popular chart stud-ies. These studies include one of the momentum oscillators (RSI, CCI, MACD, Stochastics Fast), the 14-day average price range study, that is, the ATR(14). Now let's look at a few oversold and overbought levels, that is, where oversold stocks begin to rally off a historical support level and overbought stocks begin to drop from a historical resistance level.

Examine the price chart and demand zone shown in Figure 3.3.

Proficient traders who use demand and supply zones almost always use *bracketed* trades. A common bracketed order is set up with a limit entry order, a protective stop, which is a *market order*, and a second limit order at the trade's profit target. See Table 3.1 for descriptions of a few commonly used order types. High-frequency day traders who enter doz-ens of daily trades use bracketed trades for efficiency. Trying to monitor 20 or more working trades is extremely difficult. This requires day traders

Table 3.1 Order types

Limit order	An order that triggers incrementally when a stock price is equal to the specified limit order price. This often results in incremental buying or selling as the price of the stock fluctuates above and below the specified stock.
Market order	A buy or sell order placed at a specified price. When the price is touched by the underlying, all shares are bought or sold at the current market price, regardless of the direction of subsequent price movements.
Stop order	Stop orders are used to prevent losses when the price of a long (bought) stock drops or a short (sold) stock rallies to the stop price. Protective stops use market orders; entry orders and profit targets use limit orders.
OCO 1st trgs all 1st trgs 2 OCO 1st trgs 3 OCO	OCO stands for *one cancels other*. The OCO order is used with bracketed trades in which a protective stop and one to three profit target orders may exist. When either the stop or profit target triggers, one or more other orders are automatically closed. Note that some traders use multiple profit target orders, T1, T2, and T3, for profit targets one, two, and three. Having two or more profit targets is referred to as *scaling out*.

to develop and use a series of preset order templates that include limit entries, market stop orders, and one to three limit orders as their profit targets. Day traders are *scalpers* and use established reward to risk (R:R) ratios that can range from 2:1 to 5:2, expressed in either dollars or as percentages. These ratios are used in their trading templates that are selected and entered with a few clicks of a mouse.

Returning to the demand zone and bracketed trade in Figure 3.3, notice how traders have choices in their trade setups. The typical demand zone is used to set up either a *proximal* or *distal* limit entry. The *proximal* entry places its limit entry at a price that corresponds to the opening price at the bottom of the body of the first candle that previously led to the most recent transition from a drop to a rally. If there are two previous drops and rallies near the same price points, even better. A common alternative is to use the *distal* (or "distant") price level that is located at the bottom of the candle's shadow (or *wick*)—the period's low. It's easy to see how proximal entries trigger more often than distal entries, as prices often turn before they drop to the previous low. But as you've probably already realized, if the trader is wrong about the demand zone and the order is filled and then stopped out, the proximal entry loses a bit more money than the distal entry. But if the price turns and begins to rally before the stock is stopped out, the trader stands to make more money, represented by the length of the candle's bottom shadow.

Once a bracketed order fills and the underlying stock begins to rally from an increase in buying volume, or demand, the trader can slide the protective stop up in order to limit a potential loss in the event that the stock price reverses direction. When able to slide the stop above the limit entry price, the trader can assure a profitable trade outcome. The bracketed trade's profit target can also be slid upward for more profit. Traders call this *letting the profits run*.

Now let's examine Figure 3.4. This illustrates a trade in a supply zone that is at a recent resistance level located at the top of a price chart. It is the mirror image of the demand zone.

As you can see, trading in a supply zone at resistance and at a recent historical high can result in a trade that's just as profitable as trading a stock that's rallying off a support level in a demand zone. This is an example of shorting a stock, which can be just as profitable as buying a stock that is trending upward. Many stock traders make as much, if not more, income by shorting stocks and then buying to close them at a substantially lower price. When shorting stock, traders must finance the short stock with the equity in their brokerage accounts. Typically, most brokerages permit traders to use half of the value of "big board" stocks and ETFs held in a margin account, while Over the Counter (OTC) stocks, also called *Penny* or *Pink Sheet Stocks*, have no value for margin purposes.

You should be aware that penny stock companies are rarely audited, have very little capital, are not subject to U.S. Securities and Exchange Commission (SEC) review, and often fail. Many use "pump and dump" schemes to promote stock sales. These schemes extol the virtues of these penny stock companies that are often exaggerated. Increasing stock values benefits the owners. But there are times when the increased value from stock sales is actually invested in company operations and new product development.

And there are some examples of OTC stocks that turned into viable growth companies that moved to one of the major exchanges. In any case, full-time, experienced high-frequency traders rarely invest their precious holdings in OTC stocks.

CHAPTER 4

Using the Option Chains

Examining and Using Option Chains

This chapter dives deeper into the use of option chains, examining how to:

- Use the extensive information displayed on option chains
- Use the *Greek* values displayed at each strike price and what they mean
- Use the current implied volatility (IV%) to determine buying and selling opportunities
- Understand how to use ± Price Movement values
- Evaluate the current Open Interest values when selecting one or more strike prices
- Find, copy, and paste option codes used with conditional order (stops and profit targets)
- Add two or more strikes (or *legs*) to create option strategies
- Edit quantities, prices, strikes, expiration dates, prices, etc. on the order bar
- Display risk profiles to determine how trades respond to price changes
- Set up and configure a bracketed trade
- Roll working orders up, down, and/or out
- Review and submit orders from the order confirmation dialog

At the Money, In the Money, Out of the Money Review

Examine the call and put sections of the option chain in Figure 4.1 on the following page. It is separated into two sections to make the text and numbers larger and easier to read. Notice that it is set to display

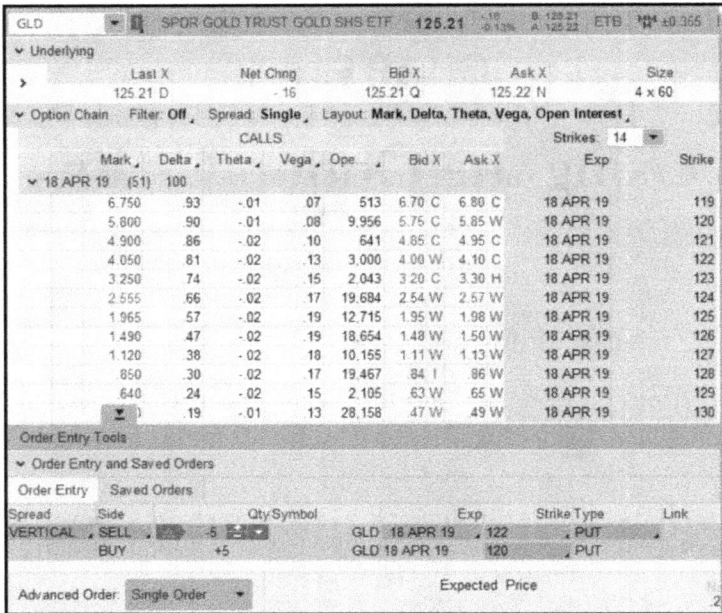

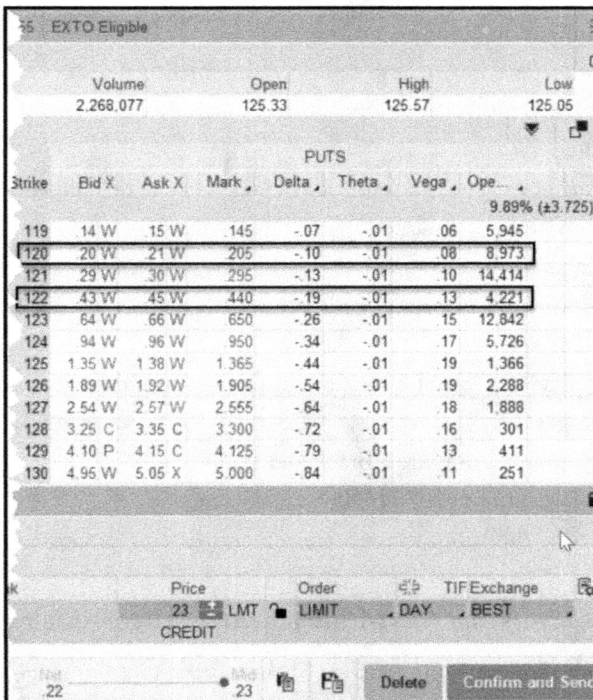

Figure 4.1 An option chain showing a bull put vertical spread

©2019 TD Ameritrade IP Company, Inc. For illustrative purposes only.

14 strikes, that is, seven strikes having values lower than the ATM strike and seven above, although only five strikes are shown in the illustration. The $125 strike is closest to the current price, $125.21, of GLD. Traders use expressions like "below the money," "near the money," "far out of the money," and so on.

Now look at the ATM strike's Delta values on the put and call sides. Notice how the Delta values of both the call and put are quite close to .50. This is typical of the Delta values that are closest to the ATM money strike. The value of Delta decreases incrementally between strikes as the strikes move farther out of the money (OTM) or deeper in the money (ITM). This is because Gamma, which is used to calculate the values of Delta, is highest ATM and declines in value as it moves farther away from the ATM strike. Also recall from Table 2.1 how each Delta's value is used to compute the change in premium values for each $1.00 change in the price of the underlying stock. This tells us that the Mark values of those strikes that are closer to the ATM strike change more than when farther OTM. You can verify this fact by looking at the difference in the Mark values from one strike to the next.

Also notice how the Mark values, or the premium traders pay or receive, increases in value as the strike prices drop on the call side of the option chain. Now examine the put side of the option chain to see how the Mark value of the puts increases as the price of the underlying decreases. Both of these moves are referred to as "moving deeper in the money."

Now look for the implied volatility (IV%) of 9.89 percent located above the Open Interest column on the put side of the option chain. This is an indication of current trading volume relative to the average trading volume over the past 12 months. The 9.89 percent IV value is quite low but will likely return to historical levels unless the enterprise that the stock represents is experiencing a decline in business operations, which may have caused a reduction in trading.

The ±3.725 is referred to as the *price movement*. This is a mathematical derivative of the IV% value and is the calculated price movement that is expected throughout the life of the option, that is, through expiration. These values are extremely sensitive to changes in trading volume. And at such a low IV% of 9.89 percent, an increase in both the IV% and the price movement values are likely. This is an excellent value for buying call options if bullish or put options if bearish, because the IV% is likely to increase in value as it returns toward its historical volatility level. When the IV% value increases back toward historical volatility levels, premium values increase.

Recall how option traders look for high volatility values when selling options and low volatility values when buying options. Experienced option traders always examine volatility values prior to trading because volatility influences premium values more than any of the other so-called option *Greeks*, that is, Gamma, Delta, Theta, Vega, or Rho. Volatility values are discussed again in the order rules narrative provided in Chapter 5.

Buying, Selling, and Buying and Selling

An introduction to several common option strategies was included in Chapter 2. These strategies bought and sold puts and calls, combined puts and calls into *vertical spreads*—an extremely heavily used options trading construct—and also described strategies that combined both call and put vertical spreads, like the extremely popular *iron condor* strategy.

Most trading platforms support up to four option legs. The iron condor, described in the Buying and Selling Put and Call Spreads section of Chapter 2, is an example of a trade that includes four different strike prices, that is, a short and long call and a short and long put.

When trading two or more different option contracts at different strikes, they are displayed on the order bar located at the bottom of the option chain. An option chain and order bar for the iron condor mentioned previously is shown in Figure 4.2.

Notice how the trade includes four "legs," a short and a long call and a short and a long put. Also be aware of how we click on the Bid cell to sell options and the Ask cell to buy options. Here are the steps you can use:

1. Click the Bid cell on the 140 call strike row.
2. Press and hold the Ctrl key while clicking the Ask cell on the 150 call strike row.
3. Press and hold the Ctrl key while clicking the Bid cell on the 115 put strike row.
4. Press and hold the Ctrl key while clicking the Ask cell on the 110 put strike row.

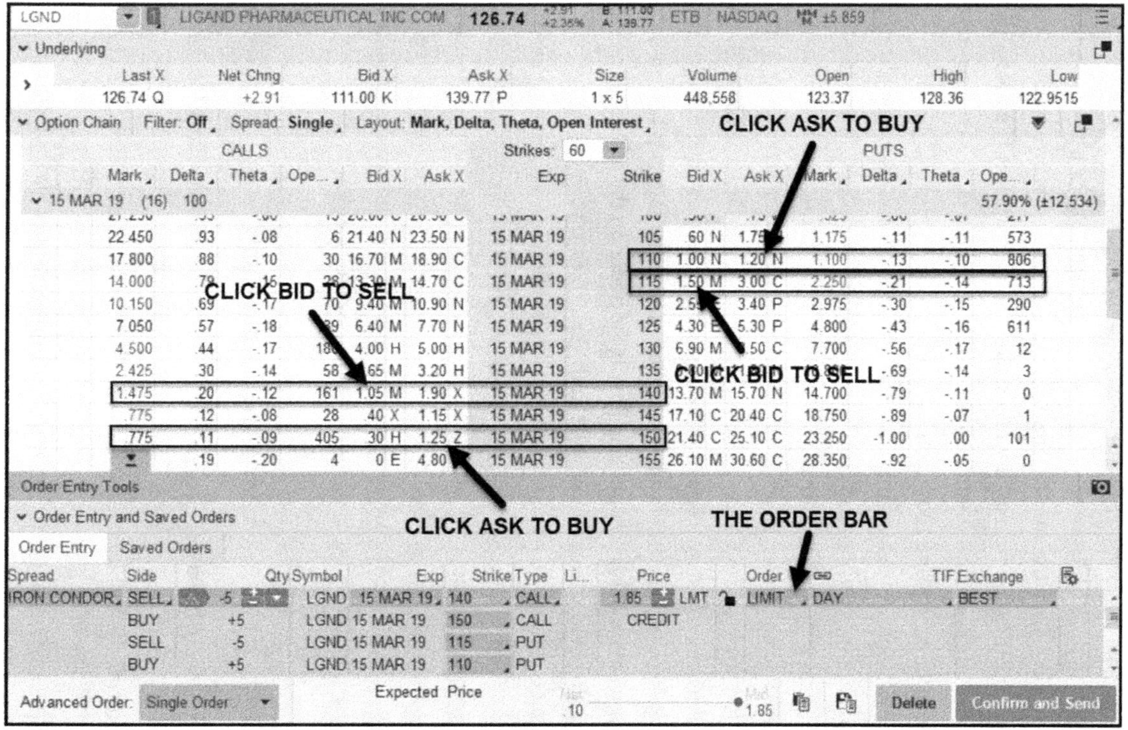

Figure 4.2 An option chain and order bar illustrating an iron condor

©2019 TD Ameritrade IP Company, Inc. For illustrative purposes only.

Notice how the short options are both at or below Delta .25. This Delta value is used because when this trade was entered, the five short puts and calls had a 25 percent or better probability of remaining OTM through option expirations in 16 days. (Find the expiration date and (16) in Figure 4.2.) Traders have used Delta values for years in the same way as *Probability ITM* is used. Although the market often makes unexpected moves, using Delta for determining the probability of a strike price to remain OTM for a successful trading outcome works more often than not. The key is to never "overtrade" by putting too much money at risk.

Being able to determine the odds of a successful outcome through option math is only one reason the popularity of options is on the rise. But unless prospective traders read a book like this one or take an option trading course, they will never know how to use option math.

Now look at the Open Interest values of each strike. The Open Interest values, which show current working trades at each strike, appear to be ample. Strong Open Interest helps working orders fill faster. When an order fills, you are probably "trading seats" with the trader on the other side of your trade. However, trades that include multiple strikes, especially four, are often difficult to fill. Some traders buy and sell multiple-leg trades two strikes at a time. In this iron condor example, this would entail selling an iron condor in two separate transactions: a vertical bear call spread—the short call and long call above, and a vertical bull put spread—the short put and long put below. Be aware that entering two separate orders increases your trading overhead because it requires you to pay two brokerage commissions.

Using the Order Bar

The following order bar is created as each of the option trades is selected (Figure 4.3).

Notice the values in each section of the order bar.

Spread: The name of the spread, in this case, IRON CONDOR
Side: This can be either SELL or BUY.
Qty: The number of contracts to buy or sell; the five can be incremented or decremented manually or preset as the default value. Notice + is BUY and − is SELL.

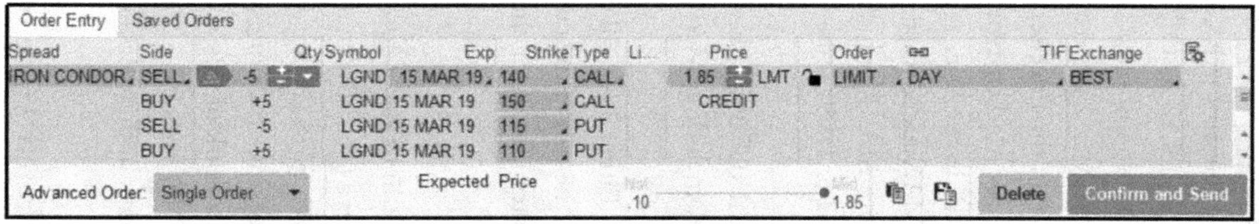

Order Entry | Saved Orders

Spread	Side	Qty	Symbol	Exp	Strike	Type	Li..	Price	Order	TIF	Exchange
IRON CONDOR	SELL	-5	LGND	15 MAR 19	140	CALL		1.85 LMT	LIMIT	DAY	BEST
	BUY	+5	LGND	15 MAR 19	150	CALL		CREDIT			
	SELL	-5	LGND	15 MAR 19	115	PUT					
	BUY	+5	LGND	15 MAR 19	110	PUT					

Expected Price .10

1.85

Advanced Order: Single Order

Delete | Confirm and Send

Figure 4.3 The order bar

©2019 TD Ameritrade IP Company, Inc. For illustrative purposes only.

Symbol: The ticker symbol of the underlying stock, ETF, financial index, and so on.

Exp: The option contract expiration date(s)

Strike: The selected strike prices of each option

Link: This section is blank unless a MARKET or STOP order is used. When a STOPLIMIT, TRAILSTOP, or TRAILSTOPLIMIT order is used, the Link section displays the following:

STOPLIMIT: MAN for Manually; requires the trader to type a stop limit order value in the Price section of the order bar.

TRAILSTOP: MARK for Market; type a trailing stop value as a MARKET order value in the Price section of the order bar.

TRAILSTOPLIMIT: MAN for Manual; type a TRAILING STOP LIMIT value line with MARK, which is a market order.

Price: The debit to be paid or credit to be received when entering an order

Order: A Limit order is the default. Other order types are selectable from a drop-down list, including Market, Stop, Stop Limit, and Trailing Stop Limit.

TIF for Time in Force (): Either good till canceled (GTC) or a Day order, which expires at the end of the current trading day

Exchange: BEST designates the use of the exchange that offers the best transaction price(s)

This order bar illustrates a limit order configured to sell five puts at the $277 strike. It also includes a protective market stop order designed to trigger if the SPY price drops to $278 (Figure 4.4). Notice the stop order is a GTC and will exist as a working order unless triggered by a drop in the price of SPY to $278. You can think of this as a "conditional order" that is triggered if the price of LGND breaches $278. If the 277 put option is not filled during the trading day, both orders expire unfilled.

Setting Up a Bracketed Trade on an Order Bar

Bracketed trades can be set up in a few different ways. For example, a trader can use the order bars at the bottom of the option chain to set up a bracketed trade. This requires the use of an advanced order type such as

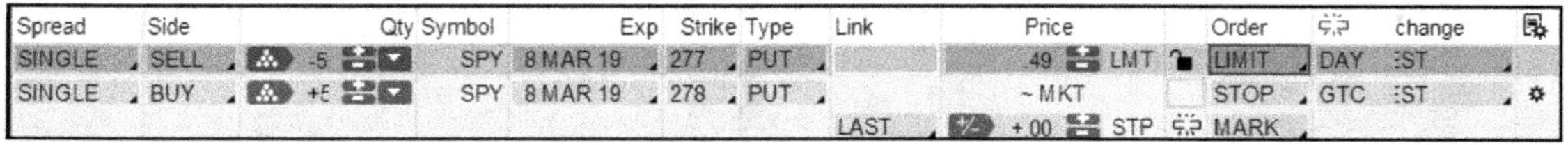

Figure 4.4 Submitting a stop order with your trade

©2019 TD Ameritrade IP Company, Inc. For illustrative purposes only.

a first triggers all order. Other selections like first triggers sequence, one cancels other (OCO), first triggers OCO, first triggers two OCO, and so on, are also available. Learn what's available on your trading platform, their meanings, and how to use them.

Trading platforms also include trade setup dialogs, or *Order Rules*, that provide access to a variety of order setups and dependencies. Be sure to examine these dialogs and the way they work on your trading platform. If unsure about how to set an order up, check with your brokerage's support team. This is why they're there, and they are usually quite helpful.

Examine the order bar in Figure 4.5. This illustrates the first step in the creation of a bracketed trade on the order bar at the bottom of the option chain. The example begins with a bull put vertical spread that sells five short puts above five long puts and collects .24 cents for $120 in premium.

Now the trader can add a profit target and protective stop. But first, the order is changed to a 1st trgs OCO, for first triggers one cancels other. This setup cancels one order when the other one is triggered. Therefore, if the profit target is used, the stop order is canceled (Figure 4.6).

Once the 1st trgs OCO is selected (#1 arrow), some trading platforms permit the trader to open either a shortcut menu (#2 arrow) or a drop-down-style menu. The menu is used to create two opposite orders— one as a profit target and the other as a protective stop. The protective stop can be configured either as a limit order or as a market order, which is entirely up to the trader. In this example, two limit orders are used (Figure 4.7).

Once the opposite order bars are added, the order column is used to configure the brackets. Notice the profit target Price is set to 15 cents and the Order type is set to LIMIT, GTC. If this 24-cent DAY order is filled, the stop orders begin working. If the MARK drops to 15 cents for a $90 profit, the order is triggered, and the OCO cancels the other side of the bracket. If the Mark rallies to 30 cents, the protective STOPLIMIT/ GTC order triggers, and the OCO cancels the profit target order. This bracketed trade works in exactly the same way as targets and stops work with stocks.

There are more variations to bracketed trades and stop order triggers, such as using a Delta-triggered stop order or a stop based on a Bid or

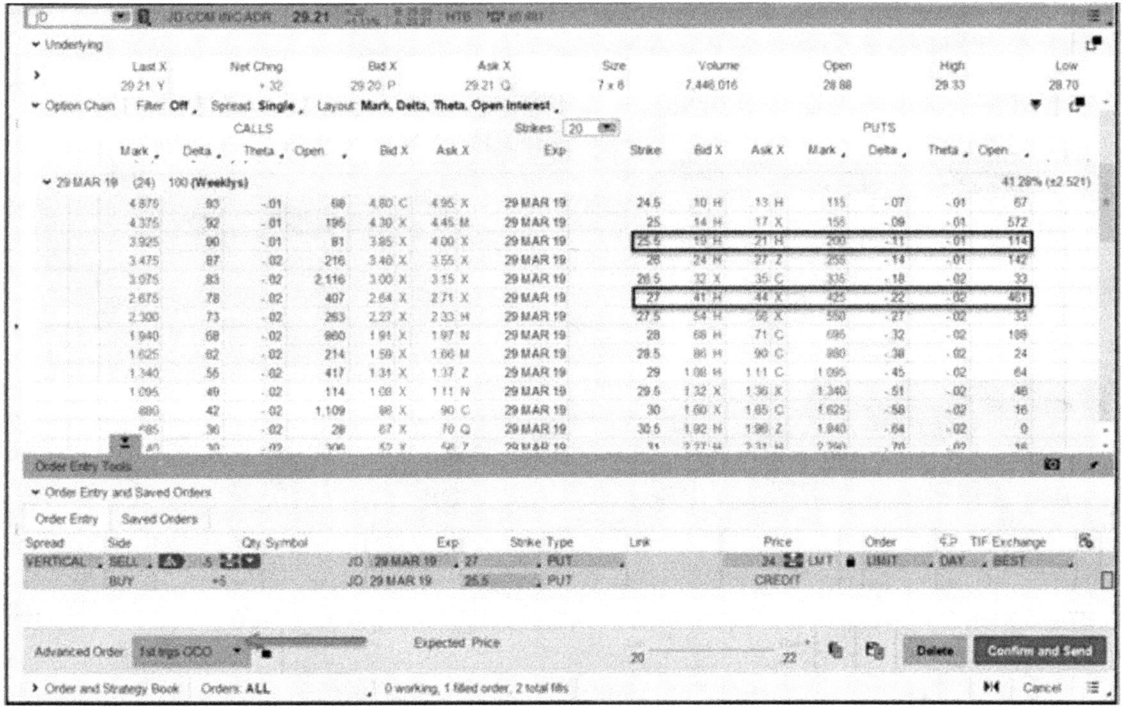

Figure 4.5 Constructing a bracketed trade on the order bar

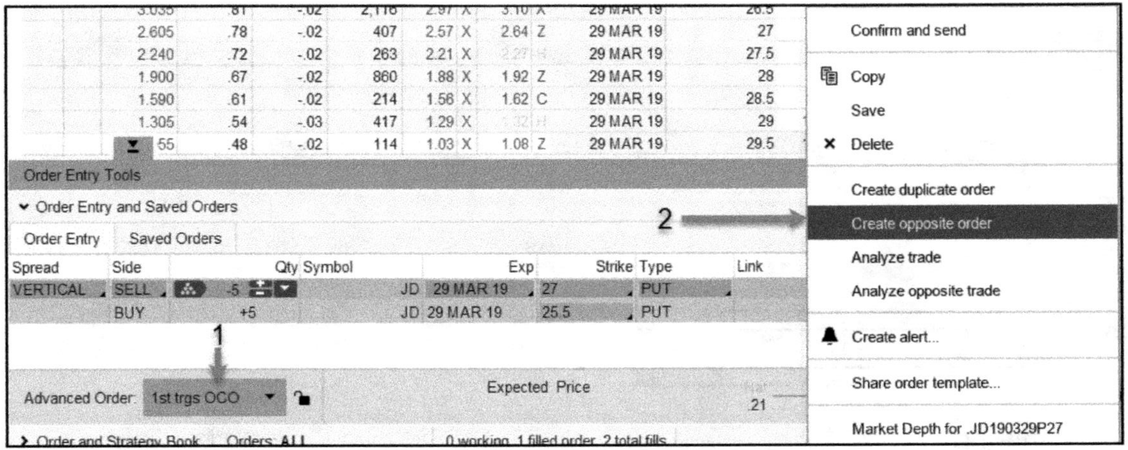

Figure 4.6 Setting the order type to 1st trgs OCO

©2019 TD Ameritrade IP Company, Inc. For illustrative purposes only.

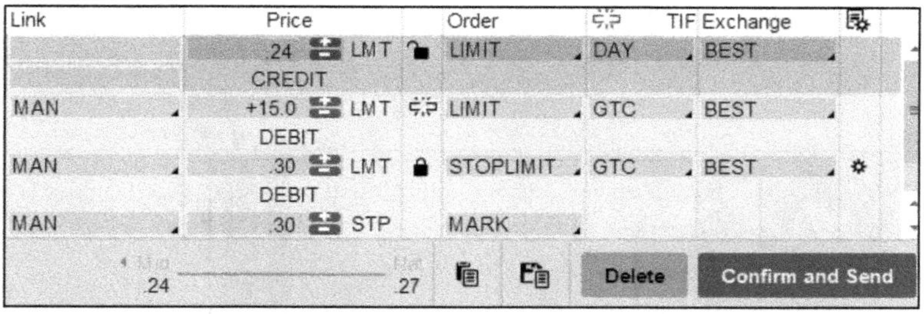

Link	Price	Order		TIF Exchange	
	.24 LMT LIMIT CREDIT	LIMIT	DAY	BEST	
MAN	+15.0 LMT LIMIT DEBIT	LIMIT	GTC	BEST	
MAN	.30 LMT STOPLIMIT DEBIT	STOPLIMIT	GTC	BEST	
MAN	.30 STP	MARK			
	.24	.27		Delete	Confirm and Send

Figure 4.7 Adding the profit target and the protective stop

©2019 TD Ameritrade IP Company, Inc. For illustrative purposes only.

Ask price value. These can be configured to either take profits or to limit losses. Every competent trader of stocks, options, or futures learns how to construct and submit bracketed trades. All include protective stops and one to three profit targets.

Examining an Order Confirmation

The order confirmation dialog should be carefully examined to confirm the order details. But high-frequency day traders, also called *pattern day traders*, often suppress the order confirmation dialog in order to expedite the submission of their trades to the market. They want their orders to enter the market as quickly as possible. And they use a series of bracketed order templates with limit orders, protective stops, and limit profit targets that permit them to scan stock charts and enter their trades with a single mouse click. Speed is essential, particularly on stocks with fast-moving price levels. They do not want to wait for the order confirmation dialog and miss an opportunity to quickly *scalp* a fast price move for a quick profit.

But most swing traders who may make two or three trades each morning to perhaps a dozen or more a week usually check their trade setups on an order confirmation dialog before submitting their trades. Swing traders got their name because they take advantage of price swings in underlying securities.

Examine the information provided in the order confirmation dialog shown in Figure 4.8. Look at each of these lines, beginning with the top line and working your way down. As you can see, this information,

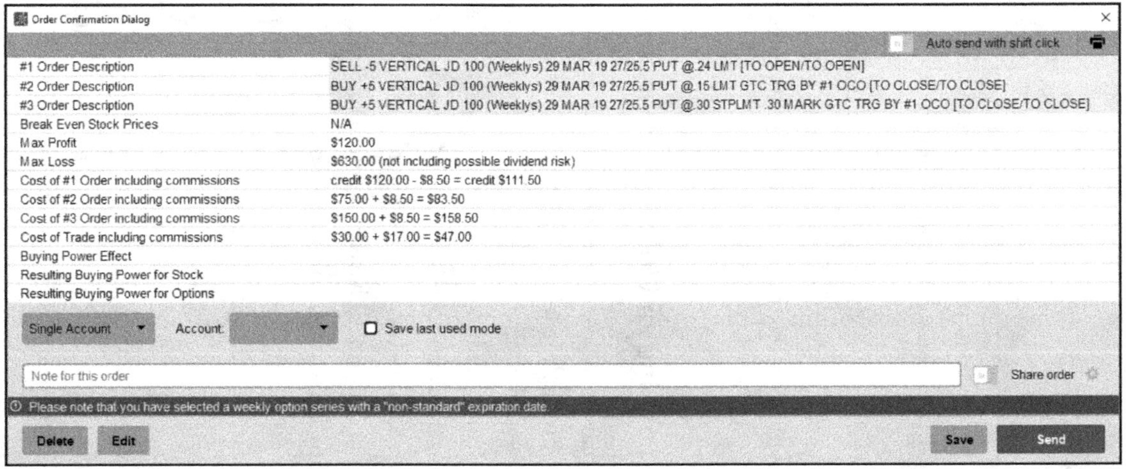

Order Confirmation Dialog		× ⬚
		⬚ Auto send with shift click
#1 Order Description	SELL -5 VERTICAL JD 100 (Weeklys) 29 MAR 19 27/26.5 PUT @ 24 LMT [TO OPEN/TO OPEN]	
#2 Order Description	BUY +5 VERTICAL JD 100 (Weeklys) 29 MAR 19 27/26.5 PUT @ 16 LMT GTC TRG BY #1 OCO [TO CLOSE/TO CLOSE]	
#3 Order Description	BUY +5 VERTICAL JD 100 (Weeklys) 29 MAR 19 27/26.5 PUT @ 30 STPLMT 30 MARK GTC TRG BY #1 OCO [TO CLOSE/TO CLOSE]	
Break Even Stock Prices	N/A	
Max Profit	$120.00	
Max Loss	$630.00 (not including possible dividend risk)	
Cost of #1 Order including commissions	credit $120.00 - $8.50 = credit $111.50	
Cost of #2 Order including commissions	$75.00 + $8.50 = $83.50	
Cost of #3 Order including commissions	$150.00 + $8.50 = $158.50	
Cost of Trade including commissions	$30.00 + $17.00 = $47.00	
Buying Power Effect		
Resulting Buying Power for Stock		
Resulting Buying Power for Options		
Single Account ▾ Account ▾	⬚ Save last used mode	
Note for this order		⬚ Share order ⚙
ⓘ Please note that you have selected a weekly option series with a "non-standard" expiration date.		
Delete Edit		Save Send

Figure 4.8 An order confirmation dialog

especially the potential profit to loss, or reward-to-risk ratio, is not particularly attractive. If the trader permits this bull put vertical spread to expire in the money, the trader would have to pay $25 per share for 500 shares of JD stock, a total of $12,500 plus commissions less the initial $120 premium credit received when the trade was filled. Once the stock is put to the trader, it can be sold to recover all but $630.00—a benefit provided by a vertical spread. Or the trader could keep and use the stock with a series of covered call options.

Finally, most traders look for much lower reward-to-risk ratios than the one displayed in the order confirmation dialog. The $120 max profit is only 19.04 percent of the max loss. Probably not an acceptable ratio unless the odds are extremely favorable for the short put to remain OTM through expiration.

#1 Order Description: The trade description including the strategy, strikes, and expiration

#2 Order Description: The trade description of the limit profit order that closes the vertical spread for $0.15 per share

#3 Order Description: The trade description of the protective limit stop order that is triggered if the premium (Mark) value breaches 30 cents

Break Even on Stock Prices: This line usually displays the stock price required to achieve breakeven, which is usually displayed when the strikes can be calculated

Max Profit: The maximum profit potential

Max Loss: The maximum loss potential excluding dividends when the stock is owned

Cost of Trade including commissions: The debit or credit paid or received when this trade is filled

Buying Power Effect: The reduction in available margin used when this trade is filled

Resulting Buying Power for Stock: The residual stock buying power in the trader's account

Resulting Buying Power for Options: The residual option buying power in the trader's account

Single Account/Account: Trader's account number(s); choose from a drop-down list

Delete/Edit: Delete the order or edit the order

Adding and Removing Option Chain Columns

Most full-featured trading applications, or *trading platforms*, include option chains, price charts, and watch lists. Some even include stock and option scanners. These scanners permit traders to set up search parameters to find and list ticker symbols that meet established parameters such as average daily trading volumes, the low-to-high price range, current volatility levels, current price trends, and so on. Some traders also include one or more oversold or overbought ranges using one of several available momentum oscillators that are often used on price charts. Three examples of popular momentum oscillators are the relative strength index (RSI), commodity channel index (CCI), and the moving average convergence/divergence (MACD). These and others, such as one of a few stochastic oscillators, are frequently viewed on price charts by technical analysts.

Regardless of how an option trader scans for his or her stock picks, once the stock is viewed on the option chain, the trader uses the information on the option chain to decide on the structure and placement of an option trade. This includes the selection of a bullish, neutral, or bearish strategy, the strike price(s), and one or more option expiration dates. For example, when a trader is bullish and buys a call on a stock trending upward, a long-term option contract is used to give the stock's price ample time to increase in value. Or, if selling an OTM put contract for a credit, the trader collects premium from the sale of the option. If the option remains safely OTM, the trader can either close the trade within a few weeks for a profit or let it expire worthless for 100 percent profit. When short options are permitted to expire OTM and worthless, the trader is not required to pay a trading commission or option exchange fees.

Examine Figure 4.9, which illustrates a typical option chain customization dialog. Notice there is a long list of available columns on the left-hand side of the dialog, while only six columns are used.

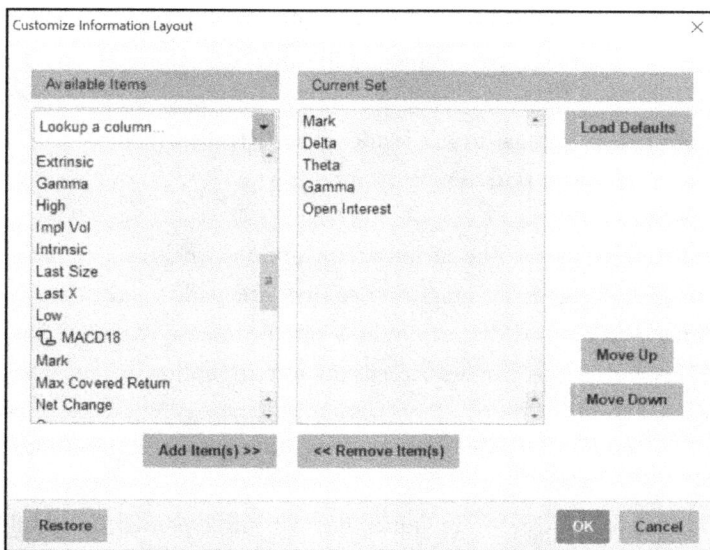

Figure 4.9 Adding/removing option chain columns

©2019 TD Ameritrade IP Company, Inc. For illustrative purposes only.

Strikes: 60			PUTS				
Strike	Bid X	Ask X	Mark	Delta	Theta	Gamma	Open...
							20.00% (±153.235)
6890	35.90 X	38.00 X	36.950	-.29	-4.78	.00	77
6900	38.30 X	40.30 X	39.300	-.30	-4.84	.00	765
6910	40.70 X	42.80 X	41.750	-.32	-4.89	.00	10
6920	43.30 X	45.50 X	44.400	-.34	-4.94	.00	38
6925	44.50 X	46.80 X	45.650	-.35	-4.94	.00	48
6930	45.90 X	48.20 X	47.050	-.36	-4.96	.00	44
6940	48.80 X	51.20 X	50.000	-.37	-4.98	.00	14
6950	51.90 X	54.20 X	53.050	-.39	-4.98	.00	155
6960	55.10 X	57.50 X	56.300	-.41	-4.97	.00	8
6970	58.20 X	61.00 X	59.600	-.43	-4.94	.00	22
6975	60.10 X	62.80 X	61.450	-.44	-4.93	.00	46
6980	61.70 X	65.10 X	63.400	-.46	-4.92	.00	21
6990	65.50 X	69.00 X	67.250	-.48	-4.87	.00	57
7000	69.60 H	73.00 X	71.300	-.50	-4.80	.00	605
7010	73.70 X	77.20 X	75.450	-.52	-4.70	.00	29

Figure 4.10 The put side of an option chain with seven column headings

©2019 TD Ameritrade IP Company, Inc. For illustrative purposes only.

Figure 4.10 shows the seven selected column headings on the put side of an option chain. Using too many columns creates unnecessary clutter. Therefore, many traders rarely use more than five or six columns on each side of the central strike column unless using a large wide-screen monitor. But there are times when we want to check one or more specific values, such as the Extrinsic (time) value remaining in an in the money short option. Adding the current Mark and Extrinsic value provides the cost to exercise the selected strike, plus commissions. Adding the Extrinsic and Intrinsic values is equal to the Mark value. (Recall that the Mark is the premium value that traders pay for options when bought or collect when an option is sold.)

This is frequently true of long-term options, such as a LEAPS options. (LEAPS stands for long-term equity anticipation securities, which are long-term options that expire in 1 year or more). When the sum of the Mark and Intrinsic values exceeds the amount option buyers must pay to exercise an in the money short option, the trade is rejected to prevent the buyer from losing money by spending more money than the option is worth. As the option approaches expiration and/or it moves deeper in the money, however, it becomes vulnerable to being exercised. So checking the Extrinsic value of a short option can be important.

In addition to extrinsic value, there is also intrinsic value. The sum of the Extrinsic and Intrinsic values is equal to the Mark (or premium) value of each option.

The analysis of the underlying stock is enhanced by examining additional values provided on its option chains. Most option chains provide a customization feature in the form of a shortcut or drop-down menu that lists available columns. In addition to an option chain's default values that include the Strike prices and the corresponding Bid and Ask columns, the customization menu lists several column headings that are easily added or removed with a few mouse clicks.

Adjusting the Number of Strike Rows

You can expand or reduce the number of displayed strikes by selecting a number from the Strike drop down, typing a number, such as 40 to show 20 strikes above and below the ATM strike, or select ALL to examine all available strike prices. Displaying ALL can be in the hundreds, especially for financial index options such as the S&P 500 (symbol SPX) or the Nasdaq 100 (symbol NDX). However, if trading within 10 or 20 strikes of the ATM price, you may want to display 40 or 50 strikes to eliminate the extra time required to scroll up and down.

Bid, Ask, and Mark

The width between the Bid and Ask price values is typically narrow on stocks with high trading volumes, and wide on stocks with low trading volumes. This is a good sign of liquidity. When trading volume is strong, trade orders tend to fill rapidly. And the narrow Bid-to-Ask price range of a heavily traded stock or index also helps to fill a trade because traders are more willing to give up a few pennies to fill a trade than to adjust their sell (Bid) or buy (Ask) prices by 10 or more cents per share to fill an order.

Wide Bid-to-Ask spreads create what is referred to as *slippage*. Slippage occurs when traders are required to slide their price up or down to finally get their trades to fill. Every experienced trader has experienced "chasing" a trade by moving a Bid or Ask price up or down to get their opening and exiting orders to fill. Of course, it's more important to close a losing trade to cut off a major loss than to open a trade.

Open Interest (Liquidity)

Open Interest is another option chain column that experienced option traders examine. Open Interest values are an important indication of liquidity. It shows the number of working trades at each strike price. High Open Interest values encourage trade entry because it indicates strong interest in the selected equity and in one or more specific strike prices. There are two Open Interest "rules of thumb" you should consider.

One- or two-strike option strategies: (10 × the number of contracts). This suggests we should use 10 × the number of contracts when trading one- or two-strike option strategies.

Examples
  Selling a cash covered put
  Buying an ATM or slightly OTM long call
  Selling an OTM put and buying an OTM put below (the bull put
    vertical spread)
  Buying an ATM call and selling an OTM call above (the bull call
    vertical spread)

Open Interest Value(s)

Example: Five contracts require an Open Interest value of 50; there should also be a few thousand in total Open Interest above, below, and on the opposite side of the option chain.

Three- or four-strike option strategies: (Open Interest of 300 at each selected strike price)

Examples: (+1 = buy one; −2 = sell 2)

Long call butterfly: +1 ATM call, −2 calls 1 strike above, +1 call 1 strike above

Iron condor: −1 OTM put, +1 OTM 2 strikes below; −1 OTM call, +1 OTM call 2 strikes above

There should also be at least 5,000 in total Open Interest above, below, and on the opposite side of the option chain.

Avoid the use of strikes that have small Open Interest values.

The "Greeks" (Gamma, Delta, Theta, Vega, Rho)

The Greeks were briefly introduced in Chapter 2 and described in Table 2.1. Here, we look at them again in substantially more detail. Although Rho can be impactual on option premium values, causing premium values to increase in value faster owing to the "cost of money," traders rarely look at this *Greek* or display it on their option chains owing to currently low interest rates. Rho has not been impactual on premium prices for some time. In any case, each of the *Greek* values mentioned earlier is described in the narratives that follow.

Gamma

Figure 4.11 illustrates how the amount of time remaining until expiration influences the value of Gamma.

To further clarify the impact of Gamma, a Gamma value of .04 changes Delta's value by .04 for each one dollar move in the underlying security, such as a stock. Because there are many factors that influence option pricing, calculations are codependent. Changes in Vega and Theta also influence the value of Gamma and its Delta derivative.

Mark	Delta	Gamma	Strike
▾ NOV4 15	**(10)**	**100 (Weeklys)**	
4.700	.79	.05	110
3.900	.73	.06	111
3.100	.67	.08	112
2.395	.60	.08	113
1.780	.51	.09	114
1.265	.42	.09	115
.845	.32	.09	116
.535	.24	.08	117
▾ DEC1 15	**(17)**	**100 (Weeklys)**	
5.200	.73	.05	110
4.425	.69	.05	111
3.700	.63	.06	112
3.025	.58	.06	113
2.430	.51	.07	114
1.900	.44	.07	115
1.455	.38	.07	116
1.080	.31	.06	117
▾ DEC2 15	**(24)**	**100 (Weeklys)**	
5.575	.70	.04	110
4.825	.66	.05	111
4.150	.62	.05	112
3.500	.57	.05	113
2.920	.51	.05	114
2.405	.46	.06	115
1.940	.40	.05	116

Figure 4.11 Gamma values with 10, 17, and 24 days remaining till expiration

©2019 TD Ameritrade IP Company, Inc. For illustrative purposes only.

Gamma values are positive and negative depending on where they are found on an option chain. For example, long calls, puts, and debit spreads have positive Gamma values. Short calls, puts, and credit spreads have negative Gamma values.

There is a Gamma-Delta-neutral option spread that uses both Delta and Gamma values to determine the number of long and short contracts required to set up the trade. A third leg used in this strategy involves shorting the underlying stock to achieve neutrality among the three legs of the spread. Each share of stock has a Delta value of 1.0—a fact that is used in the Gamma-Delta neutral spread. Each share of a shorted stock has a Delta value of −1.0. Strike prices of deep in the money puts can have Delta values of −1.0. Deep in the money calls can have Delta values of +1.0.

Delta

Delta measures the directional risk present in every option strategy. As you may recall from Chapter 2, Delta values at strike prices closest to the price of the underlying (the at the money strike price) is typically at or quite close to 0.5. The value of Gamma is the highest at this strike price. Figure 4.11 shows the Delta and Gamma values of a series of near-the-money call options that are within 10 days of option expiration.

The Delta values of call and put options change from positive to negative depending on whether the options are bought or sold. Table 4.1 shows how the value of Delta responds to buying and selling.

Table 4.1 Polarity of long and short options

Option types	Buy (+)	Sell (−)
Calls	Positive	Negative
Puts	Negative	Positive

There are some option trades that are referred to as being "Delta neutral." This happens when the Delta values of a long call and a long put are identical; hence, the sum of the two Delta values is zero, referred to as being *Delta neutral.*

Vega (Volatility)

Of all the Greeks, Vega has the greatest impact on premium values, and this makes sense because it measures current volatility—the measure of current buying and selling volumes. The value of Vega increases as volatility increases and declines as volatility decreases. Vega is tied directly to the current volatility of the underlying optionable security. Recall from the previous chapter how the Vega responds to a 1 percent change in the volatility of the underlying security. Here's an example of how Vega influences premium values.

- At a certain strike price, the current premium value is $1.50 and Vega is .20.
- The volatility of the underlying security increases by 1 percent.

- The current .20 Vega is multiplied by $1.50 + 0.20 = $1.70.
- A 1 percent reduction in volatility would reduce the premium value from $1.50 − (1 × 0.20) = $1.30.

Vega values displayed on option chains are always positive. Certain spreads can produce net negative Vega values. One example is when a trader buys near-the-money option contracts with a 4.5 Vega and sells OTM option contracts with an 8.5 Vega value. Summing the short 8.5 Vega and the long 4.5 Vega produces −4.0 Vegas.

Option traders look upon Vega as a measure of risk or reward resulting from changes in volatility. A trader's bias and the option strategy the trader uses are most often based on current volatility. Premiums are high when implied volatility is high—a good time to sell options for income. Option premiums are cheaper when implied (current) volatility is unusually low—the best time to consider buying options while they are cheap.

Looking at several option chains quickly reveals how the value of Vega increases with the extension of time. More distant expiration dates have higher Vega values than those on options that are approaching their expiration dates. In addition, Vega is also highest at those strike prices closest to the money. Look at the Vega values in Figure 4.12. Notice how the values of Vega increase relative to the time remaining till expiration and decrease as the strikes move farther OTM.

Theta (Time Value)

The *Greek* Theta on an option chain and the amount of time remaining in the underlying contract are tightly coupled. The value of Theta tells option traders how much premium value is exiting with the passage of each day. When Theta values are plotted on a graph with 90 days until expiration, the plot begins with a slight downward slope. When it reaches 30 days till expiration, the slope begins to turn downward quite rapidly. Figure 4.13 illustrates the slope of Theta from 90 days through expiration.

Notice how the value of Theta increases as the contract approaches expiration in Figure 4.14. The value exiting each of the four option chains increases with the passage of time. With nine days remaining, Theta tells us how the premium value is exiting at a rate of $0.07 cents per share

MSFT ▸ | MICROSOFT CORP COM 92.65 | ⌂ Company Profile

▾ Underlying

Last X	Net Chng	Open	High	Low
92.65 D	-1.95	93.74	93.90	92.42

▾ Option Chain | Filter: Off | Spread: Single | Layout: Mark, D...

	CALLS			Strike	PUTS			
Mark	Delta	Theta	Vega	Strike	Mark	Delta	Theta	Vega
▾ 29 MAR 18 (10) 100 (Weeklys)								24.69% (±3.155)
2.555	.67	-.07	.06	91	.790	-.32	-.06	.06
2.210	.62	-.07	.06	91.5	.935	-.37	-.06	.06
1.865	.57	-.07	.06	92	1.115	-.42	-.06	.06
1.575	.52	-.07	.06	92.5	1.335	-.48	-.06	.06
1.310	.47	-.07	.06	93	1.565	-.53	-.06	.06
1.080	.41	-.06	.06	93.5	1.830	-.59	-.06	.06
.885	.36	-.06	.06	94	2.125	-.65	-.06	.06
.715	.31	-.06	.06	94.5	2.455	-.71	-.05	.06
▾ 6 APR 18 (18) 100 (Weeklys)								23.07% (±3.884)
2.875	.64	-.05	.08	91	1.080	-.35	-.04	.08
2.520	.60	-.05	.08	91.5	1.230	-.39	-.04	.08
2.240	.56	-.05	.08	92	1.435	-.43	-.05	.08
1.950	.52	-.05	.08	92.5	1.630	-.48	-.04	.08
1.685	.48	-.05	.08	93	1.865	-.53	-.04	.08
1.450	.43	-.05	.08	93.5	2.125	-.57	-.04	.08
1.235	.39	-.05	.08	94	2.410	-.62	-.04	.08
1.040	.35	-.04	.08	94.5	2.715	-.67	-.04	.08
▾ 13 APR 18 (25) 100 (Weeklys)								21.44% (±4.226)
3.150	.62	-.04	.09	91	1.305	-.36	-.04	.09
2.760	.59	-.04	.10	91.5	1.500	-.40	-.04	.10
2.495	.56	-.04	.10	92	1.685	-.44	-.04	.10
2.200	.52	-.04	.10	92.5	1.890	-.48	-.04	.10
2.010	.48	-.04	.10	93	2.125	-.52	-.04	.10
1.765	.45	-.04	.10	93.5	2.390	-.56	-.04	.10
1.515	.41	-.04	.10	94	2.705	-.60	-.04	.10
1.310	.37	-.04	.09	94.5	2.955	-.65	-.03	.09

Figure 4.12 How time and position influence the values of Vega

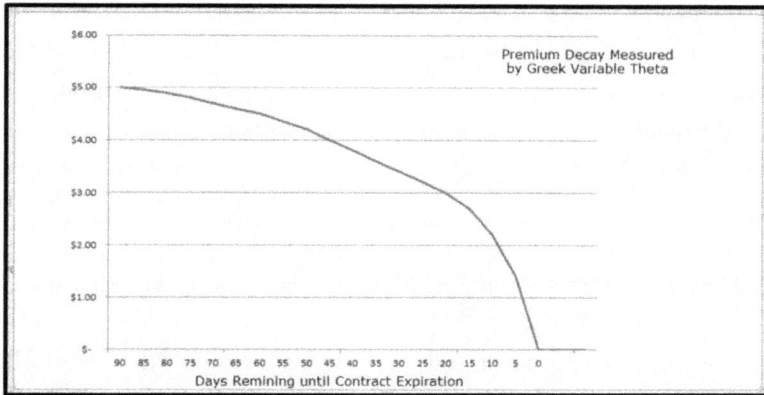

Figure 4.13 Premium declining over time as measured by Theta

©2019 TD Ameritrade IP Company, Inc. For illustrative purposes only.

Figure 4.14 Theta values at four different contract expiration dates

©2019 TD Ameritrade IP Company, Inc. For illustrative purposes only.

per day, or $7.00 per day for each 100-share contract. With 149 days remaining, Theta is only –.03, the premium value is exiting at a rate of $3.00 per day per contract.

Theta is both useful and easy to read. Option buyers pay close attention to the value of Theta. When the daily depreciation begins to signal an unacceptable loss, a buyer will enter a sell to close order in an attempt to recover what premium value may remain. Of course, it's possible to wait too long to close a trade that's soured, because nobody will want to trade chairs and take your seat. When this happens, the only benefit may be a tax write-down.

The seller on the opposite side of the same contract benefits from the rising value of Theta as the contract approaches expiration. This gives the seller several choices:

1. Let the contract expire worthless, and keep all of the original premium as profit.
2. Buy to close by paying substantially less premium than originally received.
3. Wait a little longer to exit for even more profit.
4. Roll the position to a later expiration date for additional premium income. This requires the strike price to remain far enough OTM to return an acceptable premium value.

Rho (Rate of Interest)

Rho measures each option's sensitivity to changes in current interest rates. Like Vega, interest rate changes impact longer-term options that expire in several months much more than those that expire in a matter of weeks or days. Rho is positive for long calls as higher interest rates increase the premium values of calls. Rho is negative for long puts; high interest rates decrease put premiums. (Recall that the Mark value at each strike is the premium value.)

Rho (the rate of interest) impacts premium values because it impacts the cost of carrying a trade over time. In this respect, Rho is similar to Vega. As mentioned in the preceding paragraph, increases in Rho (higher interest rates) impact longer-term options much more than short-term options. Interest rates are used in the underlying option pricing models that calculate option premium values. The pricing formulas consider option prices based on what is referred to as the "hedged value."

A "hedge" example is when a trader uses long or short options to hedge against a drop or rally in the price of a stock. Long put options are frequently bought to hedge (or offset) a portion of the loss in the price of the stock; long calls are used to hedge increases in short stocks values.

Rho is positive for purchased calls as higher interest rates increase call premiums. Conversely, Rho is negative for purchased puts, because an increase in the rate of interest decreases put premium values.

American and European Expiration-Style Options

Options have two expiration styles called American and European. The difference is in when an ITM option can be exercised. Most popular options are American-style. This is true for both put and call options. In the money American expiration-style options can be exercised for profit by buyers. European-style expiration options cannot be exercised prior to contract expiration. In fact, European-style options are automatically exercised if the option seller permits them to expire in the money. When an option seller permits his/her short options to expire in the money, the Extrinsic (time) value is completely depleted. Unless the option's buyer notifies his or her brokerage to withhold exercise privileges, the ITM short call or put options are auto-exercised by the OCC when the options are in the money by just one penny.

Exercising Options, Assigning Options, and the Function of the OCC

The Options Clearing Corporation (OCC) is responsible for clearing all option contracts that expire in the money by one penny. As mentioned in the previous paragraph, a buyer may be required to pay commissions and exchange fees that exceed his or her profit potential that may be in the pennies. When this is the case, the option buyer can notify the brokerage to withhold his or her exercise privilege to cancel an unwanted stock assignment transaction. Another important OCC function is to set and maintain option expiration schedules. Although the Chicago Board of Options Exchange (CBOE) produces options and calculates their values, the OCC is responsible for option expiration schedules.

Call Option Buyers and Sellers

When short calls are either exercised prior to expiration or permitted to expire in the money, the call option sellers are required to deliver the optioned stock to the call option buyers. In exchange, the buyers are required to pay for the stock at the option's strike price. For example, if a $50 stock option expires at $53, the option is $3.00 in the money. The buyer can pay $50 per share for the stock plus commissions. The stock is worth $53 per share. This is a $3.00 per share or $300 per option contract profit less trading overhead.

Put Option Buyers and Sellers

When a short put is exercised or expires in the money, the buyer delivers the stock to the seller, who must pay for the stock at the put option's strike price. An example of this exchange would be for the buyer and seller to trade a $55 stock option. The stock drops to $50 per share, and the buyer exercises the option on the last day of the option contract prior to market close. The buyer delivers the stock that's now worth $50 per share to the seller, who pays the buyer $55 per share for the $50 stock. The buyer earns $5 per share in profit, or about $500 per contract, less transaction costs. Because the Extrinsic (time) value is only a few pennies a share (the time till expiration is only a matter of an hour or two) the transaction fees are likely to be around $20. If the exchange includes five contracts, the buyer will earn nearly $2,500.

Option Strategy Selection and Terminology

The flexibility of options provides a broad and diverse range of trading strategies. All include buying, selling, or, more often than not, a combination of buying and selling as in vertical spreads. Option trades can include one to four strikes, call options, put options, or a combination of call and put options. They can also include one or more expiration dates. And some even include shares of stock.

Although there are descriptive names for most common options strategies, there are several names that are nonsensical, as, for instance, *Jade Lizards, Twisted Sisters, Iron Condors*, and some others. As you can see in Figures 5.9 and 6.27, the iron condor's risk profile (or risk graph) resembles a big bird with a large square body between the short put and call strikes, which are represented by two wings that drop below the zero axis on the x–y plot. It's likely that someone described the plot lines as a condor. The twisted sister is an iron condor without the usual OTM long call, and the jade lizard is an iron condor without the usual OTM long put. Risk profiles are described and illustrated in Chapter 6.

When either buying or selling options, you now know that traders always look for *liquidity*. This is seen in the trading volume of the underlying stock, as well as in the Open Interest values shown on option chains. Liquidity is extremely important when either entering or closing any kind of trade. We want demand for options that are either bought or sold. And, of course, it's more important to be able to close your options either for profit or to limit your losses than it is to fill opening orders. So *always* watch the Open Interest values. (More about this in the trading rules in Chapter 5. Open Interest values were also discussed earlier in this chapter.)

When selling call or put options, option traders consider several things. In addition to examining the underlying price charts in order to develop a trading bias—bullish, neutral, or bearish—traders also look at the amount of time remaining until expiration, current volatility, the Delta values, and, of course, the Mark values and the Bid-to-Ask spread widths. All of these and more are described in detail in Chapter 5's trading rules. But as you know from earlier narratives in this book, option traders *do not* want their short puts or calls to become in the money. Therefore, they sell their calls and puts at strikes they believe will remain OTM throughout the life of the trade. They choose option expiration dates to limit the amount of time the market has to move against their trade. Both require traders to settle for a few dollars less in premium in order to limit their risk. On the other hand, they choose stocks that currently have relatively high IV% values that are either at or exceed 40 percent. As you probably know by now, higher IV% values boost premium values, which is better for option sellers. These and several other factors give option traders an edge because they increase their probability of achieving successful trade outcomes.

In contrast, when they buy call or put options, option traders must be confident in their trading biases. They vet the underlying stock by examining the price charts over several different time intervals, that is, 3 years, 1 year, 1 or 2 hours, and perhaps 5 minutes. (Day traders may look at even lower time intervals, including tick charts that display a "candle" for each 10 to 50 trades.) When buying calls, most option traders choose stocks having upward trending prices, typically off historical support levels. (Recall the demand and support zones described in Chapter 3.) When buying puts, they consider stocks with prices trending downward off supply levels. And they choose longer contract terms that typically exceed 90 days till expiration. Some choose LEAPS options that expire in one or more years. Some who buy LEAPS options may also examine underlying fundamentals just as a buy-and-hold stock trader would.

The added time increases the option's *extrinsic values*, making them more costly when traded. But if the trader's bias is correct, the return can be enormous. In fact, trades that buy at the money calls and sell at the money puts, called a *synthetic long stock*, are very popular, because the premium paid for the long calls is offset by the premium credit received from the short puts. If the underlying rallies according to the trader's strong bullish bias, this trade can return an enormous profit. (Note that the term *synthetic* is used when one equity type is used to simulate another. In the synthetic long stock strategy, options are used to simulate the purchase of a long stock.) Entering this option strategy is relatively inexpensive. But the trader *must* be right in his or her bullish bias to achieve a successful outcome; otherwise, this trade can lead to a substantial loss.

When buying calls and puts, we want current volatility levels to be low—such as when the implied volatility percentage displayed on the option chain is at or below 15 percent. This reduces the premium values paid, making buying the calls or puts cheaper. When low volatility returns to historical levels, the premiums rise in value. Hence, the trader may sell the calls or puts for a profit. Giving the trade more time for an increase in volatility can certainly help.

Chapter 5 discusses these and other trading analytics, that is, common-sense trading rules that option traders use to enhance the probability of achieving successful trading outcomes.

Caution: Never Slide Protective Stops to Save a Bad Trade!

Most experienced traders know *never* to slide a protective stop that would potentially increase their losses. Veteran traders carefully choose their protective stop values on the basis of what they are willing to lose. But inexperienced amateurs often think a price move against them is temporary. They convince themselves that the move against them will reverse direction. But the market doesn't care. Realistically, that reversal may never occur. This can be devastating, and it happens every day! Experienced traders simply "take their medicine." They calculate the value of their stops to be affordable. And although their rules-based trades are usually successful, they also know that there will always be a few losing trades along the way. Stand on 18 in blackjack, because you'll usually win.

If your trading rules average seven winners out of every 10 trades, then a losing trade means your next trade has 7-in-2 odds for a successful outcome. Sliding stops based on hope is rarely rewarded. In fact, some traders have blown out their entire accounts because they hoped an unwanted price move would reverse direction. *Never* trade on hope, fear, or even what you hear. Trade only what you see!

CHAPTER 5

Rules-Based Trading

Option Trading Levels (Permissions)

Every brokerage has what are called *trading levels*. The levels can vary from one brokerage to another. For example, some use three levels, while others use four and even five. In this discussion, we examine four levels.

Option levels are used to protect trader accounts, but they protect the brokerage too. If a trader experiences a massive loss that exceeds his or her account value, the brokerage is stuck with the bill, because the brokerage is ultimately responsible for settling the transaction. This is why every brokerage has an active risk department, where risk managers monitor every client account and the risk of their trades. And brokerages have buffering rules, which limit the amount of money their clients are allowed to put at risk.

One buffer is the value assigned to shares of stock held within a trader's account. It's typical for a brokerage to permit traders to access 50 percent of the value of stocks and exchange-traded funds (ETFs) held within their account for buying or selling equities. For example, $5,000 worth of account equity (or margin) may be used to finance a trade when $10,000 worth of "big board" stock is deposited within his or her brokerage account.

As the option trading levels increase, the traders are permitted to use option strategies that carry higher risk. Hence, when a trader is granted level 2 trading permissions, the option strategies that are included in both levels 1 and 2 are permitted. Similarly, level 3 adds more strategies, such as vertical spreads that include short puts or short calls that carry more risk than those strategies permitted in levels 1 and 2.

Some people decide they can manage their retirement accounts better than the responsible fund managers. They are convinced that they can achieve a better return on their investments by picking their own stocks and ETFs and perhaps by trading options within a brokerage account. This is why millions of traders actively manage rollover IRA accounts held within brokerages. However, U.S. Security and Exchange Commission (SEC) rules disallow unlimited risk option trades to occur within a qualified retirement account. An example would be an option trade that includes an uncovered short call. However, dozens of option strategies are permitted, including covered calls, vertical put and call spreads, and long calls and puts. This includes the popular iron condor strategy, which is prominently described in this book. The synthetic long stock combination strategy described in a hands-on activity in Chapter 6 can also be traded in a rollover IRA account.

Option Level 1

This is the lowest option trading level. It includes *defined-risk* strategies such as covered calls and cash-secured put option trades. In both cases, if the trades achieve their largest possible loss, the trader must have sufficient equity in his or her margin account to cover the entire cost of the trade. These option trades do not add risk to the brokerage. Covered calls, for example, are short options that are covered (or protected) by the stock a trader owns. Cash-secured puts are covered by the cash the trader holds within his or her margin account.

Option Level 2

This level permits option traders who have some options trading knowledge and/or experience to add the purchase of call and put options. Long calls and puts do not require the use of account margin, although they can certainly lose money. Long calls and puts lose when the trader's bias is wrong. And if the underlying price doesn't change, time decay, especially as the long option contracts approach expiration, can erode premium values to zero. Hence, long puts and long calls require the underlying security to either rally (calls) or drop (puts) to succeed.

Option Level 3

This level adds a whole new universe of trades, including spreads. Recall the vertical spread strategies briefly introduced in Chapter 2. The Buying and Selling Put and Call Spreads paragraph introduced these and mentioned their popularity.

More examples of both put and call spreads are included in Chapter 6. As you will see, these spreads are risk-defined option strategies, which makes them extremely popular. But they can be overtraded when too many contracts are used. Also know that the risk-defined trades that are permitted by level 3 traders prevent traders from exceeding the total value of their account holdings. However, because level 3 trades include either short calls or short puts, it's possible to exceed allowable account margin levels from an unwanted move in the price of the underlying security. The added risk can exceed the brokerage's margin allowance. Because only 50 percent of the stock values held in the trader's margin account is available, it's quite possible to trigger a margin call or even an SEC Regulation T call.

Note that trading platforms can *beta weight* the current use of account margin against the S&P 500 index. A good trading platform can even beta weight simulated trades. This permits a knowledgeable trader to examine his or her margin allowance before making a defective trade.

This is also how brokerages monitor each trader's margin allowance. Brokerages use the S&P 500 index value and the current volatility rate to measure margin risk. For example, one popular brokerage does not permit clients to exceed 100 percent of their account values at 12 percent above or below the S&P 500 index value or to exceed 200 percent of the account value at 20 percent above or below the S&P 500 index value.

Option Level 4

This is frequently the highest option trading level, although a few brokerages offer five levels. The highest level requires the option traders to have several years of trading experience and/or to pass an options trading test. This level permits traders to enter strategies with undefined risk; in other words, strategies that could potentially lose a trader's entire holdings in addition to causing the brokerage to suffer a financial loss.

Trades that can lose massive amounts of money include short calls, short puts, or both. If either a short call or put on an expensive stock or a financial index becomes deep in the money (ITM) and is either exercised or permitted to expire ITM without being closed or rolled, the trader could potentially lose millions of dollars. This is why the brokerage (and SEC) require option traders to understand the risk that corresponds to short option positions. In addition, the leveraged account margin *must* be carefully monitored in order to close a threatened trade before an excessive loss becomes a reality.

Although these short option strategies carry substantial risk, they can be extremely profitable for traders who know how to trade them. This includes choosing far out of the money (OTM) strikes that have extremely low probabilities of becoming ITM and that expire within a matter of days to perhaps a week or two. Many traders thrive on short calls and puts, but they *must be* carefully monitored. And, as traders who hold the highest option trading permissions know, short (uncovered) calls are more dangerous than short cash-covered puts because the calls can exist at strikes that are hundreds of dollars higher than the OTM puts, which increases risk.

The S&P Volatility Index: Symbol VIX

The S&P 500 index includes the top 500 company stocks in the nation. It has greater following than the other equity indexes such as the Dow Jones Industrial Average and the NASDAQ Composite index and is considered to be the best representation of the health of the US stock market. This is because the S&P 500 has a highly diverse constituency and valuation weighting methodology. Hence, the S&P 500 is used by brokerages to *beta weight* the holdings within brokerage accounts relative to the current volatility of the S&P index.

The Chicago Board Options Exchange (CBOE) manages the S&P 500 volatility index, which measures current trading volume and direction—the measure of the overall price fluctuations of the 500 constituent equities within the index. When the VIX is in the low teens, trades carry considerably less risk than when VIX value begins to exceed 20. In fact, when the VIX rises beyond the mid 20's, many traders who frequently sell short puts and calls retreat to the sidelines until the VIX value drops back to more normal values in the mid-to-low teens.

Many option traders buy and sell VIX calls and puts depending on their bullish or bearish bias. When the VIX moves into the low teens, some option traders buy long-term calls. Their plan is to sell them when the VIX rises to the mid-twenties or thirties for a profit. When the VIX begins to drop from the low thirties or high twenties, traders may decide to buy long-term puts and wait for the VIX to retreat to the teens, at which time they buy to close their VIX put options for profit. In spite of the trader's style, symbol selection, and favorite options strategies, experienced traders use the rules-based trading setups described in this book.

Standard Margin

Most brokerages offer margin accounts that permit traders to use their deposits in cash and the value of equities held in their accounts as collateral when buying or selling securities, including stocks, options, futures, and foreign exchange pairs. Before margin accounts became popular, traders had what were called "type 1" accounts, in which their cash and securities, such as shares of stock, were held. However, if a trader wanted to sell one stock and use the proceeds of the sale to buy a different stock, they had to wait for the stock sale to settle before they could buy the second stock. Because it typically took three days for the stock sale to settle, the trader had to wait till the cash was available before they could purchase the second stock. After three days, the price of the second stock could have rallied by several dollars per share, causing the trader to suffer a loss or simply give up. This often meant the trader had to wait on the sidelines for a different buying opportunity to materialize.

Today's margin accounts coupled to rapid electronic communications networks permit traders to sell one stock and use the proceeds to buy a second stock within a matter of seconds. The underlying value of the margin account, which includes the credit from a recent stock sale, serves as collateral for the second trade. As already noted, standard margin accounts typically permit the account owner to collateralize 50 percent of the value of their big board stocks, where big board stocks are traded on a major exchange such as the New York Stock Exchange (NYSE) or the American Stock Exchange (AMEX). Recall from Chapter 3, over-the-counter, also called *penny stocks* and *pink sheet stocks,* are not eligible for use as account equity.

Some believe that being allowed to trade only 50 percent of the value of their securities is to protect the brokerage. But it also protects the trader. The 50 percent reserve prevents the account holder from losing their entire account holdings. If they lose every trade, they still have half their account holdings. So the reserve protects both the trader and the brokerage. The 50 percent held in reserve prevents traders from losing the entire value of their margin accounts. And the brokerage is rarely required to finance bad trades made by their clients.

Portfolio Margin

The SEC permits brokerages to offer what is called *portfolio margin* to experienced traders who meet account deposit minimums in the $100,000 to $125,000 range. Option traders who hold the highest trading levels, as in level 4 described early in this chapter, and who meet the minimum deposit requirements, may upgrade to a portfolio margin account. Brokerages grant portfolio margin accounts to incentivize traders to deposit and maintain a minimum amount of money in their accounts. Having portfolio margin permits traders to use 85 percent of the value of the stock and ETF equities held within their margin accounts instead of the usual 50 percent. However, if the account value falls below the minimum deposit requirement, it reverts to standard margin.

Margin Calls

If an option trader risks more money than is permitted by his or her brokerage by:

- Using excessive account margin
- Overtrading during a rise in the value of the VIX
- Having a short option that moves either too close to or ITM

the trader's brokerage will issue a *margin call*. This requires the trader to close either part or all of losing trades, to sell off shares of stock held in the margin accounts for cash in order to bring the account margin back within compliance, or as a last resort, add more funds or securities to the margin account to cover the overage.

Regulation T Calls

There are also Regulation T calls that are issued by the SEC, notifying an option trader that he or she has 10 days to settle a trade by delivering the required funds or shares of stock to one or more traders on the opposite side of a trade. Failure to settle punishes both the trader and the trader's brokerage, which receives a written reprimand from the SEC.

Setting Up and Scanning Multiple Price Charts

Regardless of the trading venue, that is, stocks, options, futures, or foreign exchange, it's useful to study multiple interval price charts to see how both historical and current prices have varied over different periods of time. Figure 5.1 illustrates a setup that displays four different time periods.

Notice the "personality" of the S&P 500 financial index. It has trended upward for the better part of 3 years (upper left-hand quadrant). It experienced a drop in value in late 2018 and recovered in early 2019. This can be seen on both the 3-year and 1-year price charts at the top of the quartile. The bottom left-hand 20-day, 1-hour candle chart shows a bottom at $2,722.27 and a recovery from Friday of the previous week and Wednesday of the current week when these charts were examined. The tick chart in the lower right-hand quadrant, which displays a candle for every 50 trades, began to trend downward at approximately 2:30 p.m. The S&P 500 index lost approximately $4.00 per share in the final 15 minutes of the trading day.

Notice how long VIX put and call options could be traded when reaching their low and high points. Because the VIX trades within a narrow range, this makes price actions reasonably predictable. Notice how the VIX remains in the midteens for long periods of time with what could be rewarding rallies and drops, as can be seen in the charts in Figure 5.2. However, the SPX financial index is not nearly as predictable, although a series of far OTM short-term puts, calls, and perhaps some short strangles could have been sold by level 4 traders for a substantial amount of weekly premium incomes. (More about this in Chapter 6.)

Price Trends

Every experienced trader looks for a sustained upward or downward price move. Trends were mentioned earlier in the preface of this book

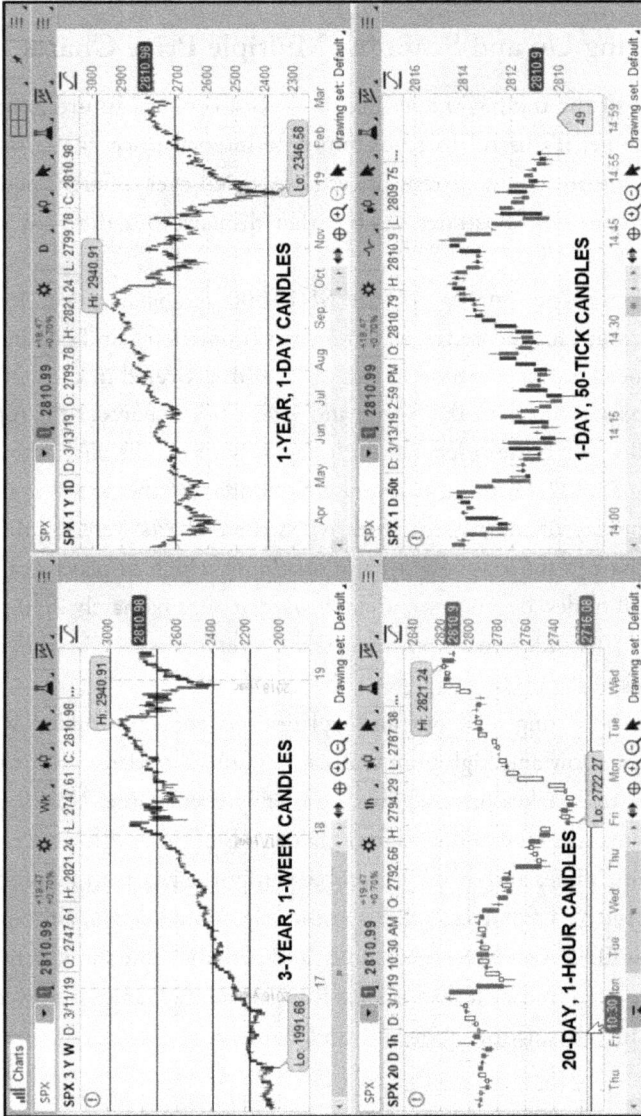

Figure 5.1 SPX price charts over four different time periods

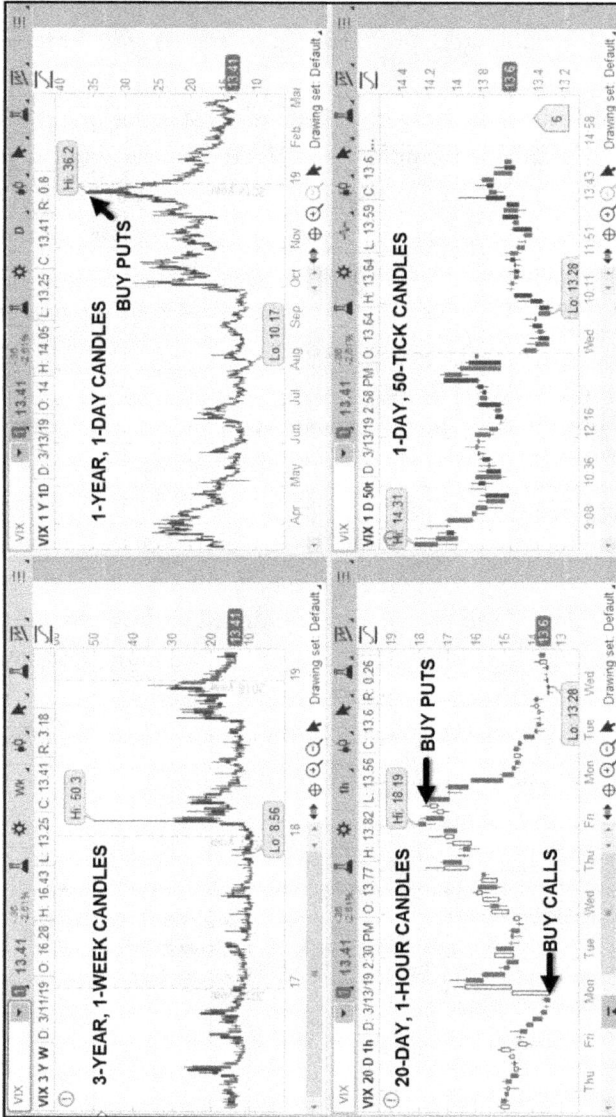

Figure 5.2 Volatility Index (VIX) price charts over the same four time periods

©2019 TD Ameritrade IP Company, Inc. For illustrative purposes only.

and again in Chapter 2. Price trends are described as a medium- to long-term series of price moves that are either predominantly upward or downward. Most traders consider a series of higher highs and higher lows to be trending upward. Traders who short stocks or buy put options look for downward-trending stock prices formed by a series of lower lows and lower highs.

Strong companies that are characterized by a series of increasing quarterly profits are good candidates to trade. The exception is when the profit takers, especially financial institutions that hold several million shares of stock, begin taking profits by dumping large quantities of shares on the market. These institutions struggle with market liquidity, because it can take several days or even weeks to exit a large position. The increase in selling creates an oversupply, drives the stock price down, and punishes those traders who also hold positions in the stock. This results in a bearish trader sentiment; individual retail traders may rush to sell, while others take advantage of the downward trend by shorting the stock, buying puts, or selling calls. When the stock hits bottom, the bulls return to buy the stock, which is now oversold and undervalued.

In spite of the sell-off, the company continued to thrive. So the price of its stock was affected by market sentiment and had nothing to do with company operations. The price trends shown in Figure 5.3 are typical. In fact, you can look at the SPX price trends in Figure 5.1 to see this sawtooth pattern, which is an accurate representation of a series of upward and downward price trends.

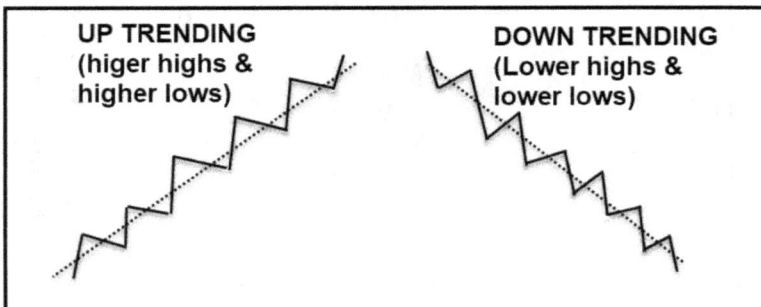

Figure 5.3 Price trends—higher highs and higher lows or lower lows and lower highs

©2019 TD Ameritrade IP Company, Inc. For illustrative purposes only.

Traders look for, trade, and profit when they find equities having sustained directional price trends. The price charts provide the keys to finding these price trends. Once the price trend is found, the corresponding option chains are used to select an appropriate option strategy—a call, a put, a vertical spread that combines a short and long put or call, and so on. And knowing where to place the trade based on the potential risk and reward is where the rules come into play. This book was written to help its readers understand and apply these time-tested rules.

Rules-Based Trading

The following is a series of option trading rules that seasoned option traders use to increase the probability of achieving successful trading outcomes. As you will see, the rules evaluate what the market is doing now as well as what is expected. But, as every trader knows all too well, the market can be fickle. So those of us who have spent several years trading the market are rarely surprised by unexpected moves. And these events can be either favorable or hurtful.

Trading rules are based on both historical and current values. The rules evaluate most of the following factors:

Long-term and current price trends (rallying, dropping, moving sideways)

Support and resistance levels (historical bottoms or tops where frequent price reversals occur)

Oversold/overbought calculations (Check momentum oscillator values; see Chapter 3.)

Daily average price movement (Examine the ATR(14) value.)

The potential for a price breakout (Examine the TTM_Squeeze on the relevant price chart.)

The current volatility level (IV%) (Compare with historical volatility [HV%] levels.)

The time till expiration (Sell inside 5 to 7 weeks; buy at or outside 90 days.)

Examine These Values on the Underlying Option Chain to Select One or More Strike Prices

Implied Volatility (IV%)

±Price Movement

Delta

Bid, Ask, and Mark

Bid-to-Ask Spread

Open interest

Theta

Vega

Selling Puts (Bullish) or Selling Calls (Bearish)

Short calls are permitted only by traders having the highest options trading permissions.

Implied volatility (IV%) (Consider IV% at or above 40 percent for acceptable premium. High IV% values increase the premium credits received by the option sellers.)

±Price Movement (The difference between the ATM strike and the selected strike of your short option should be greater than the ±price movement value.)

Time till expiration should not exceed 5 to 7 weeks. (Shorter is better to reduce risk.)

Delta at or below 0.25 (Provides a 75 percent probability of remaining OTM.)

Open Interest (2-strike trades: 10 × the number of contracts; 3+ strikes strategies: a minimum of 300 at each strike with several thousand in Open Interest at all strikes)

Theta (Theta's daily premium reduction should be sufficient to earn each short option several dollars per day.)

Vega (Mid- to high Vega values are preferred based on current high trading volume. A reduction in the value of Vega also reduces premiums, which is desirable when options are sold for credit.)

Bid–Ask spread should be relatively narrow (Narrow spreads reduce premium slippage at entry and indicate strong trading volume.)

Mark value: (Premium should be at or above 50 cents to make the risk worthwhile, although some traders accepts premium values of 30 cents.)

Buying Puts (Bearish) or Buying Calls (Bullish)

Implied Volatility (IV%) (Consider IV% at or below 20 percent in order to pay a relatively inexpensive premium debit; an increase in

IV% toward historical trading volume increases premium values. Low IV% values reduce the premium debit paid by option buyers when trading long calls and long puts.)

±Price Movement (The difference between the ATM strike and the selected strike of your long option(s) should be less than the ±price movement value except when used in a defined-risk spread and placed farther OTM as a protective long option. Vertical spreads, such as those used in an *iron condor*, are examples of these spreads. See the iron condor risk profile later and the iron condor trade example in Chapter 6.)

Time till expiration should be 90 or more days; LEAPS options that expire in a year or more are frequently used when a sustained price rally is expected.

Delta at or near 0.50 (the ATM strike price)

Open Interest (2-strike trades: 10 × the number of contracts; 3+ strike strategies: a minimum of 300 at each strike with several thousand in Open Interest at all strikes)

Theta (The daily premium reduction per share should only be a few cents per share when buying long-term options.)

Vega (Mid- to low Vega values are preferred based on currently low trading volume. An increase in the value of both Vega and volatility is highly desirable because it increases the premium value of long options.)

Bid–Ask spread should be relatively narrow. (Narrow spreads reduce premium slippage at entry and indicate strong trading volume.)

Mark value: (Premium should be affordable; find options on securities that have strong directional price trends at or above 50 cents to make the risk worthwhile.)

Trading Spreads

Vertical spreads combine an equal number of short and long calls or puts. Spreads are used within a large number of option strategies. You were introduced to the bull put spread and the bull call spread in Chapter 2. Recall how the bull put spread included an OTM short put above a long put, while the bull call spread included a long call at a strike close to the money and an OTM short call above.

The iron condor was also introduced. This popular premium collection option strategy combines a bull put spread, already described, with a bear call spread (a short call with a long call a few strikes above). There are also *calendar* and *diagonal* vertical spreads.

A calendar spread includes a long call or put that expires one expiration later than the short call or put. A diagonal spread includes a long call or long put that expires several expirations later than the short call or put. The long-term options typically expire 90 or more days later than the short-term options. Both calendar and diagonal spreads are used by many option traders.

There is also a bullish *horizontal* credit spread that combines a short ATM put that expires in 2 weeks and an ATM long call that expires in 1 week. The longer-term short put collects more premium than the shorter-term long call. If the trader's bullish bias is correct, this option strategy can be closed within a few days for a fast profit, even if the price moves sideways. If the trader's bullish bias is correct, both the call and the put return profit as the call moves ITM and the put moves OTM. But if wrong, the call loses value as it moves farther OTM and the put moves ITM. If the vulnerable put is not closed, it becomes vulnerable to being exercised.

It's always the short options, either puts or calls, included in every type of vertical spread that are the "Achilles heel." Therefore, option traders who trade spreads want to place their short options at strikes that are unlikely to become ITM throughout the life of the option contract. *They never want a short option to expire ITM!* Knowing this helps option traders configure their option trades to reduce the probability of having their short calls or puts exercised.

This is done by first developing a trading bias using a watch list of optionable securities, examining the underlying price charts and some of the available chart studies, using implied volatility and price movement values, and checking the option Greeks and Open Interest values. After time and with practice, these steps become second nature. And you learn how the foregoing option trading rules give short put and call options a 75 percent probability of remaining OTM through expiration.

Following the rules discussed within this book will help you achieve many more profitable trades than losing ones. But if you become a frequent option trader, you will occasionally suffer a loss. If you always ensure the money you put at risk is affordable, your account will continue to grow in value. Traders who never lose never trade. Every seasoned trader understands that there will always be losses. But if you use risk-defined strategies such as vertical spreads and long call or put butterfly spreads, all of which can be traded by option traders with level 3 trading authorization, you should earn a weekly income. And consider using bracketed trades by adding protective stops and profit targets that were introduced in Chapter 2 and illustrated in Chapter 4. If unsure of how to set up a bracketed trade, check with a member of your trading platform's technical support staff.

Examining Risk Profiles

Every practicing option trader is quite familiar with risk profiles. In fact, if you show a risk profile (also called *risk graphs*) to an experienced option trader, the trader can likely identify and name the underlying strategy and tell you how a change in the price of the underlying security affects the option premium value.

Risk profiles include a vertical Y axis up the left-hand side of the graph and an X-axis across the bottom. The X and Y axes converge at 0,0 at the bottom left-hand corner of the graph. When an option trade is plotted, the Y axis shows the option value, while the X-axis shows the price of the underlying stock, ETF, or index. Figure 5.4 includes an example of a bull put spread on a typical risk profile.

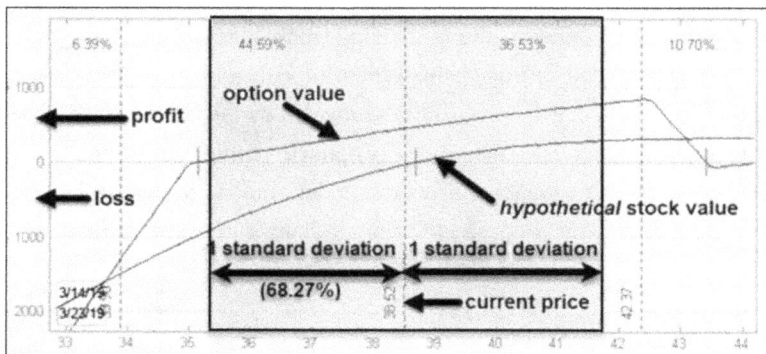

Figure 5.4 A typical bull put vertical spread risk profile

©2019 TD Ameritrade IP Company, Inc. For illustrative purposes only.

Examine the risk profile to determine the information provided. The Y axis plots the value of the option premium at different stock prices that are displayed from low to high across the X-axis. In this risk profile, if the price of the stock remains between $36 and $43, the trade will succeed. The highest profit is achieved at approximately $42.50. If the price drops below $35, the options will begin to lose value.

Notice the gray shaded area. This region represents one standard deviation, or 68.27 percent, above and below the current stock price of $38.52. Many traders use one standard deviation as the price range within which the price of the underlying security is likely to remain through the option's expiration date. However, many option traders add a bit more safety margin by using 25.00 percent rather than 31.33 percent, which is the reciprocal of the 68.27 percent standard deviation value. Also notice how the *hypothetical* price value of the underlying stock is represented by the smooth line that is plotted parallel to the premium value of option.

When Are Risk Profiles Used?

Risk profiles are available and easily accessed on every full-featured trading platform. Once the trade is constructed and displayed on an order bar, the risk profile is usually displayed in a separate window using a shortcut or by clicking "analyze" on a drop-down menu. Before confirming and then sending the trade to the market, a large percentage of traders spend the extra time required to display and view the corresponding risk profile.

This is a precise representation of how the option values are affected across a range of prices in the underlying stock. And although the trader carefully selected the option chain's expiration date and strike prices on the basis of the mathematical probabilities provided by the Greek values, Open Interest, and other essential values contained within the option chain, looking at the risk profile confirms the trader's bullish or bearish bias and plots how the option will respond to price changes in the underlying.

Risk Profile Examples

The following are seven common risk profiles. Brief descriptions of each option strategy and how it works are also provided.

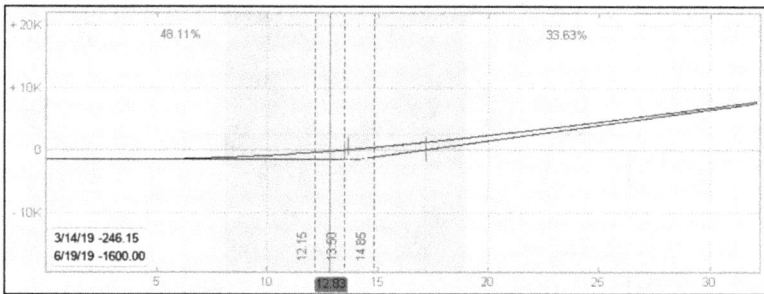

Figure 5.5 A typical long call risk profile

©2019 TD Ameritrade IP Company, Inc. For illustrative purposes only.

Long Call Risk Profile

This risk profile illustrated in Figure 5.5 represents a long call strategy that expires in 96 days. It sells five call options on S&P 500 financial index's volatility index, ticker symbol VIX, for a debit (cost) of approximately $1600. The VIX has periods of high volatility that often moves its price above $30. Notice how the risk graph in Figure 5.5 shows the option value of close to $7,000 when the VIX rallies to a value near $30. When looking at practically any one-year VIX price chart, brief rallies in volatility occur several times per year. And even at a VIX value of $25, the five long calls will net a profit close to $5,000, as shown in the long call risk profile.

Short Put Risk Profile

The risk profile illustrated in Figure 5.6 reflects the sale of five OTM put options on Boeing Aircraft stock. The trade expires in 22 days and collects $1,340 in premium when filled. When traded, Boeing stock had suffered a decline in its stock price of nearly 25 percent as a result of the recent failure of two of its popular 737 Max airliners. These events resulted in strong selling, which drove Boeing's stock from $446 to $336 within a matter of 2 days. The price of the stock finally stopped dropping and began to move sideways as stock sales declined and traders began to buy Boeing stock again. In addition, aircraft back orders for a new series of jumbo jets encouraged buyers to begin buying Boeing again in anticipation of a strong recovery. Therefore, five short put options were sold in anticipation of an increase in Boeing's stock price from fresh buying.

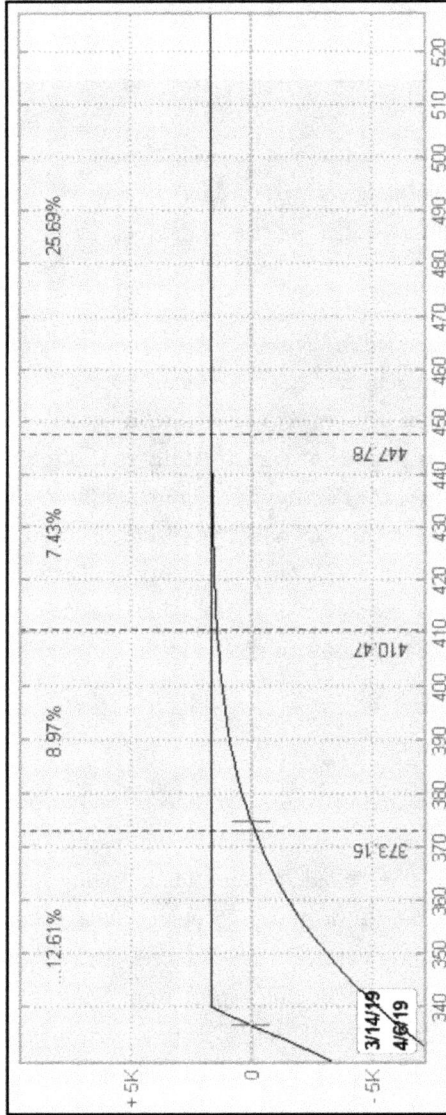

Figure 5.6 A typical short put risk profile

©2019 TD Ameritrade IP Company, Inc. For illustrative purposes only.

Short Strangle Risk Profile

The strangle is a premium collection strategy. The short calls in this short strangle option strategy can be sold only by traders having the highest options trading permissions. This short strangle example sells five call and five put options on Ligand Pharmaceutical, symbol LGND. At the time of this trade, the option chain displayed an IV% value of 50.30 percent with a price movement value of $14.19. This option trade collected $1,400 in combined premium when filled. Both strikes were placed well OTM. The call option's strike has a Delta value of −.13 and provides a credit in premium of 97 cents. The put option's strike has a Delta value of .14 and a premium of $1.60. The 50.30 percent IV% produced excellent premium values—ideal for short options. This trade expires in 35 days and has an 86 percent probability of expiring safely OTM based on the highest Delta value of .14. Notice how the risk graph shows how the premium is retained by the trader if the Ligand's stock price remains between $85 and $160.

Long Straddle Risk Profile

A long straddle buys one or more ATM long calls and long puts, making it a fairly expensive debit spread. There is also a short straddle that sells an equal number of ATM short calls and puts for a credit in premium. In this example, the IV% value on the popular SPDR S&P 500 ETF, ticker symbol SPY, was trading at the $281.54 strike. When traded, the IV% was only 15.28 percent, making buying this trade ideal because of the relatively low premium values.

Two call and put contracts were traded for a total premium debit of $2,964. This is the maximum amount of money that can be lost, making this a risk-defined strategy. As can be seen on the risk profile, the entry cost is at the bottom of the plot, which resembles a wide "V" shape. The SPY must rally above $296 or drop below $267.48 for this straddle to recover the initial premium that was paid. However, when a trader detects what may become a sustained directional move, the losing leg can be sold to partially offset the initial debit paid when this trade was originally filled. The winning leg becomes either a long call or a long put. If the SPY continues its directional price move, the trader can realize a substantial profit, especially with a few months remaining till expiration (Figure 5.8).

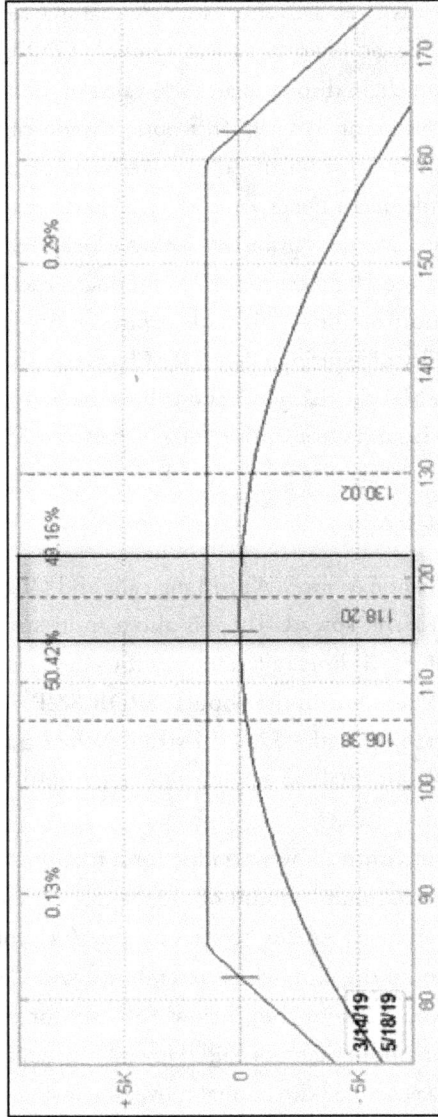

Figure 5.7 A typical short strangle risk profile

©2019 TD Ameritrade IP Company, Inc. For illustrative purposes only.

Iron Condor Risk Profile

The ever-popular iron condor option strategy was discussed in Chapter 2 and again in some detail in Chapter 4. The iron condor strategy was shown on an option chain in Figure 4.2. Here, you can examine a typical iron condor risk profile. It is similar to the short strangle risk profile illustrated in Figure 5.7, except that the long put and call options limit losses. Hence, the construction of an iron condor makes it a defined-risk strategy.

Recall how the iron condor combines a bull put vertical spread and a bear call vertical spread. Both typically expire at the same time, although it's possible to use more than one expiration as in a calendar or diagonal spread. And the puts could expire earlier than the calls. Because options are quite flexible, many adjustments can be made, although the deviations suggested here are rarely considered. Hence, most iron condors use one expiration date.

The fact that the iron condor is a defined-risk strategy is illustrated by the horizontal lines, drawn below the zero line, and created by the long calls and long puts. However, most option traders would close the threatened spread and keep the profitable one. Notice how the iron condor returns a credit when filled. This is because the short options are closer to the money than the long options. And, as alluded to earlier in this book, the long options are referred to as "buying insurance" as they cover the risk created by the short puts and short calls.

The iron condor risk profile shown in Figure 5.9 trades Five Bellows, Inc., symbol FIVE, all of which expire in 14 days. The IV% is at a high 58.32 percent with a price movement value of ±$11.083. When traded, a credit of $775 is collected. The Delta value of the short puts is at 0.16, and the Delta value of the short calls is at 0.21. The risk graph illustrates how this iron condor remains profitable, that is, the $773 credit is kept, as long as the price of the Five Bellows, Inc. stock remains between the short strikes of $105 and $130. The probability of this happening is better than 79 percent based on the .21 Delta value of the short $130 call's strike. Most traders would consider this a reasonably safe trade.

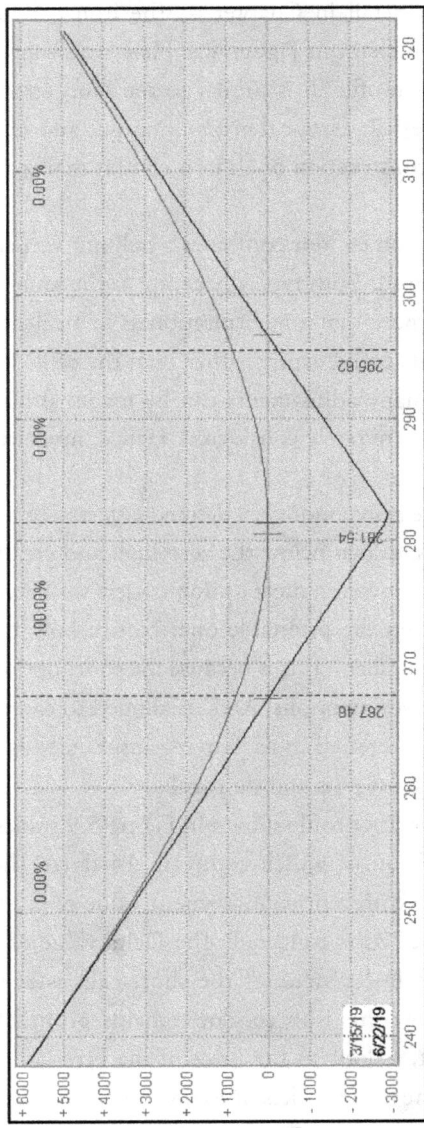

Figure 5.8 A typical long straddle risk profile

©2019 TD Ameritrade IP Company, Inc. For illustrative purposes only.

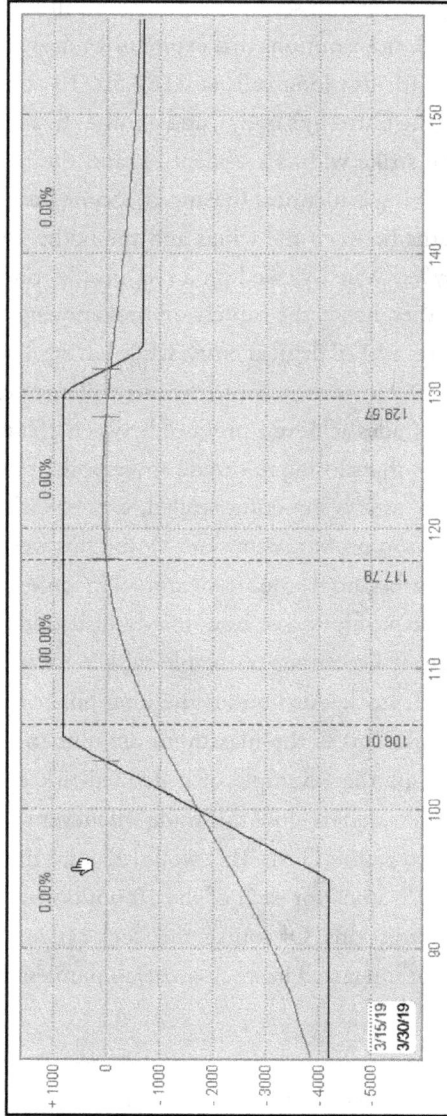

Figure 5.9 **A typical iron condor risk profile**

©2019 TD Ameritrade IP Company, Inc. For illustrative purposes only.

Long Call Butterfly Risk Profile

The long call butterfly strategy is used by many option traders. It is a limited risk strategy, as you can see by the risk profile in Figure 5.10. This butterfly trades AAPL stock options that expire in 14 days. It is a balanced long call butterfly with five long calls at $187.50, 10 short calls at the $190 OTM strike (the butterfly's body), and another five long calls at the $192.50 strike. The strike widths are identical and the number of long call options in each wing is identical (balanced). Some butterfly strategies vary the strike widths between the wings and the body. These are called *broken wing butterflies*. When viewed on a risk profile, one of the wings droops below the other, hence the expression broken wing.

This trade requires a $170 debit at entry, while having a potential maximum profit of $1,080. However, most traders are willing to close this trade when their butterfly trades achieve a profit of between 15 and 20 percent. You should also know that closing this trade at the peak of the tent-shaped plot, or "witches hat" as it is sometimes called, is rarely achieved. Hence, aiming for 20 percent in profit is common. Doing this week in and week out can add up to a substantial amount of annual income.

Examine the risk profile to see how this bullish butterfly trade has an excellent chance of becoming profitable with a small price rally in the underlying AAPL stock. Also notice the long horizontal lines at the −$170 on the Y axis. This is the maximum amount this butterfly can lose. Hence, this is another example of a defined-risk option strategy. Finally, prudent option traders close this trade whenever the central short calls are threatened to expire ITM. This would require the trader to pay for100 shares of AAPL stock for each of the 10 option contracts—a cost of $95,000 plus commissions. Of course, the stock can be sold, but most option traders are not interested in stock ownership unless they can make a substantial profit.

Broken Wing, Unbalanced Long Call Butterfly Risk Profile

The broken wing butterfly was briefly mentioned in the previous discussion. The broken wing unbalanced long call butterfly is an interesting option strategy that can profit regardless of the directional move in the underlying stock price.

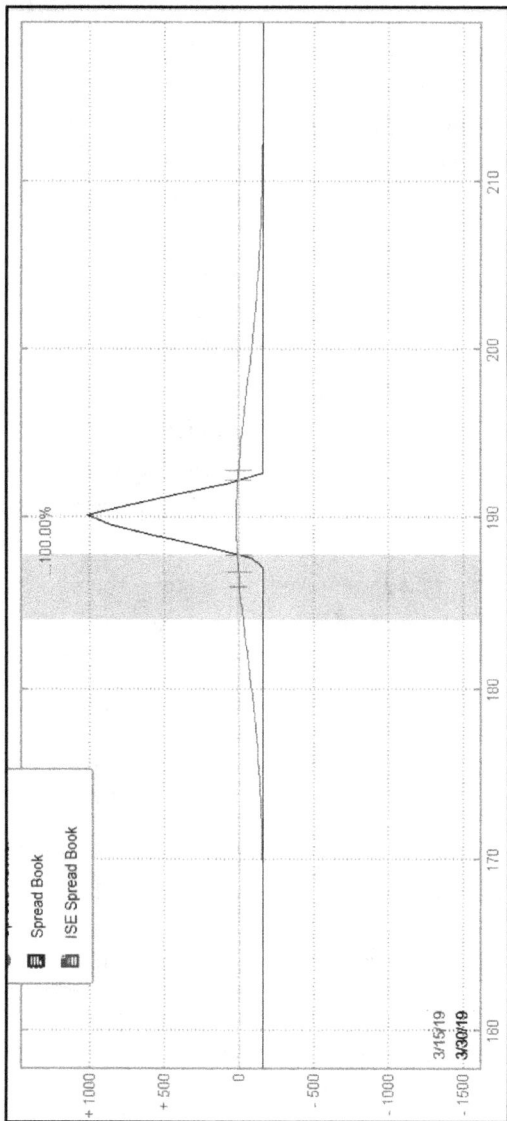

Figure 5.10 A typical long call butterfly risk profile

©2019 TD Ameritrade IP Company, Inc. For illustrative purposes only.

Using AAPL again, this butterfly strategy expires in 7 days. The IV% was 21.37 percent, and the price movement value was a meager $\pm\$4.608$ based on the short expiration of only 7 days. The trader selects all OTM call option strikes. AAPL stock is currently trading at \$186.12. The trader buys +3 calls at the 190 strike, −10 calls at the 192.50 strike, and +7 calls at the 197.50 strike. By reducing the number of long calls in the bottom wing and increasing the number of long calls in the upper wing, the trader is able to construct a credit spread rather than paying the usual debit in premium. Some traders refer to broken wing butterflies as *skip strike* butterflies, since the strike widths vary. It is unbalanced because fewer options are bought below the body than above. This configuration results in a total credit of \$50 when filled. But as shown on the risk profile in Figure 5.11, the trader can lose \$2,700 if AAPL's price rockets past the short strikes in the body to \$196.68. This loss occurs only if the price of the AAPL stock exceeds \$194.60. However, the short options at the \$197.50 strike have a Delta value of .04. The underlying math suggests a failure to keep the initial \$50 credit is a meager 4 percent, which is quite unlikely.

If Apple's stock price does move into the tent, the trader would close the trade for a few hundred dollars without hesitation. However, if all strikes remain OTM, the trader would let the trade expire worthless and keep the \$50 credit received when this trade was filled.

Rolling Up, Down, and Out

Recall from Chapter 2 how options were described as being flexible financial instruments. This flexibility is derived from the ability to:

- Move an option to a later expiration date (roll out)
- Move an option's strike price to a higher strike price (roll up)
- Move an option's strike price to a lower strike price (roll down)
- Move an option's strike price and expiration to a higher strike price at a later expiration (roll up and roll out)

The following paragraphs describe these transformations and include examples of option order bars.

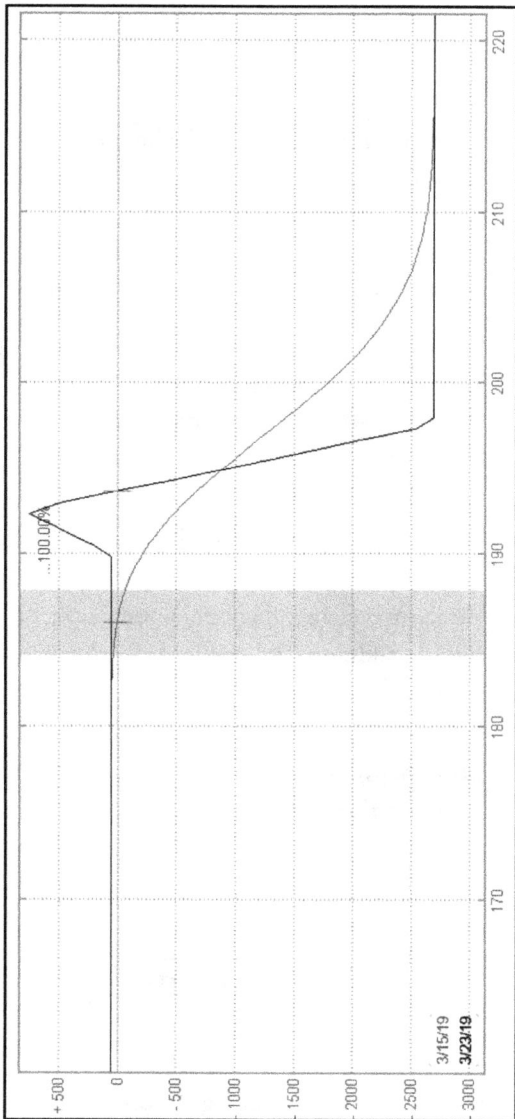

Figure 5.11 A typical unbalanced, broken wing long call butterfly risk profile

Rolling Up

Rolling up typically involves selecting a working short call option that may be threatened by an upward price move in the underlying security—usually a stock or ETF. The trader may decide to buy the current call option using the premium originally received plus some more money in order to buy to close the existing short call and simultaneously sell to open another short call at a safer strike that is farther OTM. This transaction is referred to as "rolling up."

The order bar below shows how a short $13 call is closed with a buy-to-close order and a farther OTM $16 short call is sold to replace the original call. The net cost is $1.10 per share.

Spread	Side		Qty	Symbol	Exp	Strike	Type	Link	Price		Order	oo	TIF	Exchange
DIAGONAL	BUY	+10		VIX	3 APR 19	13	CALL		1.10	LMT	LIMIT		DAY	BEST
	SELL		-10		VIX	3 APR 19	16	CALL		DEBIT				

©2019 TD Ameritrade IP Company, Inc. For illustrative purposes only.

Rolling Down

Rolling down typically involves selecting a working, cash-secured short put that may be threatened by a downward price move in the underlying security. The trader may decide to buy the current put option using the premium originally received and use additional money in order to buy to close the existing short put and simultaneously sell to open another short put below at a strike that is farther OTM. This transaction is referred to as rolling down.

The order bar below shows how a short $170 put is closed with a buy-to-close order and a farther OTM $160 put is sold to replace the original put.

Spread	Side		Qty	Symbol	Exp	Strike	Type	Link	Price		Order	oo	TIF	Exchange
DIAGONAL	SELL	-5		AAPL	17 JAN 20	160	PUT		2.83	LMT	LIMIT		DAY	BEST
	BUY		+6		AAPL	17 JAN 20	170	PUT		DEBIT				

©2019 TD Ameritrade IP Company, Inc. For illustrative purposes only.

Rolling Out

Rolling out involves either buying or selling a working option contract and simultaneously buying or selling a similar option that expires at a later date. This is frequently combined when either rolling up or rolling down and is the most common roll used by option traders because it usually returns a credit in premium.

The following order bar shows a $13 call being closed with a buy-to-close order being replaced with another $13 call that expires 21 days later. This is rolling the $13 option contract out to a later expiration date. Also notice this is a credit spread because it sells more time (Extrinsic) value resulting from a lower Theta value due to an increase in time.

Spread	Side		Qty	Symbol	Exp	Strike	Type	Link	Price		Order		TIF	Exchange
DIAGONAL	BUY	+10		VIX	3 APR 19	13	CALL		1.15	LMT	LIMIT		DAY	BEST
	SELL	-10		VIX	24 APR 19	13	CALL		CREDIT					

©2019 TD Ameritrade IP Company, Inc. For illustrative purposes only.

Rolling Up and Out; Rolling Down and Out

Rolling up and out and rolling down and out are both used to salvage a working trade that may be threatened by an unwanted price move. Both include choosing a different strike and expiration date than the original call or put option. Rolling up chooses a strike price above and is often used with short calls. Rolling down chooses a strike price below and is often used with short puts. Rolling out chooses a later expiration date for the new trade that replaces the existing trade.

The following order bar shows a $170 put being closed with a buy-to-close order and being replaced with a $160 sell-to-open put order that expires five months later. This trade produces a small 2-cent per share credit owing to the increase in time value. The example illustrates how options are simultaneously rolled down and rolled out.

Spread	Side		Qty	Symbol	Exp	Strike	Type	Link	Price		Order		TIF	Exchange
DIAGONAL	SELL	-5		AAPL	19 JUN 20	160	PUT		.02	LMT	LIMIT		DAY	BEST
	BUY	+5		AAPL	17 JAN 20	170	PUT		CREDIT					

©2019 TD Ameritrade IP Company, Inc. For illustrative purposes only.

Legging a Vertical Spread into a Long Call Butterfly

In addition to rolling trades, they can also be converted. For example, a short call can be converted into a vertical spread by adding a long call either above or below. The short call could be morphed into a diagonal bull call by buying a call below that expires at a later time, called either a diagonal or calendar spread. A vertical call spread can be transformed into a butterfly spread by adding short and long calls above or below. These adjustments are done for a few reasons. One would be to convert a losing trade into a profitable one. Another might be to reduce a potential loss by converting a vulnerable trade to a risk-defined trade.

To illustrate, consider a bull call vertical spread that includes a long ATM call and a short call two strikes above. All options expire in 3 weeks. After 1 week, the trader decides to convert this common vertical call spread into a long call butterfly. The trader does this by selling one more short call at the same strike as the first short call. Another long call is added two strikes above the two short calls. All options expire at the same time. This results in a traditional balanced long call butterfly—a very popular risk-defined options strategy.

CHAPTER 6

Hands-On Option Trading Activities

Common Option Strategies

This chapter includes 10 different trading activities that readers are encouraged to try in simulation in order to learn how options work in the market through hands-on experiences. Most option trading platforms include a trading simulation feature in order to "paper trade." This is an excellent way to experiment with trade setups, entries, and outcomes. If you find several strategies that you understand and that consistently return profits, it's time to go live with real money.

Managing Working Trades

Many investors are familiar with the success offered by options. But most are not familiar with how options work. One very successful investor I know became fascinated with the opportunities offered by options; over a period of a few years he read six different option trading books. But he was still reluctant to enter an option trade because he didn't know how to manage a working option trade. He didn't know how to repair a broken trade. That same trader finally read one of my option books, which includes both order rules and hands-on trading activities with trade management tips. With the book on his desk, he began trading options! And I'm pleased to report that after trading options for 2 years, he increased the value of his brokerage account by several million dollars.

If you've read, understood, and used the rules in this book, you should now know how to choose an appropriate option strategy. After reading the following hands-on activities, you should also learn how to manage them. The trade management sections, located at the end of each of the following hands-on trading activities, discuss how to respond to both planned and unwanted price moves in the underlying optioned security. Some responses to troubled trades require traders to either close or salvage a working trade.

Salvaging a failing trade may include rolling working option positions up, down, and/or out. One salvage method rolls a defective trade to a later expiration and reconfigures the initial strategy into a completely different one. An example would be to convert a vertical spread into an iron condor or perhaps a long call butterfly. Always count the cost before rolling or legging a working strategy into another. Study the order confirmation dialog. Will the conversion provide a better outcome? Is it safer? How much will it cost? Strategy conversions may cost more than simply closing and walking away from a losing trade. Always calculate the cost.

Emotion

As you will see, making live trades with real money can create a range of emotions, including, but certainly not limited to, apprehension, hopefulness, and even regret. And once a trade begins to return a profit, it may be time to close it. But greed often encourages traders to let a trade work a little longer for more profit only to have the price reverse direction and turn a winning trade into a losing trade. This happens hundreds of times each day. So set a reasonable profit goal and stick to your plan.

Almost every option trader finds strategies they understand and that work quite well in simulation. But going live often creates a whole range of unexpected feelings, like second guessing trades that consistently worked in simulation. Or regretting the money you put at risk and rushing to close a trade prematurely to recover your money that's presently working in your favor.

Books have been written about the bad trades that were made by some of the world's most famous, successful traders. Expect to lose some of your trades. If you trade small and trade often, you'll minimize your financial risk. Over the long haul, the odds are in your favor when you use your trading rules. Remember, your odds of achieving successful trade outcomes are typically better than 70 percent, which is extraordinary!

The typical Las Vegas casinos make fortunes with only 54.5 percent favorable odds. And with these comparatively low odds, their patrons, who unwittingly gamble with 45.5 percent winning odds, frequently leave the casinos flat broke. So always use your trading rules and use those option trading strategies you've tested and understand. The odds are in your favor.

The common saying "It takes money to make money" is especially true for those who trade the market. Being able to trade 5 to 10 or more option contracts can return thousands of dollars. But if you can only afford to trade one contract at a time, it may take many months or even years to increase the value of your brokerage account. However, once you've grown your brokerage account and have settled on several high-probability option strategies, you can begin earning a few thousand dollars each week in option premium income.

And never risk more money than you can afford to lose. If you do, your trading days will likely come to an unpleasant end! You'll be either sufficiently discouraged and give up or simply out of the money you need to continue. So trade small and trade often.

You should also learn how to use protective stops and profit targets. And learn how to set and use trade alerts, as described in Chapter 4.

Finally, only *trade what you see*! Use your price charts, chart studies, and option trading rules. Understand and use the Greeks. Never trade what you hear, hope, or fear. Operate your trading as a business, develop a trading schedule, make a list of your favorite strategies that you understand well, and go to work. If you do, you may be amazed by your success!

Some of the trade examples on stocks or exchange-traded funds (ETFs) that sell for a few hundred dollars per share may not fit your account size. Even though options are much less expensive, the risk may be too high. There are hundreds of inexpensive stocks and ETFs that you can use with the examples in this chapter. Find a few dozen highly traded, optionable securities that fit your account size. Then test each of the strategy examples in simulation using the trading rules that accompany each.

Covered Call

If you are presently a stock trader, you should consider the covered call strategy. This strategy sells a reasonably short-term out-of-the-money (OTM) call option for every 100 shares you hold in your brokerage account. The options are typically placed several strikes above the at-the-money (ATM) price of the underlying stock. The premium received when the short call options are sold is like found money.

Structure (Applying Your Trading Rules)

NOTE: The positive and negative Delta values were described in Chapter 4. There you saw how short calls and long puts both have negative Delta values. For simplicity, *absolute* (unsigned) Delta values are included in the trade setup structure listings. Just remember, the absolute Delta values of calls decrease and values of puts increase as their strike prices rise in value. The Delta value of a short call, although negative, is written .25 rather than $-.25$.

> Trader Bias: Bullish to neutral
> $+n \times 100$ Shares of Stock
> $-n$ OTM CALL OPTION
> Option Expiration $<$ 56 days
> IV% $\geq$ 40 percent
> $\pm$ Price Movement: $<$ Short Call Strike $-$ ATM Strike
> Short Call Delta $\leq$ .25
> Short Call Open Interest: $10 \times$ Number of short call contracts
> Premium $\geq$ 50 cents per share (depending on personal rules)

Goals

This is an exceptionally simple premium collection strategy. If a trader owns 100 or more shares of stock in his or her brokerage account, selling an OTM call for each 100 shares held in the trader's account is an extremely simple trade that collects the premium less brokerage commissions and exchange fees.

Description

Because the stock covers the vulnerability of each short call option, the trader collects premium when the calls are sold; for instance, suppose the trader owns 1,000 shares and the short call's premium at a Delta .30 is 50 cents per share. This returns $500, which is $50 per contract for 10 contracts. Note that the trader *must* be willing to sell the stock if its price rallies above the strike of the short call option by one penny. However, if only a few days remain, the short call may be closed for a few cents per share before the underlying stock is called away. Being exercised on a rallying stock is not a loss because the trader profits from the increase in the stock price plus the premium received when the short call options were initially sold.

If the price of the stock remains below the strike of the short call, the trader may repeat this trade to collect premium several more times. The strike price of the short call is adjusted as necessary each time the trade is repeated. The follow-on trades would always adhere to the trader's option trading rules listed in the above structure information.

Many amateur stock traders are unfamiliar with the earning power provided by options, including this simple covered call strategy.

Chart Analysis

The trader originally bought 500 shares of LULU in July 2018 for $50 per share. The stock is now trading at $141.79, which is off its $164.79 high that occurred five months ago in October 2018. Although LULU has dropped $23 per share from its high, the trader is confident that LULU stock will recover based on its recent earnings of $2.85 per share. The trader recently read this book and decides to try a short-term covered call on his 500 shares of LULU's stock.

The trader checks the LULU price charts to determine the current price trend. Four charts in Figure 6.1 show a sustained upward price trend with a recent pullback over the past month. After performing a chart analysis over four different time intervals, the trader believes that LULU is approaching a demand zone and expects a bounce and gradual price increase. Hence, a mild rally is likely to occur. The trader decides to examine a LULU stock option chain that expires in 3 weeks.

Using the Option Chain

Armed with his or her trading rules, the trader carefully examines the LULU option chain. First, the IV% and price movement are checked.

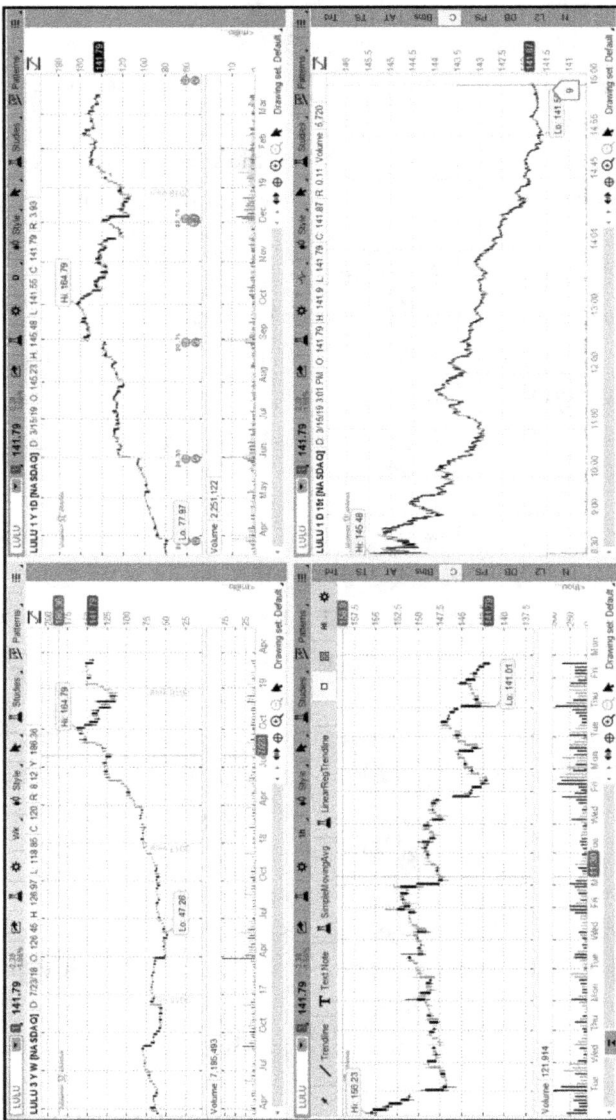

Figure 6.1 Scanning four LULU price charts

©2019 TD Ameritrade IP Company, Inc. For illustrative purposes only.

Perfect! Selling a short call that expires in 20 days and has an IV% value of 63.80 percent is excellent. The price movement is at ±$17.43. The trader looks at the $160 call with a premium value of $2.295. And the spread between the current $141.79 stock price and the $160 strike is $18.21, which is greater than the price movement calculation. However, the currently high implied volatility value of 63.81 percent is likely to decrease along with the current price movement value. This will reward the trade as the premium values retreat over the coming week. This is an example of selling volatility.

The trader sells five $160 call options for $2.20 per share and collects $1,100 in premium less about $10 in brokerage and exchange fees. Notice the arrows in Figure 6.2a and the following descriptions:

1. This shows the trader that 20 days remain till option expiration.
2. This is the current implied volatility (IV%) value and ±Price Movement calculation.
3. This points to the Delta value (.22), which is used to select a reasonably safe strike price. The .22 Delta value at the 160 call has a 78 percent probability of remaining OTM through expiration.

(Order Bar): The three arrows on the order bar show, from left to right, the number (Qty) of option contracts, the Strike, and the Price (premium value).

Covered calls are sometimes used to buy stock for a discount. In the order bar shown in Figure 6.2b, notice how the stock and short call options are traded together. The $141.79 per share stock price is discounted by the option premium, reducing the cost of the stock to $139.51 per share. Of course, the trade must fill at this price. Frequently, premium slippage created by wide Bid-to-Ask spreads requires traders to nudge their Bid or Ask price up or down in order to fill their trades.

Another Possibility: Adding One or More Puts to the Covered Call

It's also possible to boost the amount of premium received from a covered call by either selling an OTM put or combining the covered call with a bull put spread comprised of an OTM short put and a long OTM put a few strikes below. The option chain used with the covered call showed

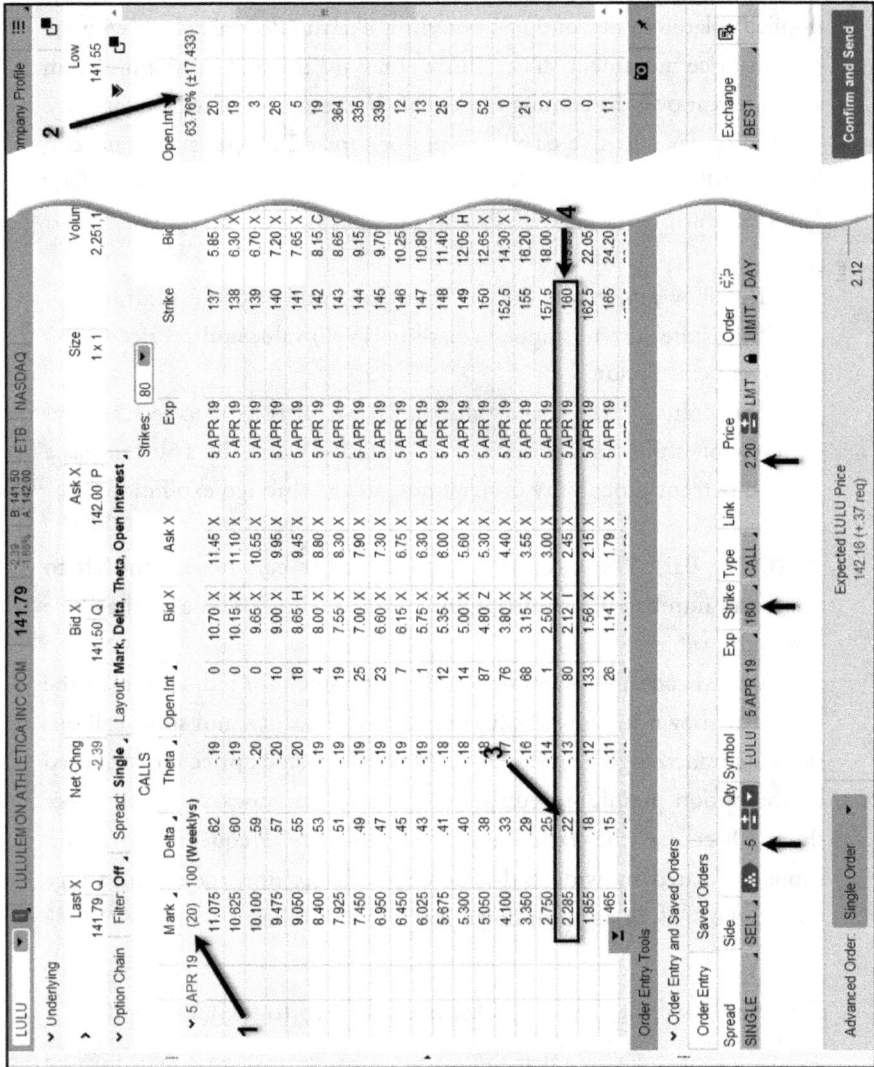

Figure 6.2a Examining a LULU option chain

©2019 TD Ameritrade IP Company, Inc. For illustrative purposes only.

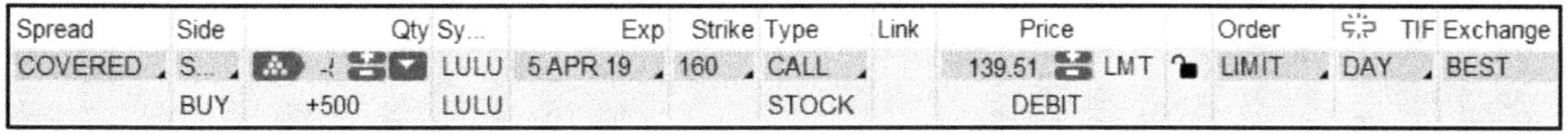

Spread	Side	Qty	Sy...	Exp	Strike	Type	Link	Price	Order		TIF	Exchange
COVERED	S...		LULU	5 APR 19	160	CALL		139.51 LMT	LIMIT		DAY	BEST
	BUY	+500	LULU			STOCK		DEBIT				

Figure 6.2b Simultaneously buying stock and selling call options

©2019 TD Ameritrade IP Company, Inc. For illustrative purposes only.

a short put at the 120 strike with a Delta value of .14, and strong Open Interest of 414, and a Mark value of $1.87 in premium. This trade would be called a covered strangle. The short put in isolation is a cash-covered put, sometimes called a cash-secured put. The addition of five short puts at the 120 strike adds $935 in premium to the trade. This is something an experienced option trader would certainly consider.

Instead of using a covered strangle, this trade could also include a bull put spread by adding a long put below the short 120 put. This could be done by buying a put two strikes below at the 110 strike. With a Delta −.06 and an Open Interest value of 221, this deducts $0.76 in premium from the trade. Figure 6.3 shows the put side of the LULU option chain. Notice how the strikes of the bull put vertical spread are outlined at the 120 and 110 strikes. Because the five 120 short puts return $1.87 per share and the five 110 long puts cost around 76 cents, five contracts included in the bull put would earn $1.11 per share, or an additional $550 to the covered call trade.

The decision to use a short put without the long put below is based entirely on how much risk tolerance the trader has. Also be aware that the addition of the long put reduces the amount of margin used to finance the cash-covered put. This may be sufficient incentive to add the long put and prevent a possible margin call.

It's important to know how to beta test the level of margin currently being used to ensure you remain within your brokerage's margin guidelines. Most full-featured trading platforms provide a beta testing facility. Some can even beta test simulated trades, working trades, or both against the S&P 500 index value. For example, *price slices* are set up at the −12 percent, −20 percent, 0 percent, +10 percent, and +12 percent levels to see how the trader's working trades, simulated trades, or both reduce available margin. In any case, you can contact your brokerage's technical support group, and they should be happy to walk you through the beta testing process.

Examining the Order Rules

Each of the order rules were considered in the above trade.

> Time to Expiration: These short options expire in 20 days, well within the 56-day rule for short options. (Remember, less time is always better when selling options.)

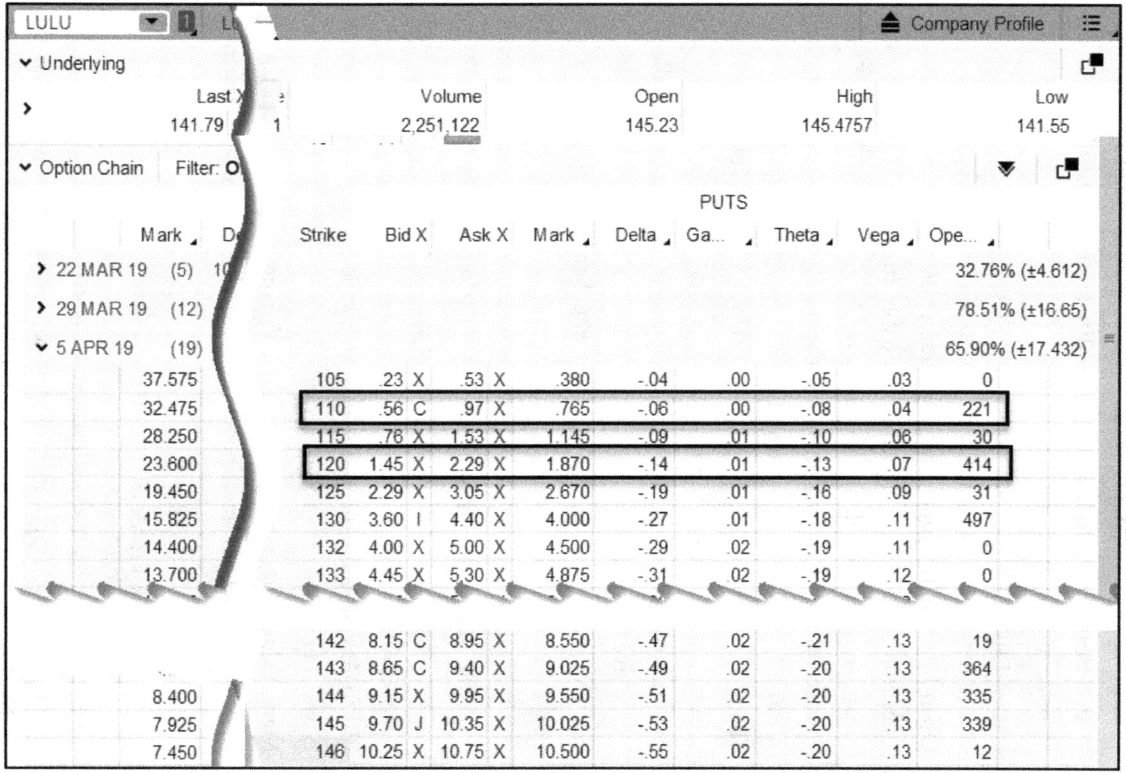

Underlying

Last X	Volume	High	Open	Low
141.79	2,251,122	145.4757	145.23	141.55

Option Chain Filter: O

PUTS

Strike	Bid X	Ask X	Mark	Delta	Ga..	Theta	Vega	Ope..
105	23 X	53 X	.380	-.04	.00	-.05	.03	0
110	56 C	.97 X	.765	-.06	.00	-.08	.04	221
115	.76 X	1.53 X	1.145	-.09	.01	-.10	.06	30
120	1.45 X	2.29 X	1.870	-.14	.01	-.13	.07	414
125	2.29 X	3.05 X	2.670	-.19	.01	-.16	.09	31
130	3.60 I	4.40 X	4.000	-.27	.01	-.18	.11	497
132	4.00 X	5.00 X	4.500	-.29	.02	-.19	.11	0
133	4.45 X	5.30 X	4.875	-.31	.02	-.19	.12	0
142	8.15 C	8.95 X	8.550	-.47	.02	-.21	.13	19
143	8.65 C	9.40 X	9.025	-.49	.02	-.20	.13	364
144	9.15 X	9.95 X	9.550	-.51	.02	-.20	.13	335
145	9.70 J	10.35 X	10.025	-.53	.02	-.20	.13	339
146	10.25 X	10.75 X	10.500	-.55	.02	-.20	.13	12

Mark:
22 MAR 19 (5) 32.76% (±4.612)
29 MAR 19 (12) 78.51% (±16.65)
5 APR 19 (19) 65.90% (±17.432)

37.575
32.475
28.250
23.600
19.450
15.825
14.400
13.700

8.400
7.925
7.450

Figure 6.3 The LULU option chain—adding a bull put spread to a covered call

IV%: The IV% was at a high 63.76 percent, ideal for selling options.

± Price Movement: Subtracting the ATM strike from the strike of the short 160 call ($160 − $142 = $18) is greater than the $17.433, although not much. However, the exceptionally high IV% is likely to retreat toward its historical volatility level, which will reduce the price movement value.

Delta of the 160 short call: The Delta of the short call's strike is .22 and within .25 Delta value rule.

Open Interest: The Open Interest value of 80 is sufficient for a single option trade, especially with reasonably strong Open Interest values on both the call and put sides of the option chain. The Open Interest rule is 10 x n, where n is the number of contracts required for a 1- or 2-strike option strategy.

Theta: The value of Theta is presently at −.13. This results in a $1.30 daily decline in premium value, or a total $6.50 per day for five contracts. Theta represents the daily profit received by the seller of the five short calls.

Vega: With a Vega value of .10, a 1 percent change in volatility changes the Bid and Ask values by .10. A 5 percent drop in IV% with a .10 Vega value results in a 50 cent per share drop in premium value at the 160 strike. This is why option sellers choose high IV% to take advantage of the likelihood of the current IV% moving back toward historical levels.

Bid-to-Ask Spread: The Bid-to-Ask spread is 33 cents, which is reasonably narrow for a $141 stock.

Mark Value: The Mark value of $2.285 is much better than the 50 cent ($50 per contract) benchmark used by many option traders.

Checking the Risk Profile

The risk profile in Figure 6.4 illustrates a covered call and plots both the stock and the option premium relative to the prices shown across the X axis. Notice that the standard deviation, often represented by the Greek symbol sigma (σ), is well below the short call's $160 strike price. Also recall that one standard deviation is 68.27 percent above and below the current price, $141.79, of the underlying LULU stock.

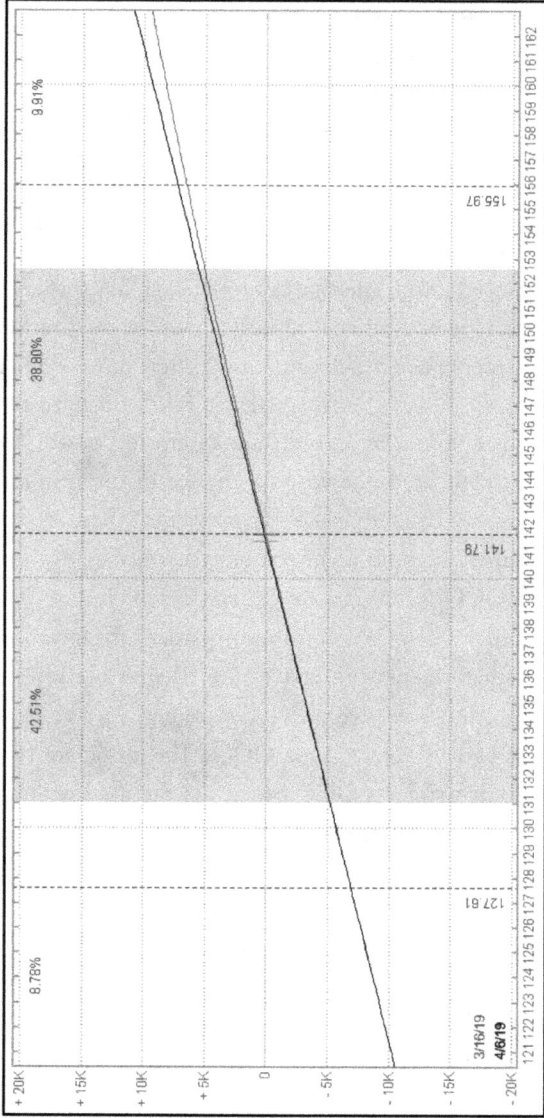

Figure 6.4 A covered call risk profile

©2019 TD Ameritrade IP Company, Inc. For illustrative purposes only.

Checking the Order Bar

The order bar at the bottom of Figure 6.2 illustrates a single LIMIT DAY order. A LIMIT order will only trade five option contracts at or below the specified $2.20 Bid price. It's possible to nudge the price up by 5 or 10 cents, but using the default price value will likely fill. Also, notice the Advanced Order box is a Single Order. There are several other order types available in the drop-down list. Orders that include spreads often use:

Blast All: Confirm and send all orders currently on the order bar.

First triggers sequence: The first order triggers a sequence, or *series* of orders within a "bracketed" order that includes a limit entry, a GTC protective stop, and one or more GTC limit orders for profit. This order type ensures that all orders within the bracket become working orders once the primary limit entry order is filled.

First triggers all: When the first order is filled, all remaining orders that comprise a bracketed trade are submitted as working orders. Working orders are filled when a change in the primary security price moves to an established trigger value, where triggers are set on the Mark, Bid, Ask, Delta, or a chart study.

First triggers OCO (One Cancels Other): Often used to close a working stop order when the opposite stop order is triggered, i.e., closes a profit target when a protective stop triggers or closes the profit order when the protective stop order triggers.

First triggers two OCO or three OCO: These operate in the same way as the first triggers OCO order, but are used with two, three, and four-leg option trades that include multiple brackets that correspond to each leg within the trade. Each OCO pair works independently.

OCO: The one cancels other is used with trades having two legs, like a long or short straddle or strangle. When one leg fills based on a profit target, the opposite leg is canceled.

Reviewing the Order Confirmation Dialog

A confirmation dialog was described and illustrated in substantial detail in Chapter 4. The order confirmation shown in Figure 6.5 describes the

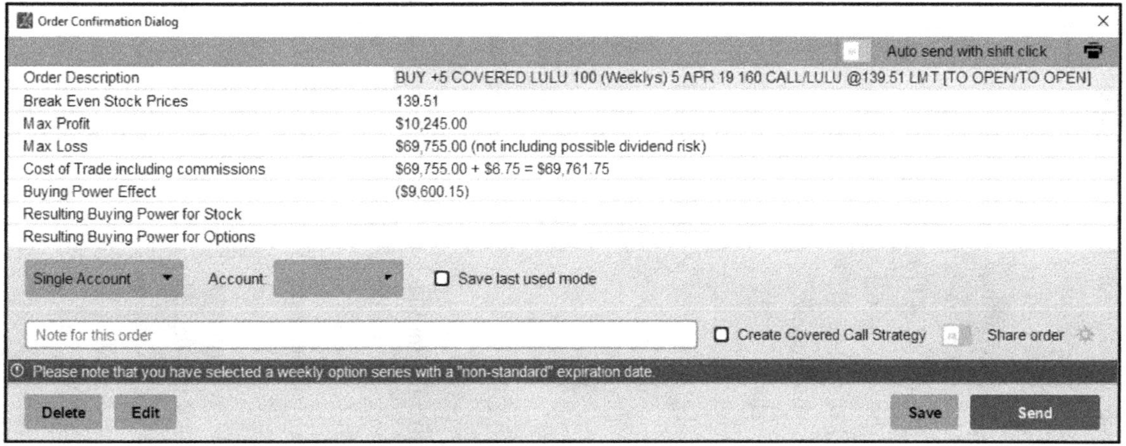

Order Confirmation Dialog ▦   ☐ Auto send with shift click   ⎙   ✕

Order Description	BUY +5 COVERED LULU 100 (Weeklys) 5 APR 19 160 CALL/LULU @139.51 LMT [TO OPEN/TO OPEN]
Break Even Stock Prices	139.51
Max Profit	$10,245.00
Max Loss	$69,755.00 (not including possible dividend risk)
Cost of Trade including commissions	$69,755.00 + $6.75 = $69,761.75
Buying Power Effect	($9,600.15)
Resulting Buying Power for Stock	
Resulting Buying Power for Options	

Single Account ▾   Account: [▾]   ☐ Save last used mode

[Note for this order]   ☐ Create Covered Call Strategy ⊞   Share order ✿

ⓘ *Please note that you have selected a weekly option series with a "non-standard" expiration date.*

[Delete] [Edit]   [Save] [Send]

Figure 6.5 A Covered Call Confirmation Dialog

©2019 TD Ameritrade IP Company, Inc. For illustrative purposes only.

121

five LULU stand-alone short calls on the first line. It also provides profit and loss information and the effect on the trader's margin account on the Buying Power Effect line. And, of course, it displays the cost of the trade, including commissions. Once satisfied with this information, the trader can send the order to the market by clicking the Send button. If the trade requires adjustments, click Edit to return to the order bar to make your changes. For example, you might want to bump the price up a few cents, or change the number of contracts.

If, after looking at the Max Profit and Max Loss information, you are not satisfied with the level of risk or the amount of available income in your trade setup, click Delete to cancel the trade setup and continue your search for an acceptable trade.

The Max Loss value of $69,755 shown in the confirmation dialog in Figure 6.5 may discourage a trader from entering this trade. However, this loss would occur only if the value of the LULU stock were to drop to zero. Although this is possible, it is highly unlikely.

Trade Management

1. The price of LULU stock remains below the $160 strike for the entire 20-day period, and the trader lets the five short calls expire OTM and worthless and keeps the $1,100 premium received when the trade was originally filled. The trader can sell another five OTM calls at a strike having a Delta value at or less than .30 if sufficient premium exists. (The trader prefers a .25 Delta, but because the short calls are covered by stock, the trader is willing to accept a Delta .30 for slightly more premium income.)

2. The price of LULU stock drops. The trader lets the short call options expire OTM and worthless. The original $1,100 premium is retained, but the price drop of the LULU stock loses value. The trader keeps the stock and sells another round of OTM short calls. The trader could consider buying puts to hedge against a further drop in the stock price. Buying protective puts at the same time that call options are sold is referred to as a *collar*. (This is a popular hedging strategy that uses options to reduce the amount lost when the price of a stock drops.)

3. The trader receives an alert message on his or her cell phone when the price of LULU stock breaches $159. Only 2 days remain until option expiration. The trader, concerned about the short $160 calls becoming ITM, rolls them up and out by choosing the $165 strike that expires in 10 days. The longer time till expiration returns a few cents in premium. The stock value has increased by approximately $20 per share in the trader's favor. The trader sets a new $164 alert and will continue to monitor the status of the short calls.

4. The price of LULU stock moves to $162 and is now ITM by $2.00. The trader wants to keep the LULU stock, so to prevent being exercised, the options are bought back for close to $5.00 per share. Although the trader loses approximately $3.00 per share on the short call options, the $22 per share increase in the price of the stock more than offsets the cost of the buy-to-close order for the ITM options.

5. The price of LULU stock moves to $162, and the short $160 calls are now $2.00 ITM. The option buyer exercises the LULU short options and pays the $160 per share strike price for the stock that's now worth $162 per share. Our trader's brokerage deposits $160 per share in our trader's account and delivers the LULU stock to the buyer.

Cash-Covered Short Puts

A short put was described in the above covered call trade as a way to increase profit. Here, the cash-covered put is described in isolation. Recall how the cash-covered short put strategy simply sells one or more out of the money short calls. The trader covers the potential risk with cash or stock held within his or her margin account. This typically includes 100 percent of the cash value and 50 percent of the stock value held within the trader's margin account as security.

As mentioned in the preceding covered call discussion, traders must avoid overextending the available margin value held within their brokerage accounts. If they do exceed the allowable margin, the brokerage will issue a margin call. If the account is not brought back within compliance, the brokerage will do what is necessary to increase account margin, such as selling shares of stock to bring the account back within compliance.

Structure (Applying Your Trading Rules)

Trader Bias: Bullish to neutral

−1 or more OTM PUTS

Option Expiration < 56 DAYS (Less time is better for safety.)

IV% ≥ 40%

±Price Movement: < ATM Strike − Short Put Strike

Short Put Delta ≤ .25 (Lower is even better for safety when enough premium is available.)

Short Put Open Interest: 10× Short Put Contracts

Premium ≥ 50 cents per share (depending on personal rules)

Goals

This is an exceptionally simple and extremely popular premium collection strategy. The trader's goal is to sell one or more OTM put options and collect at least 50 cents per share in premium ($50 per contract) less brokerage commissions and exchange fees.

Description

The short put options are placed at a strike price that is sufficiently far enough OTM to have at least a 75 percent probability of remaining OTM through expiration. This encourages the trader to select a strike that has a Delta value of .25 or less. Moreover, option traders who sell short puts on expensive stocks, ETFs, and financial indexes often choose strikes that are two standard deviations OTM (Delta .045) and that expire in a matter of a few days. This is when Theta has begun to accelerate the drop in premium values. Option traders want the short options to expire out of the money and worthless. When short options expire out of the money, the trader avoids paying brokerage commissions and exchange fees. Hence, the trader is able to keep the net credit premium credit received when the trade was originally filled.

Chart Analysis

Because we're using the same price chart and option chain as the above covered call, you can refer to the price charts contained in Figure 6.1.

Using the Option Chain

The option chain in Figure 6.6 is the same one used in Figure 6.2, except that it is modified to show the short put option at the $120 strike. The order bar shows a premium credit of $1.45 per share, which is the value of the Bid. Now look at the put option's Mark value on the $120 strike row. The Mark value is midway between the Bid and the Ask. The trader can adjust the option price to perhaps $1.85. If filled, which is likely, the trade returns more profit. Therefore, the trader types over the 1.45 Price value with 1.85. This is another example of *slippage*.

Note that if the trader had entered a spread, the trading application uses the Mark values which sums the Mark values and usually rounds to the closest five-cent increment, although there are also strike widths with other values that range from penny increments to several dollar increments. Most option traders know that if given enough time, a reasonable price offer is likely to fill, so they let their price offers work for a while. With enough Open Interest, which is 414, this trade may fill within a matter of minutes. If it doesn't, the trader can reduce the premium amount offered in five-cent increments until it does. Or if the offer nears the minimum acceptable premium value to warrant the risk, the trader will either close the trade or let it expire when the market closes at the end of the day.

Examining the Order Rules

Each of the order rules was considered in the preceding trade.

> Time to Expiration: This short option expires in 19 days, well within the 56-day rule for short options. (Remember, less time is always preferred when selling options to reduce risk.)
>
> IV%: The IV% was at a high 65.99 percent, ideal for selling options.
>
> ±Price Movement: Subtracting the strike of the short $120 put from the $142 ATM strike ($142 − $120 = $22) is greater than the $17.432 price movement value. Also recall that exceptionally high IV% values are likely to drop back to their historical volatility levels, which will reduce the price movement value as well as the premium values of the LULU options.

LULU | LULULEMON A

Underlying

	Last X		Volume		Open		High		Low
	141.79 Q		2,251,122		145.23		145.4757		141.55

Company Profile

Option Chain Filter: **Off** Spread:

5 APR 19 (19) 100 (Weeklys)

Mark	Delta	Ga...
32.475	.95	
28.250	.90	
23.600	.87	
19.450	.81	
15.825	.74	
14.400	.71	
9.475	.57	
9.050	.55	
8.400	.53	
	.51	

PUTS

65.99% (±17.432)

Strike	Bid X	Ask X	Mark	Delta	Ga...	Theta	Vega	Ope...
110	.56 C	.97 X	.765	-.06	.00	-.08	.04	221
115	.76 X	1.53 X	1.145	-.09	.01	-.10	.06	30
120	1.45 X	2.29 X	1.870	-.14	.01	-.13	.07	414
125	2.29 X	3.05 X	2.670	-.19	.01	-.16	.09	31
130	3.60	4.40 X	4.000	-.27	.01	-.18	.11	497
132	4.00 X	5.00 X	4.500	-.29	.02	-.19	.11	0
140	7.20 X	8.00 X	7.600	-.43	.02	-.21	.13	26
141	7.65 X	8.30 X	7.975	-.45	.02	-.20	.13	5
142	8.15 C	8.95 X	8.550	-.47	.02	-.21	.13	19
143	8.65 C	9.40 X	9.025	-.49	.02	-.20	.13	364

Order Entry Tools

Order Entry and Saved Orders

Order Entry Saved Orders

Spread	Side	Qty	Symbol	Exp	Strike	Type	Link	Price	Order	TIF	Exchange
SINGLE	SELL	-5	LULU	5 APR 19	120	PUT		1.45 LMT	LIMIT	DAY	BEST

1.45 ——————— 1.87

Advanced Order: Single Order

Delete Confirm and Send

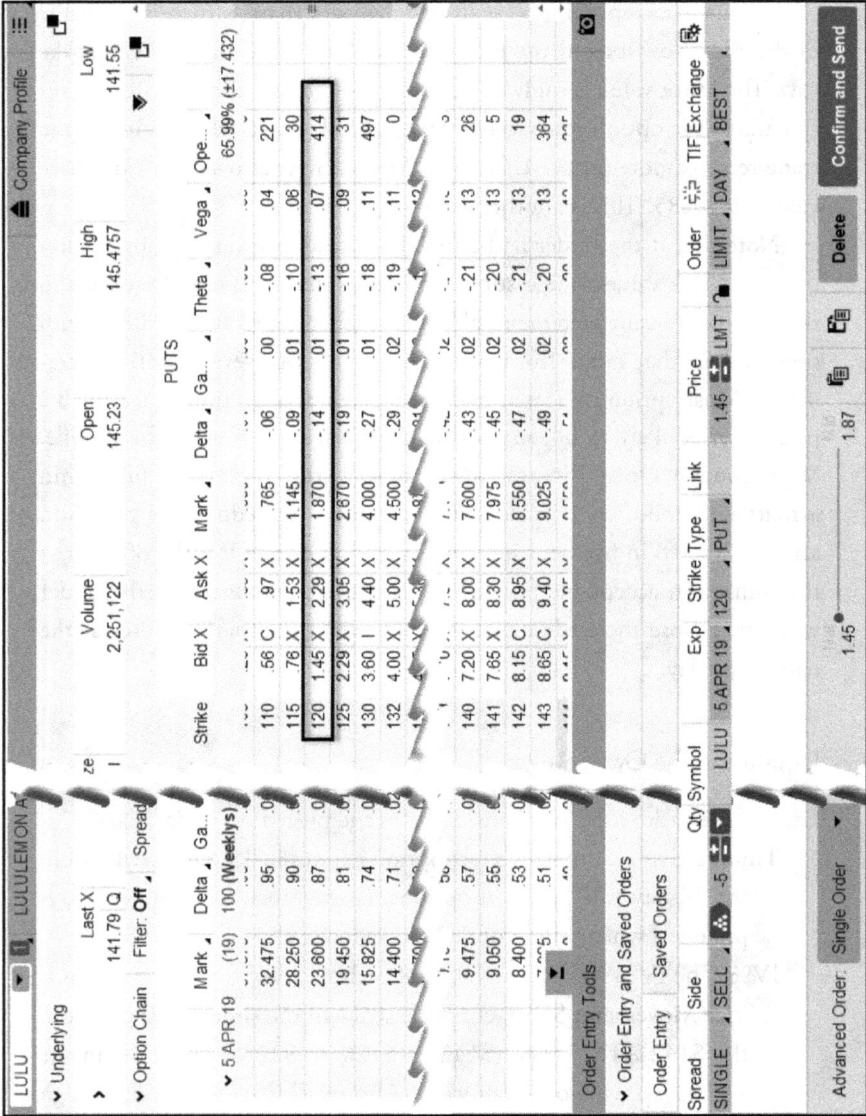

Figure 6.6 A cash-covered short put option chain

©2019 TD Ameritrade IP Company, Inc. For illustrative purposes only.

Delta of the 120 short put: The Delta of the short put's strike is at a safe .14, well within Delta .25 value rule.

Open Interest: The Open Interest value is at 414, which is more than sufficient for a single strike option trade, especially when good Open Interest values exist above, below, and on the opposite side of the option chain. Recall the Open Interest rule of $10 \times n$, where n is the number of contracts required for a one- or two-strike option strategy.

Theta: The value of Theta is presently at $-.13$. This results in a daily reduction of $1.30 in premium value, or a total of $6.50 per day for five contracts. Theta represents the daily profit received by the seller of the five short puts.

Vega: With a Vega value of .07, a 1 percent change in volatility changes the Bid and Ask values by .7 cents. A 5 percent drop in IV% with a .7 Vega value results in a 35-cent per share drop in premium value at the 120 strike—the reason option sellers choose high IV% to take advantage of the likelihood of a swing in IV% back toward historical levels.

Bid-to-Ask Spread: The Bid-to-Ask spread is 83 cents, which is a bit wide, but not so wide as to discourage the trader from entering this trade. Also notice how the higher Open Interest of the 120 put strike has a slightly narrower Bid-to-Ask spread compared with the put strikes immediately above and below, which have lower Open Interest values.

Mark Value: The Mark value of a $120 put is $1.87, an enticing value for this far OTM short cash-covered put.

Checking the Risk Profile

The short put risk profile illustrates how the strike of this far OTM short put trade is well outside the gray shaded area that represents one standard deviation (68.27 percent). The initial credit received less commissions and exchange fees initially received is the maximum amount this trade returns (Figure 6.7).

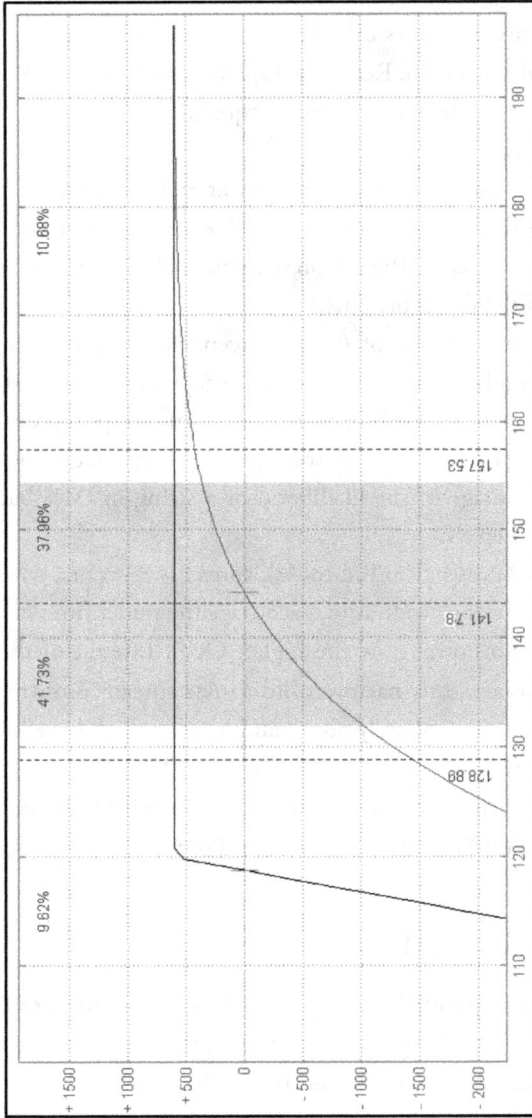

Figure 6.7 The short put risk profile

©2019 TD Ameritrade IP Company, Inc. For illustrative purposes only.

Checking the Order Bar

The order bar shown in Figure 6.8 is also included near the bottom of the option chain in Figure 6.6. Notice that the price, #1, has been adjusted to within a few cents of the Mark value. Also look at the Bid and Mark values shown on the horizontal line designated by #2 and #3 on the order bar. These values reflect the Bid and Ask values displayed on the 120 put strike row on the option chain. When you change the Price value, the blue dot moves along the horizontal line with the price change.

Reviewing the Confirmation Dialog

The short put's confirmation dialog is illustrated in Figure 6.9. It shows a Max Profit of $925. This is the gross value, because it doesn't deduct brokerage commissions and option exchange fees.

The Max Loss is the cost of the LULU stock that would be assigned if the $120 strike becomes ITM without trader intervention. If the option is exercised and the stock assigned, and in the unlikely event that LULU goes bankrupt within the next few weeks, the hypothetical loss would be $59,075. You can do the math yourself by multiplying the $120 strike price by the 500 shares included in the five option contracts. Then subtract the $925 Max Profit value to obtain the $59,075 shown on the Max Loss line. Although this outcome is remotely possible, it's highly unlikely.

Trade Management

1. The short put is monitored through expiration. The trader has picked a far OTM strike having a Delta value of .14. The trader views this trade as having a probability of expiring ITM of about 14 percent, meaning the probability of a profitable outcome is 86 percent. The trader prefers to let this trade expire OTM worthless to avoid having to pay closing commissions.
2. LULU's stock price drops to $122 with five days remaining till expiration. The downward price trend and with only $2.00 away from the ATM strike of the short put, and with just 5 days left till expiration, the trader rolls the short puts down and out to the $110 strike and out 12 days to the next expiration. The $110 strike has a Delta value of .24. With 12 days remaining, the trader sets a new $112 alert.

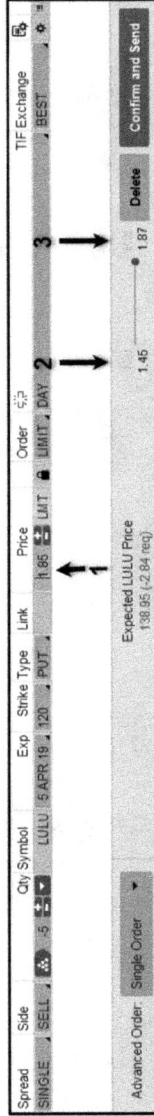

Figure 6.8 The short put order bar

©2019 TD Ameritrade IP Company, Inc. For illustrative purposes only.

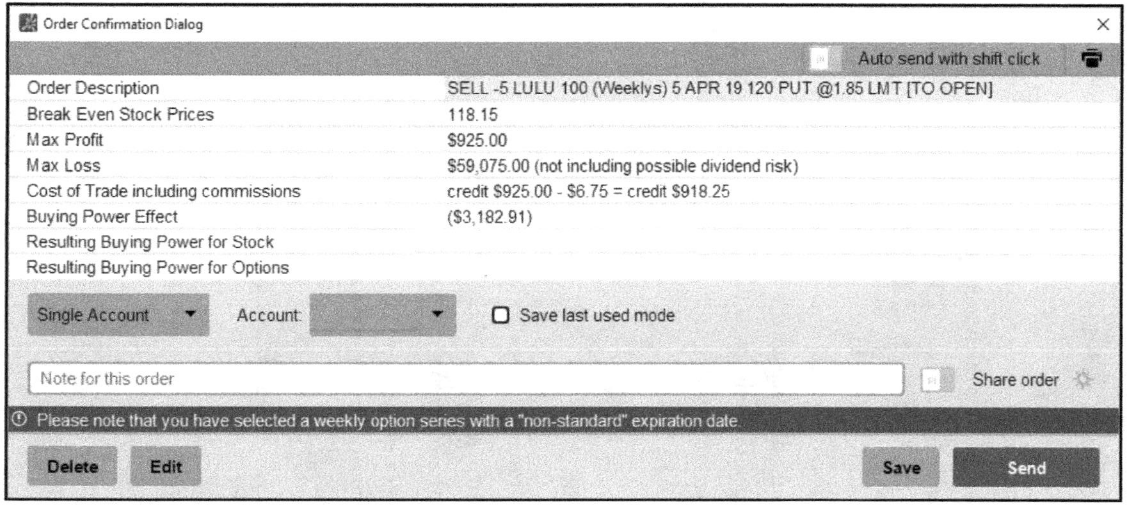

Figure 6.9 The short put confirmation dialog

©2019 TD Ameritrade IP Company, Inc. For illustrative purposes only.

3. If the price of LULU stock begins to reverse direction, the trader will let the options expire worthless. But if the price continues to drop, the trader may buy five puts one strike below the short puts and examine the possibility of adding five OTM bear call spreads. The new long puts and the bear call spread above creates an iron condor.

4. LULU's stock price drops to $122 with 5 days remaining till expiration. The trader rolls the five $120 short puts out 1 week and simultaneously sells five more $120 short puts. Then he or she buys five long $125 puts and five long $115 puts. All options expire together in 12 days. This creates a long put butterfly. The trader plans to close the butterfly within several days to a week if the price of LULU continues to drop and begins to return a small profit.

5. LULU's stock price drops to $122 with 5 days remaining till expiration. The trader decides to cut his or her losses and closes the five short puts for a loss.

Bull Put Spread

The bull put spread is a popular, reasonably short-term bullish option strategy that earns a credit when entered. It is a risk-defined vertical spread because the difference between the short and the long put is the maximum amount that this trade can lose when both the short put and long call are permitted to expire ITM.

Structure (Applying Your Trading Rules)

Trader Bias: Bullish

$-n$ PUTS

$+n$ PUTS, 1 or more strikes below

Option Expiration $\leq$ 56 Days (Shorter is better when sufficient premium exists.)

IV% $\geq$ 40% (Higher IV% is better to increase the credit earned when this trade is filled.)

$\pm$Price Movement: < ATM strike – short put strike

Short Put Delta $\leq$ .25

Open Interest at both selected strikes: $10 \times$ the number of option contracts; a few thousand at all strikes above, below, and on the call side of the option chain.

Goals

This is an example of a long OTM put option covering the vulnerability of a short put option. The trader expects the underlying stock to experience a strong rally so he or she can keep the premium received when this trade is filled. The trader's bullish bias expects the price of the underlying to experience a sustained upward trend.

Description

The foregoing goals paragraph explained how this is a bullish, risk-defined options trade. The premium collected from the short put is more than the premium paid for the long put below, making it a credit spread. The same vertical spread is used at the bottom half of an iron condor, which is explained in even more detail later in this chapter. Both the short and long put options typically expire on the same date, so the trade uses a single option chain.

If the underlying security begins to drop in price, the spread may be either closed or rolled. If the trader believes the price drop is temporary and the rally will resume, the bull put spread may be retained. However, if the trader is unsure of how much and how long the pullback will last, closing the short put may be prudent. And if the price experiences a sustained downward drop, the long put could achieve a profit.

Chart Analysis

The following chart analysis shows how the price of Arista Networks stock dropped to a recent historical support level to form a demand zone at price support. The two support levels also form a double bottom chart pattern, which often signals a price reversal. The strategy can include a limit entry order with a protective stop and one or more limit sell orders as profit targets. When you are unable to monitor your working trades in real time, consider using this type of bracketed trade.

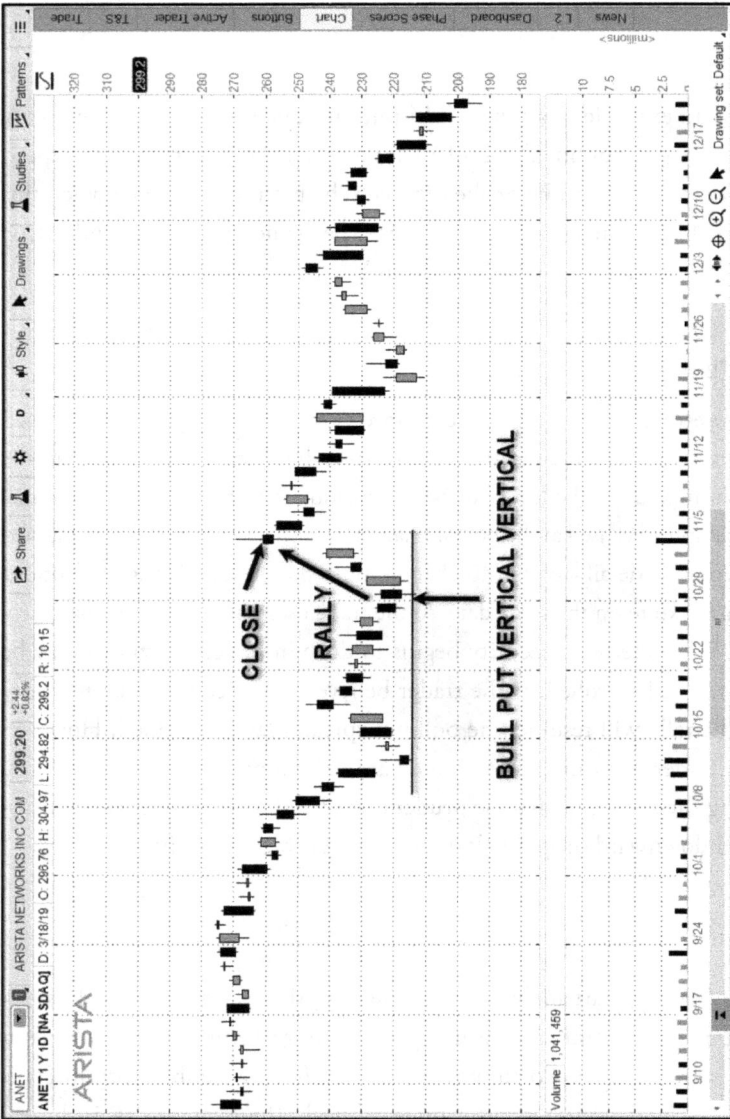

Figure 6.10 A chart pattern used to predict a price rally off a support level

Using the Option Chain

The option chain in Figure 6.11 illustrates the strikes used and their corresponding values. Notice how the short put is placed at the 280 strike, which has an acceptable Delta value of .22, Open Interest of 102, and an attractive Mark value of $3.537. Both strikes have Open Interest values that are well above the 10 × rule for one- or two-strike spreads.

The long put is four strikes below at $270 with 137 in Open Interest. The trader must pay the $1.99 debit listed in the 270 strike's Mark column. When filled, the trader expects to receive approximately $1.50 in credit per share, or $750 less the brokerage commissions and exchange fees for five contracts.

The $10 strike width between the short put and the long put below multiplied by the 500 shares comes to a potential loss of $5,000 less the $750 credit collected when this trade was filled. The maximum risk is $4,250 plus transaction fees. But the probability of this trade suffering loss is 22 percent compared with a 78 percent probability of retaining the $750 credit.

The trader might also consider using either a bracketed trade or at least a protective stop order that would trigger if the short put is threatened. Refer back to the bracketed trade example in Chapter 4 to review this process.

Examining the Order Rules

Each of the order rules was considered in the preceding trade.

Time to Expiration: This short option expires in 30 days, which is within the 56-day rule for short options. (Less time is always preferred when selling options.)

IV%: The IV% was at 31.49 percent, which is reasonable for a vertical spread that simultaneously buys and sells options. A higher IV% would simply increase the premiums of both strikes, which would return more premium credit at entry owing to the relatively higher premium value of the short put compared to the long call below.

±Price Movement: Subtracting the strike of the short $270 put from the $295 ATM strike is $25, while the price movement is $21.536. This meets our price movement rule by $3.46.

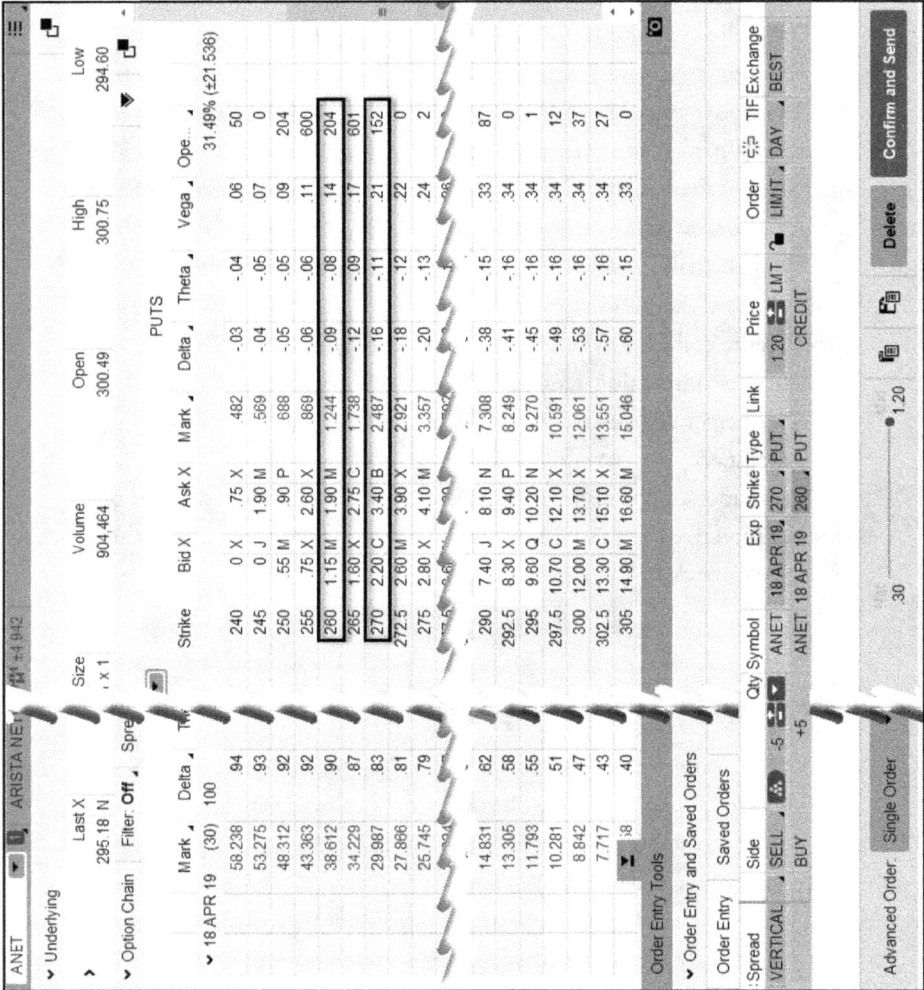

Figure 6.11 The bull put vertical spread on an option chain

Delta of the 270 short put strike is at a safe .16, which is below the Delta .25 value rule.

Open Interest: The Open Interest value at the 270 and 260 strikes are 152 and 204, both well within the 10× rule for one- and two-strike option trades, especially when good Open Interest values exist above, below, and on the opposite side of the option chain.

Theta: The Theta value is currently benefiting the short 270 put by 11 cents and reducing the value of the long 260 put by 8 cents. Because this trade depends on the short put for profit, the 3-cent difference favors this short strategy.

Vega: The Vega values are .21 for the short 270 put and .14 for the long 260 put. A 1 percent change in volatility changes the Bid and Ask values by 21 and 14 cents, which changes the overall premium by 35 cents. The trader benefits from a drop in volatility and a decline in the value of this short put spread.

Bid-to-Ask Spread: The Bid-to-Ask spread is $1.20 at the $270 strike. This is only 4/1000ths of the $295 stock price. Considering the price of the stock, this should not discourage the option trader from attempting to fill this bull put vertical spread, especially with good Open Interest values.

Mark Value: The net Mark value of $1.20 is worthwhile and will return a premium credit of $600.

Checking the Risk Profile

As can be seen from the following risk profile, if the price of the ANET stock remains above the strike of the $270 short put and expires ITM, the trader keeps the original premium as profit. But if the price of ANET stock drops below $270, the trade begins to lose money all the way down to $4,400, which is the maximum loss that can occur. Also notice how the shaded area represents one standard deviation, or 68.27 percent, above and below the current price of the stock (Figure 6.12).

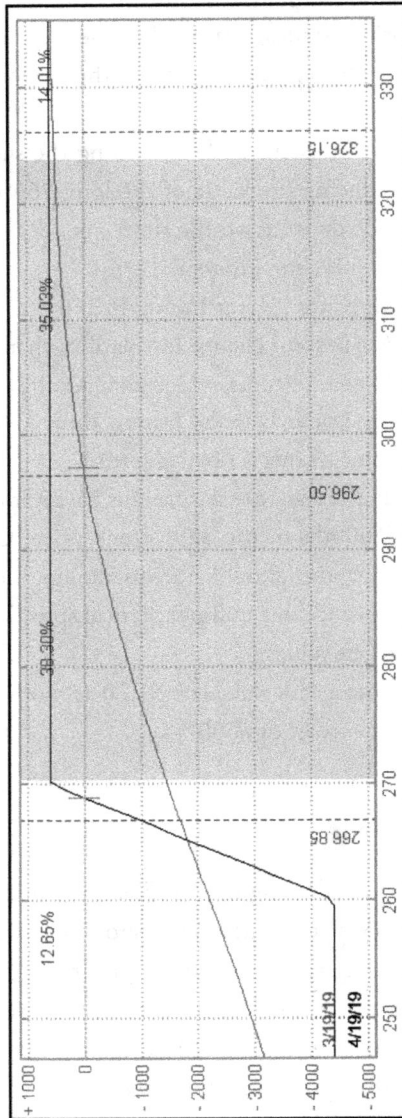

Figure 6.12 A bull put risk profile

©2019 TD Ameritrade IP Company, Inc. For illustrative purposes only.

Checking the Order Bar

The order bar shown in Figure 6.13 describes the trade by listing the short (sell) and long (buy) options. Notice the expiry, strike prices, option type, and price per share, in this case a credit. This is a limit order that will fill for $1.20 per share for each of the five contracts. This is a total of $600 less the brokerage commission and exchange fees.

Reviewing the Order Confirmation Dialog

The confirmation dialog describes the trade and shows the potential profit and loss in addition to the cost of the trade including commissions. Also shown is the Buying Power Effect, which is the reduction in margin that's available to the trader. The Resulting Buying Power for Stock and for Options (values omitted) shows the trader how much equity remains for additional trades (Figure 6.14).

Trade Management

1. If the price of the ANET stock remains above the $270 strike of the short put, the trader can let the options expire OTM and keep the original $600 in credit less transaction fees received when this trade was filled.

2. If the price of ANET drops to within a few dollars of the short put's $270 strike, the trader may wish to close the five short puts and keep the five long puts. This depends on how much time remains till expiration. Also, the trader must consider whether the long put's premium is dropping in value faster from the effect of Theta's reduction in time (Extrinsic) value. Theta's value is compared to how much this put spread is gaining from an increase in the five puts' premium from both a rise in volatility (Vega) and an increase in premium value as the long puts become closer to the ATM strike price.

3. If both the short and long puts of the bull put spread are left to expire ITM, the trader will lose the $10 per share strike width for all 500 shares—a loss of $5,000.

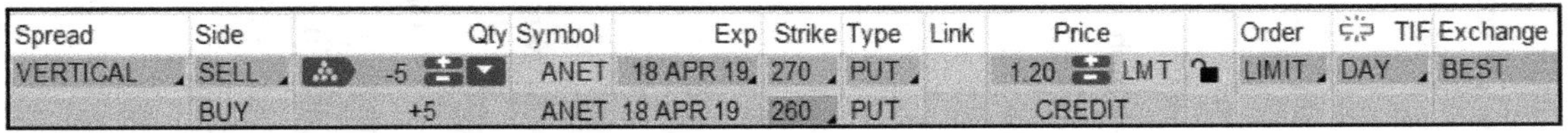

Spread	Side		Qty	Symbol	Exp	Strike	Type	Link	Price			Order	TIF	Exchange
VERTICAL	SELL	♦	-5	ANET	18 APR 19	270	PUT		1.20	LMT	♪	LIMIT	DAY	BEST
	BUY		+5	ANET	18 APR 19	260	PUT		CREDIT					

Figure 6.13 The bull put vertical spread order bar

©2019 TD Ameritrade IP Company, Inc. For illustrative purposes only.

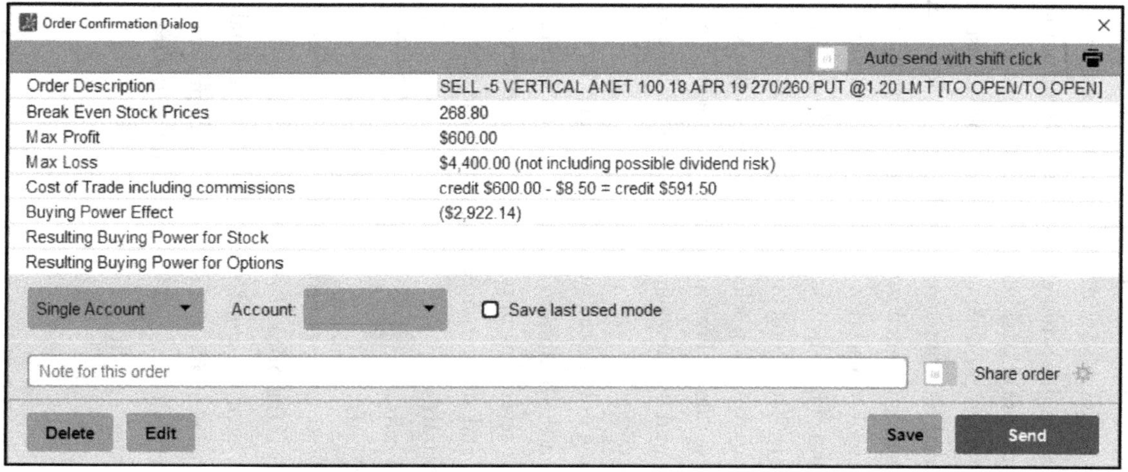

Figure 6.14 The bull put order confirmation dialog

4. If the ANET stock price is permitted to drop between the short and long puts, say to $265, the 500 shares of ANET stock could be put to the trader, who must pay $270 per share for ANET stock. The trader would pay $135,000 for the assigned stock, which is sold for $130,000, a net loss of $5,000 plus commissions and exchange fees.

5. If the $270 short put is too close to the ITM price for comfort, the entire bull put spread could either be rolled out and down or simply closed for a loss to cut what could become an excessive loss.

6. This threatened bull put spread could also be rolled out and down and simultaneously legged into a long put butterfly that expires one or two expiration dates later. If rolled down and out, the next available expiration might be considered depending on premium costs. The current short and long puts would be moved down by $5 or $10. The strike and expiration selections depend on the Mark, Delta, and Open Interest values. Five more short puts would be added to the existing five, and five new puts might be bought one strike above the 10 short puts.

7. A broken wing unbalanced butterfly might also be used. This would skip a strike at the bottom to construct a credit spread. The structure could include seven long puts at the $260 strike, ten short puts at the $255 strike, and another three long puts at the $245 strike.

+3 $245 puts
−10 $255 calls
+7 $260 puts

This butterfly structure returns a credit. The credit would be retained by the trader if the price of ANET stock reverses direction and begins to rally, or if the short puts in the $255 central body remain OTM through expiration. If the ANET stock price moves down and into the butterfly's "tent area" on a risk profile, the trader could close the butterfly for a profit.

Bull Call Spread

As indicated by the name of this frequently used option strategy, option traders consider this vertical debit spread strategy when they have a bullish bias and expect the selected equity to experience a strong price rally over the next few months. The trade includes buying one or more call options at a strike price at or slightly OTM and a short OTM call several strikes above to reduce the debit paid for the long call.

Structure (Applying Your Trading Rules)

> Trader Bias: Bullish
> $+n$ LONG CALLS
> $-n$ SHORT CALLS above
> Option Expiration $\approx$ 100 days
> Delta of short call: $\leq -.25$
> Delta of long call: $\approx .50$
> IV% $\approx$ 30 percent or less to reduce the debit paid when opened
> $\pm$ Price Movement: $<$ Short Call Strike $-$ Long Call Strike
> Open Interest at both selected strikes: $10 \times$ the number of option contracts

Goals

This is an example of using long option to cover the vulnerability of an equal number of short options, almost like the covered call in which stock is used to cover the vulnerability created by the short OTM calls. The trader expects the underlying stock to experience a rally. Instead of spending thousands of dollars to buy several hundred or several thousand shares of stock, the trader buys call options for a fraction of the cost. The short calls are sold at an OTM strike having a Delta value at or less than .25 to offset the cost of the long call options.

Description

The preceding goals paragraph explained how option traders can buy long call options for much less money than buying a stock itself. If the trader's bullish bias is correct, the long calls move deeper ITM and become more valuable as the stock price rallies. When the long calls are deep in the money at a strike with a Delta value above .65, the premium value of the long call options increases substantially.

The short call's option premium also contributes value, but at a slower rate owing to being farther OTM and having a lower Gamma value (recall how Gamma controls the value of Delta and increases to its highest value when it is ATM). Given enough time till expiration, the short calls can be rolled up for additional premium and to prevent the strike of the short calls from becoming ITM and vulnerable to being exercised. When the long call is sufficiently deep ITM, the short calls can be closed and the long calls either exercised, depending on the remaining Extrinsic (time) value, or simply sold for a profit in option premium.

Long-term bull call spreads can also sell two or more OTM short calls for additional premium income. But the prudent trader always checks the risk profile and confirmation dialog to see the potential results before rolling the short calls farther OTM.

Chart Analysis

The following chart analysis shows how Alibaba Group Holdings stock, symbol BABA, experienced a double bottom at support on a one-day per candle chart. The double bottom chart pattern often indicates the presence of a demand zone, where selling has driven the stock price down. Sufficiently low stock prices encourage traders to begin buying again, followed by an increase in the price of the stock. The resulting upward trend is illustrated in Figure 6.15 by the upward pointing arrow labeled RALLY.

Using the Option Chain

The trader finds an oversold stock within a demand zone. A rally is anticipated because the Boeing stock price is currently trading at a "bargain basement" price. After examining the price chart, the trader begins examining the Boeing Company (BA) option chains in search of a bullish option strategy because all indications are that an upward price breakout is about to occur.

The trader settles on the option chain shown in Figure 6.16. A bull call vertical spread that buys five calls at the 380 strike and sells five calls at the 430 strike fits the bill. The net debit to enter this trade is $8,365 plus commissions and exchange fees. Although this may sound

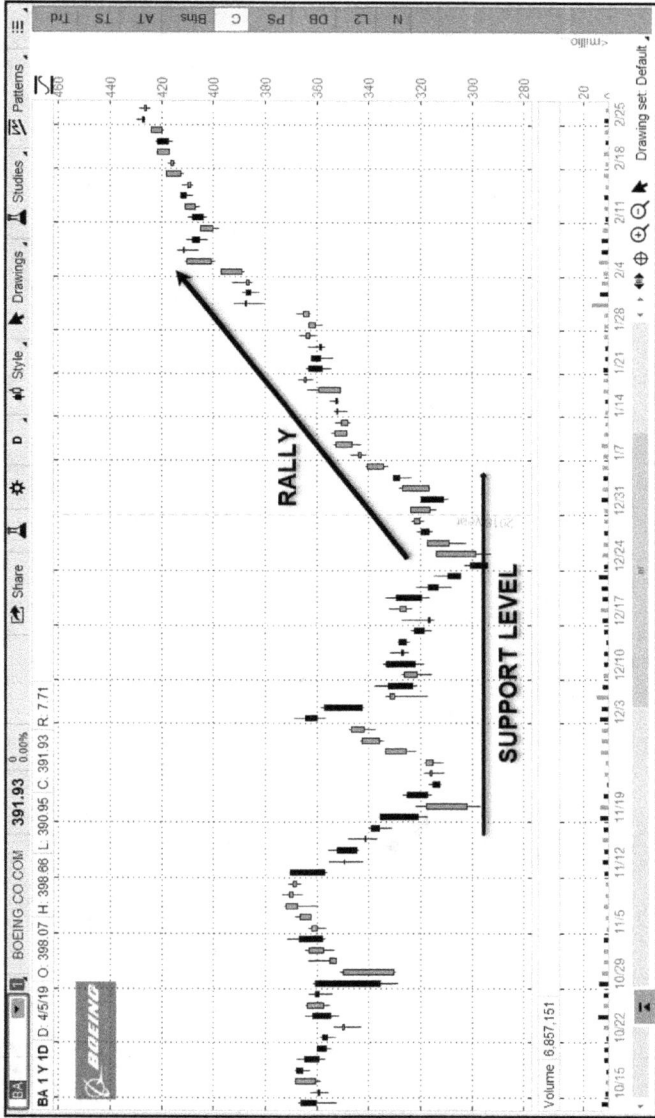

Figure 6.15 The underlying bull call vertical spread price chart

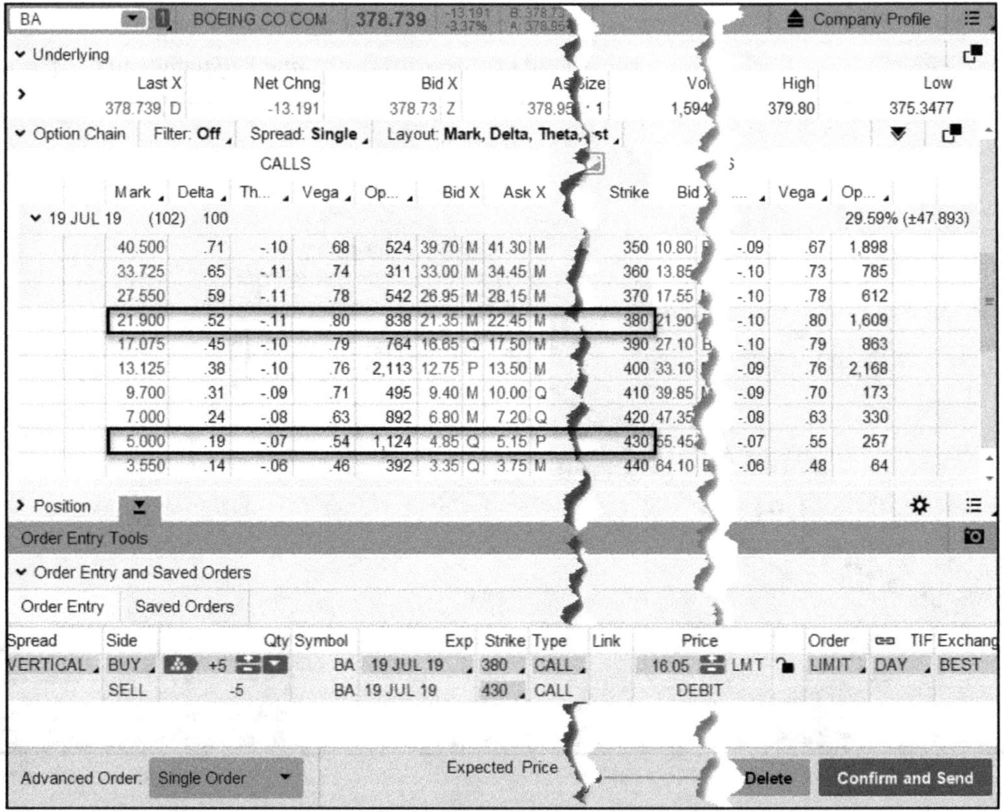

Figure 6.16 The bull call vertical spread on an option chain

©2019 TD Ameritrade IP Company, Inc. For illustrative purposes only.

expensive, the trade has a potential return of $16,635 in profit if the trader's bullish bias is correct and the price of Boeing stock bounces off support and rallies.

As can be seen by the price chart, the trader's bullish bias was correct. The price of Boeing stock rallied from $300 per share to more than $420 per share. However, a prudent trader would likely close this trade when it achieves a profit in the 60% range. You can examine several price charts to see how rallies often hit resistance and then begin trending downward for several months. This actually happened to Boeing's stock price when it discontinued production of the 737 Max in April 2019.

Examining the Order Rules

Each of the order rules was considered in this bull call vertical spread.

Time to Expiration: An option contract that expires in 102 days is selected to give BA's stock price ample time to rally. And, as shown on the BA price chart, the trader's bullish bias was confirmed.

IV%: The IV% was at 29.59 percent, which is reasonable for this trade, although an even lower IV% would be better. As you probably know by now, a lower IV% reduces the premium required to enter this trade. Of course, this trade simultaneously buys and sells options. Notice the .19 Delta value of the short call is only .19, while the Delta value of the long call is.52. This is a difference of .33. Recall how higher IV% increases the premiums of the long calls more than the OTM short call owing to the difference in Delta values.

±Price Movement: Subtracting the ATM 380 strike from the strike of the short 430 call is 50, which puts the short call outside the range of the price move by a few dollars and complies with our price movement rule.

Delta of the 430 short call strike is at a safe .19, which is six points below the Delta .25 value rule.

Open Interest: The Open Interest values are excellent. The 430 short call's strike has an impressive Open Interest value of 1,124, while the long call's 380 strike is at 838. Both are likely sufficient to fill a working trade order.

Theta: Theta attacks the long strike at 11 cents per share per day, while the 430 short call only loses 7 cents per share per day. If the price of BA stock remains where it is, this punishes the option trader by the 4-cents-per-day difference. But the combination of a price rally in concert with an increase in BA's stock price and in volatility from fresh buying will reward this trade.

Vega: The Vega value of the long call is .80, which is .26 higher than the short call's .54 Vega. An increase in the price of the stock will increase the net premium by $26 per option for each one percent increase in IV%. An increase in volatility rewards the long call by one-third more than the loss in premium value of the short call. This is a primary goal of the spread between the long and short calls.

Bid-to-Ask Spread: The Bid-to-Ask spreads are 30 cents at the 430 strike and $1.10 at the long call's 380 strike. This illustrates how the higher Open Interest value of the short call decreases the Bid-to-Ask spread of the short call.

Mark Value: This is a debit spread that requires the trader to pay a net premium of $16.05 per share for 500 shares—a total of $8,365, as shown on the order confirmation dialog in Figure 6.19. But as you can see by both the order confirmation dialog and the plot on the risk profile, a strong price rally can return a maximum profit of $16,635, which is nearly two times the cost of the original investment.

Checking the Risk Profile

Notice the potential profit value, represented by the horizontal plotline above and to the right-hand side of $430 on the X axis. The risk profile also shows how BA's stock price must exceed $397 to achieve breakeven. With 102 days remaining until expiration and with a strong upward price trend, this is quite possible (Figure 6.17).

Checking the Order Bar

The order bar in Figure 6.18 was also included at the bottom of the option chain in Figure 6.16. As shown, the VERTICAL spread buys one or

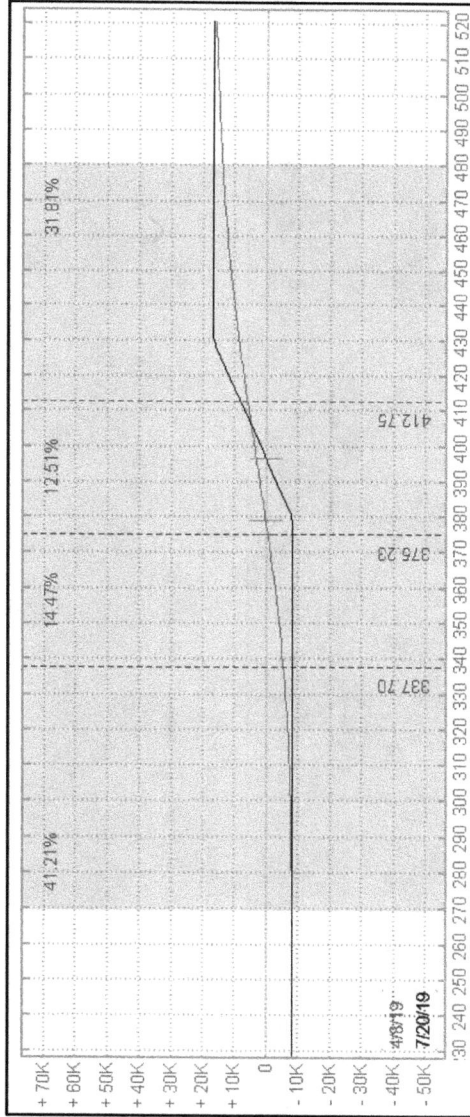

Figure 6.17 The bull call vertical spread risk profile

©2019 TD Ameritrade IP Company, Inc. For illustrative purposes only.

149

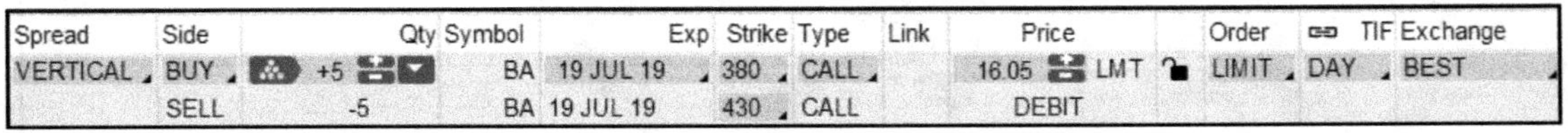

Spread	Side	Qty	Symbol	Exp	Strike	Type	Link	Price	Order	TIF	Exchange
VERTICAL	BUY	+5	BA	19 JUL 19	380	CALL		16.05 LMT	LIMIT	DAY	BEST
	SELL	-5	BA	19 JUL 19	430	CALL		DEBIT			

Figure 6.18 The bull call spread order bar

©2019 TD Ameritrade IP Company, Inc. For illustrative purposes only.

more long calls at or very close to the money and sells an equal number of calls at an OTM strike. Our trade example shows five contracts.

Also included in the order bar are the symbol, expiration date, the strikes, and the type of option, which in this case are calls. The Price shown is a $16.05 per share debit. Being a limit order (LMT), the trade is required to fill at or below $16.05. Also notice this is a DAY order. If not filled during the current trading day, the order expires when the market closes.

Reviewing the Order Confirmation Dialog

The bull call spread order confirmation dialog is shown in Figure 6.19. The order description tells the trader what is about to happen when the Send button is clicked. Unless you are a rapid-fire day trader, be sure to confirm the trade setup before sending it.

Also notice the Break Even Stock Prices, Max Profit, Max Loss, and the Cost of the Trade including commissions. And be sure to check the Buying Power Effect to make sure you do not exceed your margin limit.

Trade Management

1. If the trader's bullish bias is correct and the price begins to rally, as shown on the price chart in Figure 6.15, the bull call spread begins returning a profit according to plan. Once it increases above the $3,765 breakeven value, the trader should monitor the working trade to ensure the rally continues. The bull call vertical spread is closed when the price achieves a satisfactory profit. Option traders who specialize in debit spreads often set their profit percentage goals to the 50% to 65% range.

2. If BA's stock price begins to drop, the trader would close the long calls to collect what premium might remain and (if a level 4 option trader) keep the short calls until they expire worthless. If not a level 4 trader, the trader is required to close both the long and short calls and accept the loss.

3. Another possibility is to buy five inexpensive calls several strikes farther OTM than the original short calls. This vertical spread is risk-defined

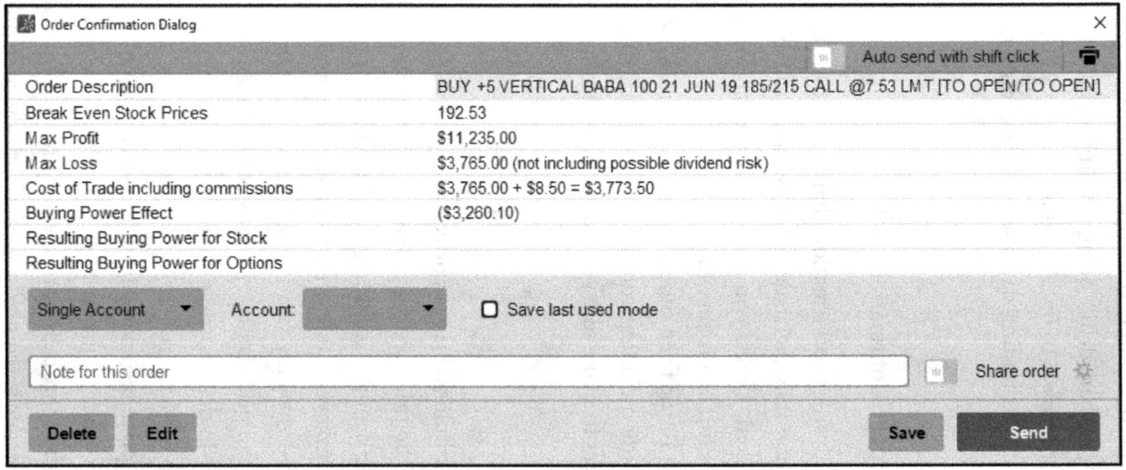

Figure 6.19 The Bull Call Vertical Spread Order Confirmation Dialog

©2019 TD Ameritrade IP Company, Inc. For illustrative purposes only.

and becomes a bear call vertical spread. However, this would be done only if the premium paid for the new long call is considerably less than the amount of premium that remains in the short call.

4. If the trader uses a protective stop and a profit target and the BA stock rallies according to the trader's bias, the trader would slide both the protective stop and profit target up and, if possible, beyond the trade's limit entry to lock in profit.

5. The trader could also roll the short call up to a higher strike in order to collect several hundred dollars more in premium income. The trader's plan may include rolling the short puts several times in order to collect more premium income.

Diagonal Bull Call Spread

This is a bullish option strategy that uses two different option chains: one is used to buy call options that are either at or very close to the ATM strike price and expire in 90 or more days. In fact, long-term equity anticipation securities (LEAPS) options are often used. (Recall that LEAPS options expire in a year or more.) The strategy also sells an equivalent number of short call options that expire within 56 days (7 weeks) or less.

Structure (Applying Your Trading Rules)

> Trader Bias: Neutral to mildly bearish
> +n ATM CALLS that expire in 90 or more days
> −n OTM CALLS that expire in 56 or fewer days
> IV%: ≥ 40%
> ±Price Movement: < Short Call Strike − ATM Strike
> Short Call Delta: ≤ .25
> Delta of long call: ≈ .50
> Short Call Open Interest: 10× Short Call Contracts
> Trader Bias: Bullish

Goals

The diagonal bull call spread is a premium collection strategy that succeeds when the price of the underlying stock rallies according to the trader's bullish bias. The trader collects additional premium by selling a series of short-term OTM calls having Delta values of .25 or less. The combination of buying profitable long calls and collecting additional premium each time the short calls are rolled can achieve a substantial profit.

Description

The trader begins by scanning his or her watch list for high trading volumes that exceed an average daily trading volume of a few million shares. Among these, the trader begins to check the corresponding charts for upward trending stocks. The trader also looks for an oversold stock with a price that's near a historical support level near the bottom of a short interval price chart. The corresponding long-term option chain should have an IV% value in the teens or low to mid-20s. This reduces the amount of premium required to buy the long options. And a return to historical volatility levels above an IV% of .50 will result in an increase in the current option premium.

The short calls should be at a Delta value at or below .25. The short calls should expire within a month or two. Although the premium may be substantially less than that of the long calls owing to the difference in their Deltas and relative time values, the trader would like to find a short call strike having at least a 50-cent Mark value to offset the cost of the long call.

If the trader's bullish bias is validated by a rally and the IV% value begins to move back toward historical levels, the long calls will become profitable. The trader should hold the position until it achieves a satisfactory profit of 50 to 60 percent and then close the trade.

Chart Analysis

The preceding one-hour interval candlestick chart shows a month's worth of price data. However, the trader would also look at a one-year, one-day per candle and perhaps the three-year, one-week per candle charts to become familiar with the underlying security's behavior. As you can see, the QQQ, which is a derivative of the highly traded NASDAQ financial index, has been trending upward for some time. The NASDAQ is the heaviest traded index in the world, averaging 1.8 billion trades a day and listing 3,300 stocks, with a heavy emphasis on technology stocks. Many option traders follow the NASDAQ 100, which is comprised of the top 100 technology stocks (Figure 6.20).

Using the Option Chain

As you can see in the option chain illustration shown in Figure 6.21, the long 183 call uses options that expire in 302 days, while the five short calls expire in 28 days. The term *diagonal* is used when two different expiration dates are used within a spread. Note that calendar spreads also exist. The term calendar usually refers to spreads that are separated by one expiration date. The separation is typically 1 week in weekly options or 1 month when only monthly options exist for a symbol. Note that monthly options expire on the third Friday of the month. If you examine your option chains, you can see that monthly options usually have more trading volume (Open Interest) than weekly options. This is a good reason to examine the monthly expiration option chains when searching for a trade setup.

Because the long calls are kept for a much longer period of time, the short calls are often rolled out to a new expiration date and up to a farther OTM (and safer) strike. If the price of the QQQ is rallying according to the trader's bullish bias, the five long calls increase in value as they move deeper ITM. So as the long calls increase in value, the short calls continue to contribute additional premium to this trade.

Of course, the QQQ *must* continue to rally for it to return a profit. If it begins to drop in value, the trader should consider closing the trade before he or she experiences a major loss. More about this in Trade Management and Possible Outcomes below.

Examining the Order Rules

Each of the order rules was considered in this diagonal bull call trade. Of particular interest, notice the strong Open Interest values, which affect the corresponding Bid-to-Ask spreads.

Time to Expiration: The long calls expire in 302 days, while the short calls expire in just 28 days. This is reducing the premium value of

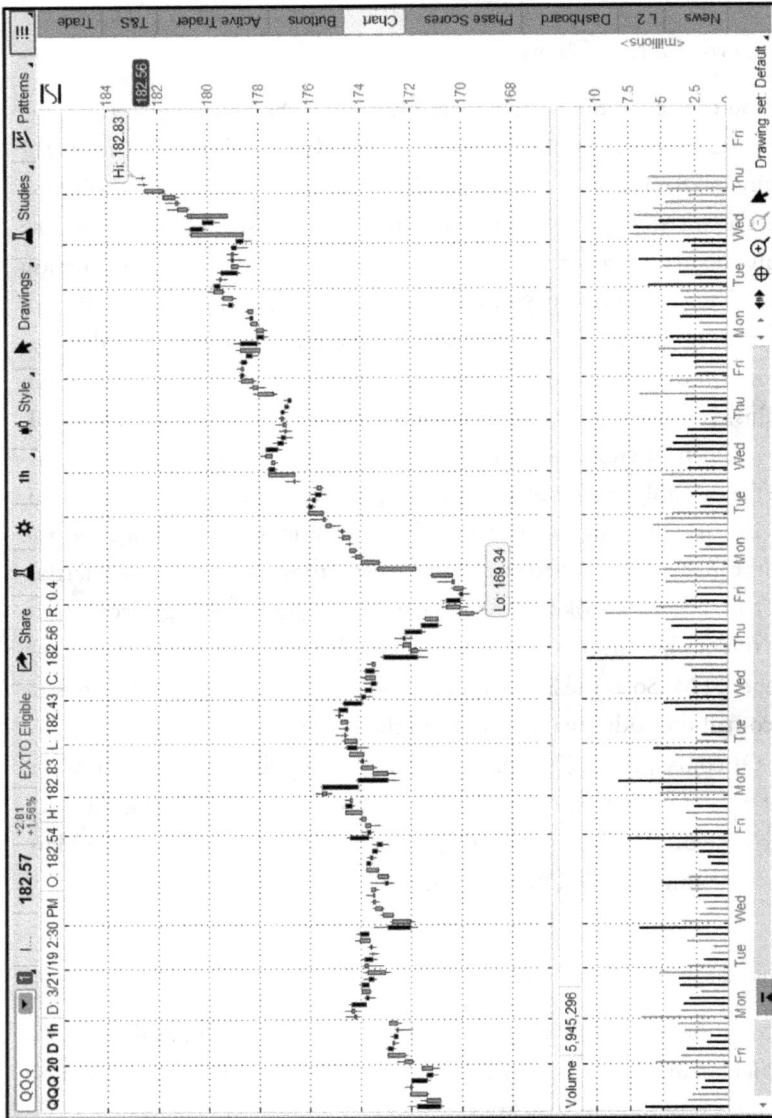

Figure 6.20 Use a rallying stock or ETF with a diagonal bull call spread

©2019 TD Ameritrade IP Company, Inc. For illustrative purposes only.

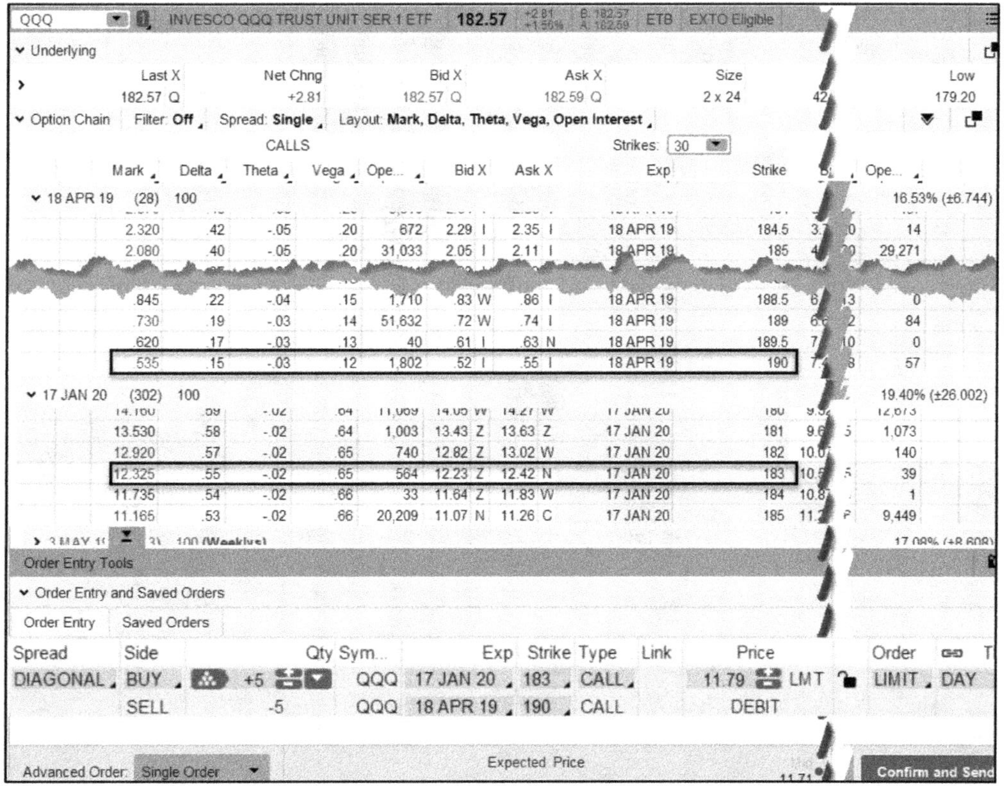

Figure 6.21 Setting up a diagonal bull call spread using two expiration dates

©2019 TD Ameritrade IP Company, Inc. For illustrative purposes only.

the short calls by roughly one-third faster than that of the long calls. This increases as the short call options draw closer to expiration.

IV%: The IV% for the long call is at a reasonably low 19.40 percent, which is ideal when purchasing a long call or put option. Low IV% reduces the premium value, which reduces the debit the trader must pay when the trade is filled. The 16.53 IV% for the 28-day five short calls is far below the 40 percent or more traders prefer when selling premium. However, the dominant, long-term options are where this trade earns its money, so the trade must favor the long call, as the short calls are simply along for the ride by contributing small amounts of premium to this trade.

±Price Movement: With the price movement at $6.744, subtracting the ATM 183 strike from the 190 strike is $7.00. This puts the short call's 190 strike at 25 cents above the price movement value. Although 25 cents is quite close, it is acceptable.

Delta of the 215 short call strike is at a safe .15, 10 points below the Delta .25 value rule. This gives the short calls an 85 percent probability of remaining OTM through expiration.

Open Interest: The Open Interest values are exceptionally strong. The 190 short call's strike has an impressive Open Interest value of 1,802, while the long call's 183 strike tells traders there are currently 564 working option trades. These liquidity values should expedite the execution of this diagonal option trade at the selected strikes.

Theta: The Theta value of −$0.02 at the strike of the long calls is currently $2.00 per day per contract or $10 per day for the five long call contracts. The −$0.03 Theta value at the five short call strikes is reducing the premium values by $3.00 per contract or $15 per day. This currently benefits the trade by $5.00 net profit per day. And, as can be seen by the long call's Vega value, an increase in volatility will reward the long calls much more than the short call's loss in premium value.

Vega: The Vega values are .65 and .12 for the long calls and short calls, respectively. Hence, a 1% increase in implied volatility increases the long call's current premium by 65 cents per share. The short calls would respond with an increase in value 12 cents for the same 1 percent increase in volatility. This rewards this spread by 53 cents per share—a net increase in value of $265 for a meager 1 percent uptick in volatility. This helps us understand the importance of buying options when volatility is low.

Bid-to-Ask Spread: The Bid-to-Ask spreads are quite narrow owing to the heavy trading volume. The short calls have only a three-cent spread. The long calls have a 19-cent spread. Although there may be some minor slippage, 19 cents is quite reasonable for high-priced options that expire in more than 300 days.

Mark Value: This is a debit spread that requires the trader to pay a net premium of $11.79 per share for 500 shares—a total of $5,895 as shown on the order confirmation dialog in Figure 6.24. However, because the diagonal spread will be rolled several times throughout the life of the trade, the maximum profit and loss data cannot be computed.

Checking the Risk Profile

The risk profile shows the initial cost of this diagonal bull call spread. Notice how this call spread moves from the debit paid when opened to a profit of approximately $2,000 when the QQQ price moves to $190. But, as you know, this is not the end of the story. Each time the five short calls are rolled up and out by a few weeks, more premium is earned. To see how each works, the trader would examine the underlying risk profiles each time the trade is updated with new short calls (Figure 6.22).

Checking the Order Bar

The order bar shown in Figure 6.23 was also included at the bottom of the option chain illustrated in Figure 6.21. This shows the trade as a DIAGONAL spread with the buying and selling actions, the quantity, symbol, and two expiration dates that correspond to each of the call contracts and their strikes. The cost is shown as a $11.79 debit. The net value

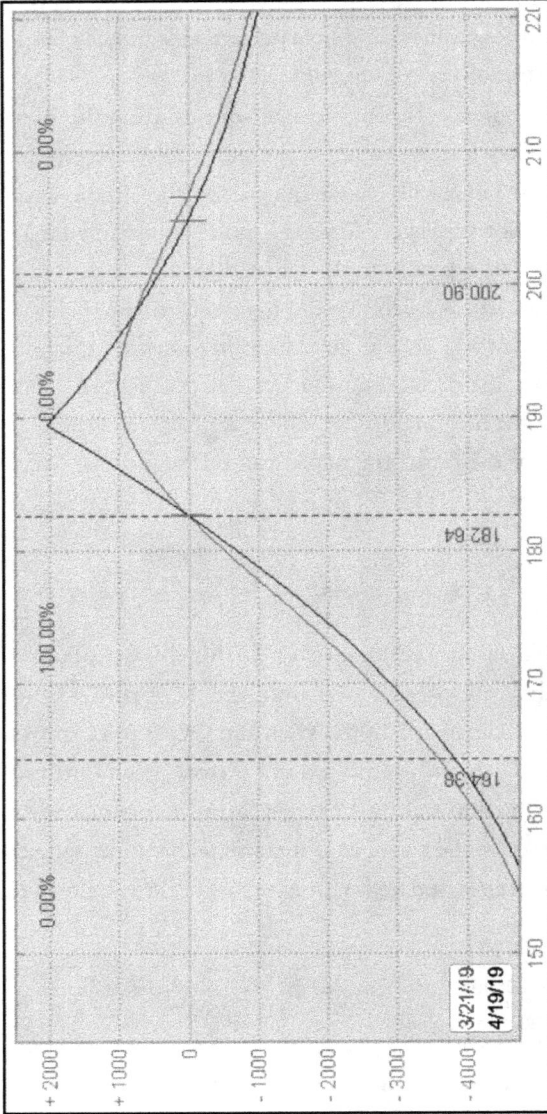

Figure 6.22 The initial diagonal bull call spread risk profiles

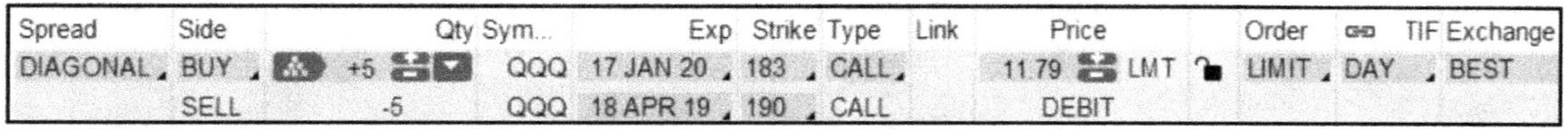

Spread	Side	Qty	Sym...	Exp	Strike	Type	Link	Price	Order	TIF	Exchange
DIAGONAL	BUY	+5	QQQ	17 JAN 20	183	CALL		11.79 LMT	LIMIT	DAY	BEST
	SELL	-5	QQQ	18 APR 19	190	CALL		DEBIT			

Figure 6.23 The initial diagonal bull call spread order bar

is shown as $5,895 in Figure 6.24, the order confirmation dialog. This value is easily derived by multiplying the $11.79 net debit by 500 shares, which equals the $5,895.

Reviewing the Order Confirmation Dialog

The order description, the cost of the trade, and the effect on the trader's buying power are all displayed on the dialog shown in Figure 6.24. Because several unknown variable values exist in this trade, some information, such as Max Profit and Max Loss, cannot be computed.

Trade Management

By now you have likely understood that option trades, including this diagonal bull call spread, succeed when the trader's bias is validated by a price movement. But the trader can also lose when a bullish or bearish bias is wrong and the trade moves in the opposite direction. This happens to millions of traders every day. The key is to minimize the amount of money put at risk. As an active trader, *never* trade more than you can afford to lose.

As shown by the plot of the risk profile, diagonal bull call spreads carry risk. In fact, every trade you ever make, regardless of whether you're trading stock, options, futures, or the forex, can "turn on a dime." But if the trader applies the trading rules, the odds of successful trading outcomes are in the trader's favor.

1. If the price of the QQQ ETF begins to drop, it's probably time for the trader to cut his or her losses and exit the trade.
2. Those option traders who have level 4 trading permissions would likely keep the short calls until they expire worthless. Lower level traders could buy a cheap OTM long call above the short call in order to retain the premium left in the short calls.
3. The trader may wish to set an alert. Knowing when the price of QQQ begins to drop is important. This causes the long calls to move OTM and lose premium value faster than the short calls return profit. Although a drop in the price of QQQ benefits the short calls,

Order Confirmation Dialog   Auto send with shift click   ✕

Order Description	BUY +5 DIAGONAL QQQ 100 17 JAN 20/18 APR 19 183/190 CALL @11.79 LMT [TO OPEN/TO OPEN]
Break Even Stock Prices	N/A
Max Profit	N/A
Max Loss	N/A
Cost of Trade including commissions	$5,895.00 + $8.50 = $5,903.50
Buying Power Effect	($3,560.26)
Resulting Buying Power for Stock	
Resulting Buying Power for Options	

Single Account ▸   Account ▸

Note for this order

☐ Save last used mode

☐ Share order ⚙

Delete   Edit   Save   Send

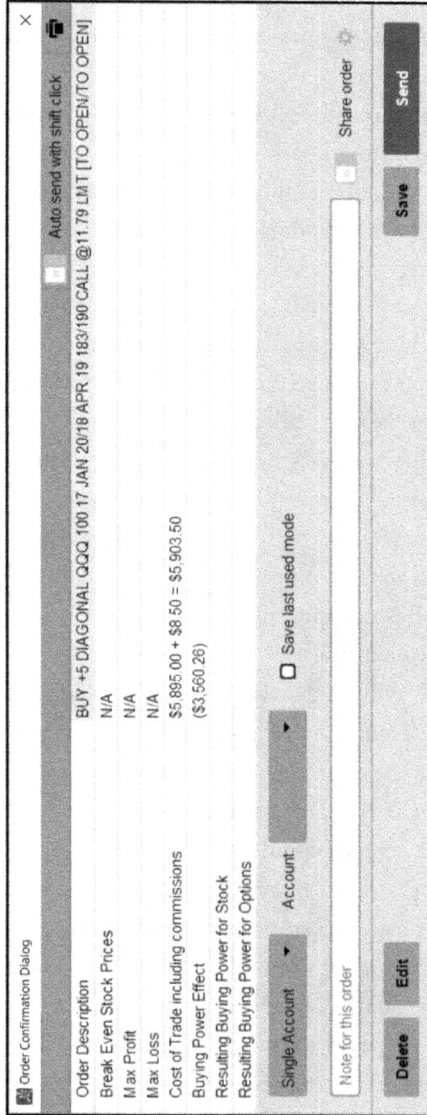

Figure 6.24 The diagonal bull call spread order confirmation dialog

they cannot offset the greater loss suffered by the long calls owing to their higher Delta value.

4. If the price drop is sustained for a period of time, buying put options could return a profit. But if the price drop is temporary, buying the puts would be throwing good money after bad, which would add to the trader's total loss.

5. It's always quite possible that the pullback is temporary. With ample time remaining in the life of the QQQ options, the price of QQQ may return to the dominant upward price trend. So don't panic during what may be a temporary market correction. Recall how price pullbacks are extremely common. Traders who look at chart patterns refer to short-term reversals in an upward price trend as a "bull flag." Many see the bull flag as a buying opportunity for a quick profit, because the long-term upward trend is likely to continue.

6. Another similar pattern, called a cup and handle, is a formation that drops, then rallies half-way back to the dominant trend, moves sideways for a few price intervals, and then returns to the dominant trend line. However, chart patterns are as random as the market, so using technical analysis on price charts should always consider both historical and fresh support and resistance levels as well as oversold/overbought momentum.

7. If a temporary pullback in value does not violate the trader's risk level, consider giving the diagonal long call trade a few dollars in working room, especially when several months remain till expiration. However, if using a protective stop, let it trigger, especially when the price reversal could last for several months from what appears to be a long-term market correction. Recall from Chapter 4, we *never* slide protective stops for a greater loss.

8. The best outcome is for the trader's bullish bias to be validated by a long-term continuation in QQQ's upward price trend. By keeping the option in play and rolling a half-dozen short call options, this trade could potentially earn $8,000 to $10,000. Don't let greed get in the way of taking a reasonable profit, because the trend could begin to move sideways and then drop. Short time increases Theta's value—the option buyer's enemy. When satisfied with the earned profit, close the trade.

9. High-frequency selling and buying price action is often a sign of indecisiveness. This is when the institutional traders begin taking profits, which would drive QQQ's price downward from high-volume selling. These same institutions wait for the QQQ to reach a support level and then buy back into QQQ in anticipation of another rally from renewed buying.

Iron Condor

The iron condor was discussed briefly in Chapter 2 and covered in some detail in Chapter 4 to illustrate how vertical spreads are used. The iron condor is quite popular among option traders because it collects premium from both calls and puts. And it is a risk-defined strategy that is easy to understand by anyone who knows how options work. This includes you, the reader, because you now know enough to try a few of the trades described in this book. Try them in simulation to gain confidence in what to trade, how to trade, and how using your trading rules increases your successful outcomes.

Structure (Applying Your Trading Rules)

Trader Bias: Neutral to mildly bearish

$-n$ OTM CALL OPTIONS

$+n$ OTM CALL above

$-n$ OTM PUT OPTIONS

$+n$ OTM PUT OPTIONS below

Option Expiration: < 56 days (One to three weeks till expiration is better.)

IV%: $\geq$ 40 percent (Traders seek higher IV% to increase premium values.)

$\pm$ Price Movement: < Short Call and Short Put Strike − ATM Strike

Delta of Short Call and Short Put Strikes: $\leq$ .25

Open Interest: $\geq$ 300 at all four strikes when trying to fill all four strikes in a single trade.

or

Open Interest: $\geq$ 10$\times$ at all strikes if the vertical put and vertical call spreads are traded in two separate transactions

Goals

The iron condor combines a bull put spread (described earlier in this chapter) and a bear call spread. Both short options are closer to the money than the long options, resulting in two vertical credit spreads. Having two credit spreads in a four-strike strategy can earn twice as much money as selling a single bull put spread or a bear call spread independently.

Description

You may recall from Chapter 4 how the iron condor returns a net premium from both the short call and the short put vertical spreads. The premium is calculated by the total difference in the long and short options. If the Mark value of the short put is $1.00 and the Mark value of the long put below is 50 cents, each put option would return $50 in premium less transaction fees. If the same Mark values exist for the call options, then the entire trade would return $1.00 in profit for the call and put spreads for a total of $100. Ten contracts would return $1,000 less the transaction costs in commissions and exchange fees.

There are some nicknames for these vertical spreads. The "chicken" iron condor uses narrow strike widths of perhaps one or two strikes. The strike values correspond to the stock price. This reduces the risk but gives up premium. The "big-boy" iron condor may separate the short and farther OTM long options by three or more strikes. This increases the net values in premium but increases the risk. Just like any vertical spread, if the short option expires ITM, the trader will be exercised, and the spread width corresponds to the amount of premium put at risk.

There are two variations to the iron condor. One combines a bear call spread with a short cash-covered put. This eliminates the cost of the long put and returns more premium. But the short put is more vulnerable because it is not covered by a farther OTM long put. This is referred to as a jade lizard.

The other is the bull put spread with an OTM short call. This can only be traded by level 4 traders who are permitted to trade uncovered calls. This trade, often referred to as a twisted sister, carries more risk if the short call drops in the money and is exercised. This is because the short calls that were originally OTM are at a higher strike price and more expensive than the short puts below. Therefore, if the short call is exercised, the loss can be substantial.

Finally, if both vertical spreads of an iron condor remain OTM through expiration, the trader would let them expire worthless. If one of the spreads becomes vulnerable, the trader would close the losing side and keep the profitable spread as described later within the iron condor's trade management description.

Chart Analysis

The LULU price chart in Figure 6.25 shows the price movement in a series of "range-bound" swings, i.e., indecisiveness on the part of market traders. This series also exists in longer-term LULU price charts, which establishes a common occurrence that exists for this particular stock. The option trader believes the iron condor to be the ideal strategy for premium income. The current IV% is at a high 97.91 percent, price movement of only ±$15.659, strong liquidity exists with high Open Interest values, and an iron condor expiring in just six days will most likely expire OTM and worthless.

Using the Option Chain

The option chain illustration in Figure 6.26 shows a series of OTM calls and OTM puts. The trader's selected strikes are outlined and described on the order bar. Notice how the iron condor earns two credits from a bull put vertical spread at the 127 and 123 strikes and from a bear call vertical spread at the 165 and 170 strikes. The order bar shows five contracts being sold for a credit of $2.37. This earns the trader $1,185 in premium income less commissions and exchange fees. Exchange fees for a four-strike strategy can add up, especially when several contracts are involved. This five-contract example includes 20 exchange fees plus the usual brokerage commission. The cost of the trade is included in the order confirmation dialog shown in Figure 6.29.

Figure 6.25 LULU 1-hour interval candlestick price chart

©2019 TD Ameritrade IP Company, Inc. For illustrative purposes only.

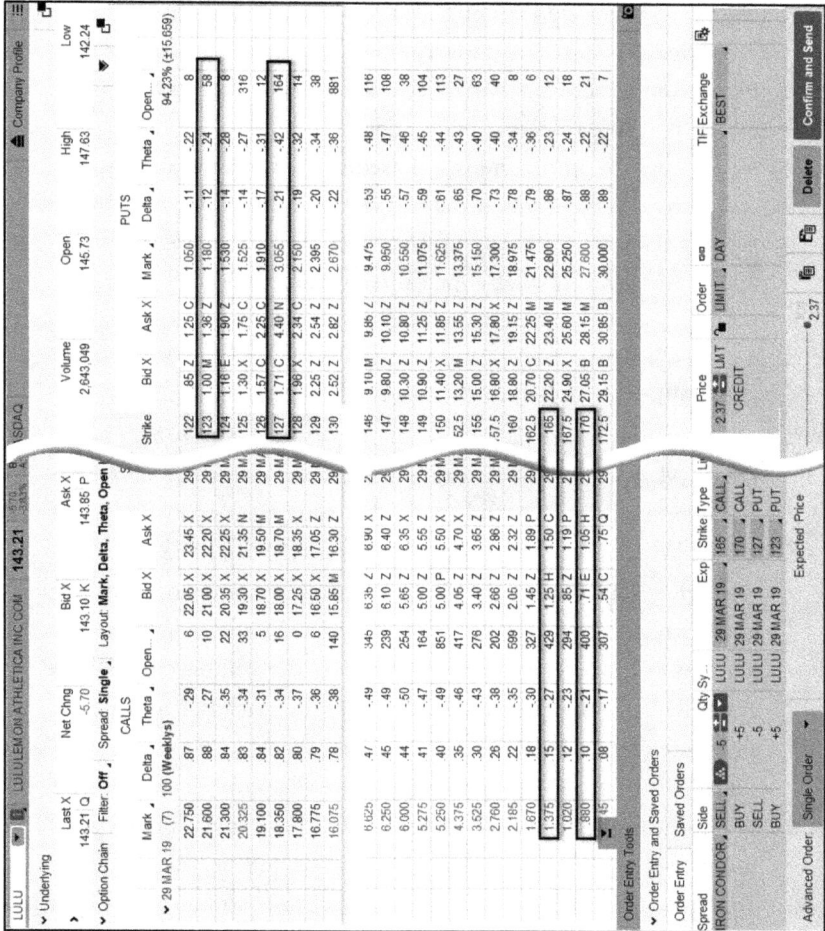

Figure 6.26 LULU option chain with an iron condor

©2019 TD Ameritrade IP Company, Inc. For illustrative purposes only.

Checking the Order Rules

Several of the order rules included in the following list were mentioned in the above option chain narrative.

Time to Expiration: The two spreads within this iron condor expire within 7 days. The short time frame benefits the short options that exist within this iron condor. This strategy should earn the trader more than $1,100 in one week. Being able to find an opportunity like this one each and every week, along with a few other trades, can earn option traders a living wage.

IV%: Because the iron condor is a credit collection option strategy, the current IV% of 94.23 percent favors this credit spread by returning more than $1100 in profit, even after deducting the transaction fees. And the high Open Interest values boost IV% and the premium values up and down both Mark columns.

±Price Movement: The price movement value of $15.659 makes it reasonably easy to find OTM short options well beyond the computed price movement. Notice the short put strike is $16 below the ATM strike, while the strike of the short call is $22 above the ATM strike. Both are within our price movement rule.

Delta of the 165 short call strike is at a safe .15, and the 127 short put strike is at a Delta .21. Both short options meet our .25 rule and have high probabilities of expiring OTM and worthless. The good news is that it is unlikely that the trader will have to pay the 10 exchange fees required to close one of the spreads, because both should remain OTM over the remaining six days till expiration.

Open Interest: The Open Interest values are all above 50. Because the two vertical spreads work independently, they can each be isolated into two separate two-strike vertical spreads. Hence, the two-strike 10× rule can apply to each. Because all four strikes have Open Interest values higher than 50, they meet our rules.

Theta: With only 6 days remaining until expiration, Theta is beginning to take its toll on premium values. Theta is reducing the premium values of the short and long puts by .42 and .24 cents per day, while the premium values of short and long calls are exiting .27 and .21 cents per day. With all other factors remaining constant, these values will be higher tomorrow. However, other factors, such as Vega (volatility) and changes in the price of the stock will also impact option premium values. These price changes constantly update the trader's position statements. The net difference in the long and short options is displayed. Hence, the put spread would drop 18 cents (.42 − .24), and the call spread would drop 6 cents (.27 − .21). But this is considering Theta in isolation, without considering the other variables that constantly impact option premiums.

Vega: The net Vega values impact the changes in option premium more than the other Greeks. Although not shown in Figure 5.26 in order to save space, the net Vega value between the short and the long puts was 3 cents (and 1 cent, respectively). Like the Gamma values, Vega values are also highest at the money (closest to the price of the underlying stock). This shows how changes in volatility affect options that are closer to or ATM more than those that are either farther OTM or deeper ITM. Also recall how Delta values increase as they become deeper ITM, although the incremental values between strikes decline.

Bid-to-Ask Spread: The Bid-to-Ask spreads are all reasonable with the exception of the 127 short put option, which is the closest to the ATM strike. This could create slippage, requiring the trader to give up a few cents per short put to be filled. In fact, the wide spread may encourage the trader to separate this iron condor into two orders: a bull put and a bear call. It is much easier to be filled when trading a two-strike spread than trying to simultaneously fill four strikes. The trader would not want to lose this profitable trade by being rejected because of the five short puts. So paying another $5.00 in brokerage commissions is reasonably inexpensive considering the overall profit potential of this iron condor.

Mark Value: This is a credit spread that is rewarded by the currently high IV% of 94.27 percent. Recall the terms "big-boy" and "chicken" spreads mentioned earlier. Big-boy spreads are wider than chicken spreads. In this trade, the bull put spread is a good example of using a big-boy spread that has a five-strike separation (strike width) between the short and long put. The bear call spread illustrates a chicken spread with only a three-strike separation. The difference in the bull put Mark values is $1.87, while the net Mark value of the bear call spread is only $.495 cents. This is a typical example of how a higher risk returns a higher reward.

Checking the Risk Profile

The risk profile in Figure 6.27 shows the $1,185 profit above the zero line. And the trader can also see what would happen if LULU's stock price drops below the $123 short puts or rallies above the $165 short calls. The trader's job is to prevent this from happening. If one of the short strikes is threatened by either a rally or a drop, the trader knows that one of the vertical spreads must be closed to limit a possible loss. Also check the "wings" of the graph. Notice how a risk-defined spread limits the losses. As shown, breaching the higher priced call spread loses a few hundred dollars more than for a price drop beyond the put spread. The trader can also see how this trade would still return a small profit even if the put spread becomes entirely ITM.

The iron condor risk profile shown in Figure 6.27 is quite typical. The "drooping left wing" shows how the bear call vertical spread is farther OTM than the bull put spread. Notice how the flat lines of the wings represent the maximum possible losses that correspond to either a substantial price drop from $143.21 to $127 or a price increase to $165.

Checking the Order Bar

The order bar confirms the iron condor trade structure (Figure 6.28). It displays the number of option contracts bought and sold, the symbol, expiration dates, strike prices, the option type (CALL or PUT) and the $2.37 net credit, which when multiplied by 500 shares is the $1,185 shown on the order confirmation dialog before transaction fees. Also notice this is a limit order and only fills at or above $2.37 per share. Recall that it may become necessary to split this trade as two vertical spreads owing to the wide Bid-to-Ask spread of the short 127 puts.

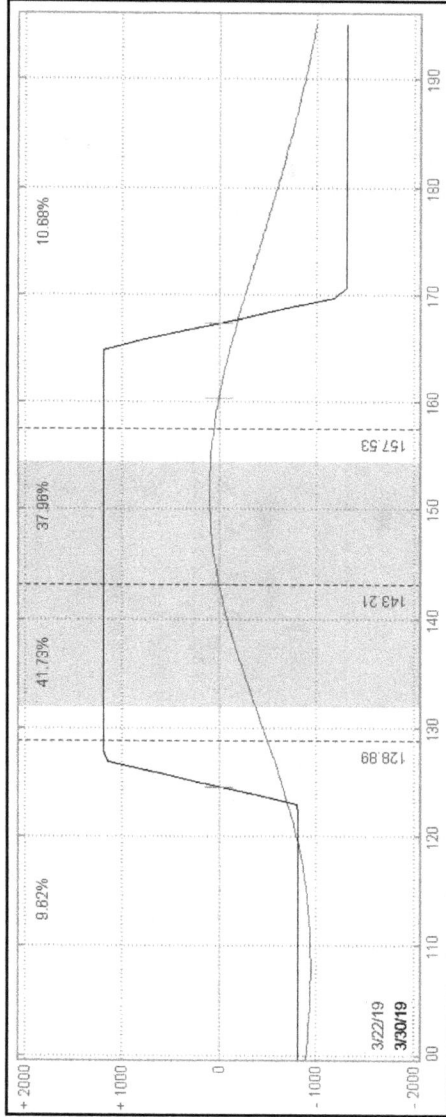

Figure 6.27 The LULU iron condor risk profile

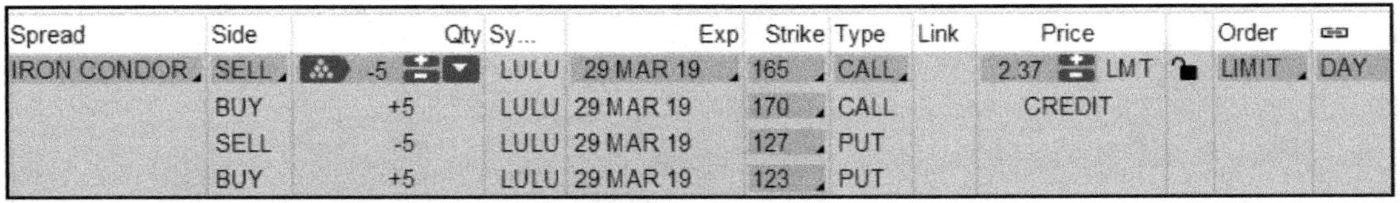

Spread	Side		Qty	Sy...	Exp	Strike	Type	Link	Price		Order	⊟
IRON CONDOR ▾	SELL ▾	❖	-5	▣ ▶	LULU	29 MAR 19	165 ▾	CALL ▾		2.37 ▾ LMT ◨	▚	LIMIT ▾ DAY
	BUY		+5		LULU	29 MAR 19	170 ▾	CALL		CREDIT		
	SELL		-5		LULU	29 MAR 19	127 ▾	PUT				
	BUY		+5		LULU	29 MAR 19	123 ▾	PUT				

Figure 6.28 Examining the iron condor order bar

Reviewing the Order Confirmation Dialog

The iron condor's order confirmation dialog shows the maximum profit as the amount received when traded, although it doesn't reveal the commissions (Figure 6.29). It also shows a maximum loss of $1,315, which happens only if the trader permits one of the vertical spreads to expire ITM. As shown on the risk profile, the worst case would be to let the bear call spread expire ITM.

Trade Management

1. Because the short options within this iron condor were placed at strikes that should remain OTM through expiration, the trader is likely to retain the credit in premium as profit until the options expire worthless.

2. If LULU's stock price either rallies or drops within a dollar of one of the short options above or below, the trader would immediately close all five vulnerable short options of the threatened vertical spread. If the long option has appreciated in value, it should reduce the debit paid when the threatened spread is closed. If the trader believes the price will continue to move through the remaining long option and move it ITM, he or she may wish to keep it and sell it when it returns more profit in premium than was paid when it was opened.

3. When the price of the underlying stock has moved away from either the iron condor's bull put spread or bear call spread, the trader may be able to add another short-term vertical spread for a few more dollars of premium when: a) there are only a matter of days until option expiration and b) when the premium justifies the risk of adding another spread. When the bull put is on the safe side and the premium of a cash-covered short put is worthwhile, the trader may consider adding it to your iron condor and letting it expire worthless for additional premium income.

4. The trader may wish to set two protective stop orders or alerts for each of the short options. This would notify the trader when either the short call or short put is within a dollar or two of a LULU price move. The specified stop amount relies on the price of the underlying security. The stop might be $1.00 above or below for a $50 stock, or perhaps as much as $5.00 for a $500 stock.

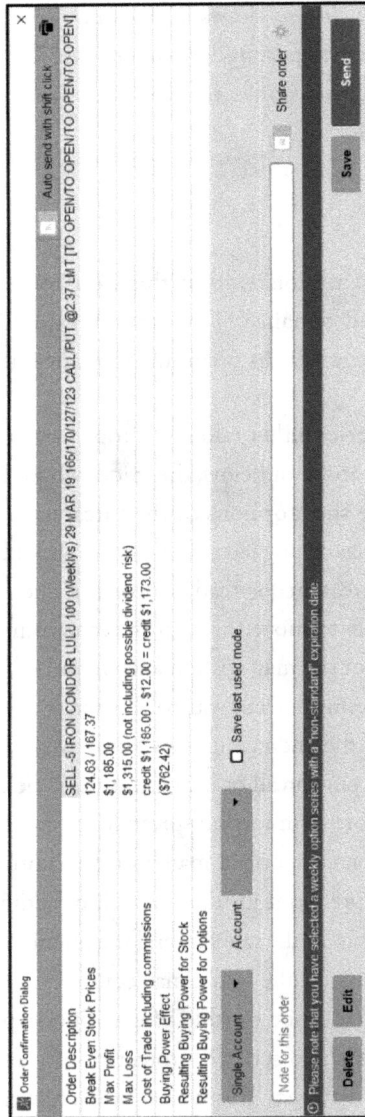

Figure 6.29 The iron condor order confirmation dialog

©2019 TD Ameritrade IP Company, Inc. For illustrative purposes only.

Synthetic Long Stock

Synthetic strategies use options to simulate the purchase or sale of a stock, ETF, or similar security. This option strategy buys calls and sells puts that are either at or within a strike of the current ATM price. This makes the synthetic long stock one of the most bullish strategies used. And, of course, it is always used on a stock or ETF trending upward. If the trader's bullish bias is confirmed by a strong, long-term upward price trend, both the call and put options can return a substantial profit. Many traders use LEAPS with the synthetic long stock. One reader of my book *The Only Options Trading Book You'll Ever Need* grew his account five-fold using the synthetic long stock strategy—his personal favorite. Once you finish this strategy's description, you may want to try this trade in simulation to see if it works for you. But *always* be sure to choose the ticker symbol of an uptrending stock or ETF. Because being wrong can be devastating.

Structure (Applying Your Trading Rules)

> Trader Bias: Bullish
> +n ATM CALL OPTIONS
> −n ATM PUT OPTION
> Option Expiration > 90 days (More time is better; LEAPS options are often used.)
> IV% ≤ 30 percent (Lower is better to reduce premium debit paid when traded.)
> ±Price Movement: (Not critical for two long options when low IV% exists)
> Long Call Delta ≈ .50
> Short Put Delta ≈ .50
> Open Interest: ≥ 300 at each of the call and put strikes

Goals

The trader's goal is to receive a substantially larger credit in premium income than originally paid when this trade is filled. If a bullish trader pays $275 to enter a synthetic long stock, the trader may close the trade for several thousand dollars if and when the price of the underlying security rallies according to the trader's bullish bias. In fact, if the price rallies over a period of a year on LEAPS options, it's possible for this trade to return more than 10 times the original premium paid. This is why many option traders use this strategy when they have a strong bullish bias on a particular security. But their bullish bias *must be right*!

Description

A typical price chart and an option chain on PayPal Holdings stock are included for your examination. The trader analyzed a sequence of long-to-short-term price charts and is confident the price of PayPal stock will continue its upward price trajectory. Recent pullbacks are seen as temporary "bull flags." This global market sentiment also influenced thousands of other popular stock prices.

The PayPal stock has been trending upward for many months, with a few short-term pullbacks as shown by the one-year chart in Figure 6.30, which includes a series of one-day candles. The option trader decides to take advantage of the current bull flag, i.e., the short-term pullback, and buy a synthetic long stock consisting of five long calls and five long puts—both at the money. The trader's reliance is on both an overall market recovery due to a brisk economy as well as PayPal's performance. The debit in premium paid for the five long calls is substantially offset by the premium received from the sale of the five short puts. This reduces the debit to a meager net debit of 55-cents per share.

Chart Analysis

Notice the bullish trend was interrupted by a $15 drop in October only to waver as the entire market experienced the pullback mentioned previously in this strategy's Description paragraph.

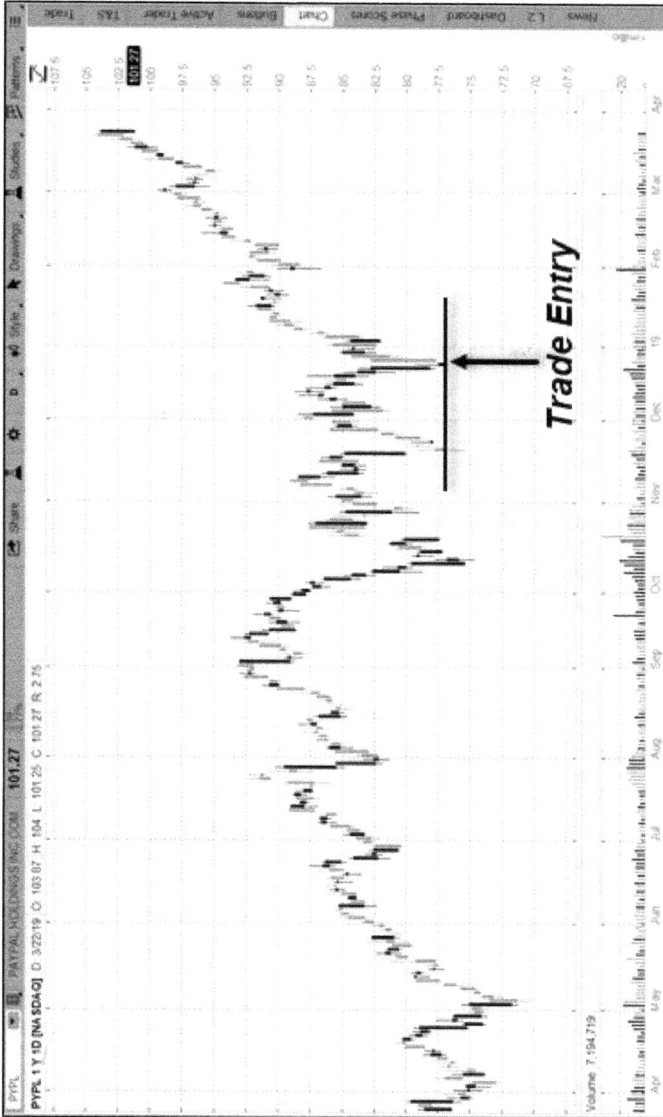

Figure 6.30 Looking for a long-term uptrending stock

©2019 TD Ameritrade IP Company, Inc. For illustrative purposes only.

Using the Option Chain

Check the long-term PayPal option chain that expires in 300 days contained in Figure 6.31. The net premium value is only 55 cents, which sums the combined Mark (premium) values of the calls and puts of $9.30 and −$8.75. Trading 500 contracts comes to a debit of $275 in premium plus commissions and option exchange fees for ten contracts.

This strategy usually trades calls and puts at the identical strike, i.e., both the calls and puts would be at either the $100 or the $105 strike. In this example, the trader deviated by one strike, which increased the debit paid when filled. If both the call and the put were placed at $105, the trade would return a credit of $875. However, some traders prefer not to sell ITM options, which would have been the case in this trade. Another alternative would be to place both the long calls and short puts at the $100 strike, which would become a debit spread that costs approximately $1,538. Hence, the trader is compelled to place the short put at the $100 strike and the long call at the $105 strike to minimize the entry cost and to place the short put OTM.

Applying the Order Rules

Time to Expiration: The synthetic long stock example shows 300 days until these two options expire. This amount of time, and often even a longer time, is common for the long synthetic stock. As mentioned earlier, LEAPS options are often used with this strategy.

IV%: Because the synthetic long stock includes both a long call and a short put, it usually has a small entry cost and often returns a small credit. The IV% is not a major factor at the time the trade is entered, and a swing in volatility is neutralized by having both long and short options. As you likely know by now, an increase in the IV% value increases the premium of the long call options while reducing the premium value of the short puts. The current IV% of 29.18 percent is reasonable for this trade and will likely increase in value as it returns toward its historical levels.

PAYPAL HOLDINGS INC COM **101.27**

> Underlying

Last X	Net Chng			Bid X		As
101.27 Q	-2.88			101.10 K		101.4

> Option Chain   Filter: **Off**   Spread: **Single**   Layout **Mark, Delta, Theta**

CALLS

Mark	Delta	Theta	Vega	Op...	Bid X	Ask X
21.550	80	-.02	26	1,001	21.10 X 22.00 I	
19.850	77	-.02	28	579	19.55 X 20.15 M	
17.950	74	-.02	30	2,454	17.55 X 18.35 M	
16.400	70	-.02	32	624	16.15 X 16.65 M	
14.700	67	-.02	33	561	14.30 X 15.10 M	
13.200	64	-.02	35	1,050	12.85 X 13.55 N	
11.825	60	-.02	36	8,610	11.50 X 12.15 M	
9.300	52	-.02	37	3,179	8.95 N 9.65 M	
7.375	45	-.02	36	3,204	7.10 C 7.65 M	
5.500	37	-.02	32	5,938	5.30 M 5.70 M	
4.175	30	-.02	32	1,073	3.85 M 4.50 M	
1.570	15	-.01	.1	100	.35 Z 1.5 h	
1.060	11	-.01	.17	1,079	.91 M 1.21 I	
.09		-.01	15	79	.73 I 1.06 I	

PUTS

Strike	Bid X	Ask X	Mark	Delta	Theta	Vega	Op...
85	3.40 M	3.75 M	3.000	-.20	-.01	26	3,774
87.5	4.10 M	4.35 M	4.225	-.23	-.01	28	925
90	4.80 Z	5.30 M	5.050	-.26	-.01	30	4,468
92.5	5.55 N	5.90 M	5.725	-.30	-.01	32	736
95	6.45 Z	6.95 M	6.700	-.33	-.01	33	805
97.5	7.20 M	7.90 M	7.550	-.37	-.01	35	479
100	8.50 P	9.00 M	8.750	-.41	-.01	36	1,144
105	10.70 X 11.35 M		11.025	-.49	-.01	37	238
110	13.75 M 14.35 M		14.050	-.57	-.01	36	20
115	17.05 M 17.60 M		17.325	-.66	-.01	33	78
120	20.75 A 21.35 M		21.050	-.73	-.01	30	81
...	31.50 P 34.40 C		32.950	-.0	.00	3t	
140	36.30 M 40.55 H		38.425	-1.00	.00	00	0
145	41.30 T 45.60 H		43.450	-1.00	.00	00	0

Order Entry Tools

> Order Entry and Saved Orders

Order Entry   Saved Orders

Spread	Side		Qty	Symbol	Exp	Strike	Type	Link
COMBO	BUY		+5	PYPL	17 JAN 20	105	CALL	
	SELL		-5	PYPL	17 JAN 20	100	PUT	

Expected Pr...

Price		Order	TIF Exchange
55 LMT	DEBIT	LIMIT DAY	BEST

1.15

Advanced Order: Single Order

Delete   Confirm and Send

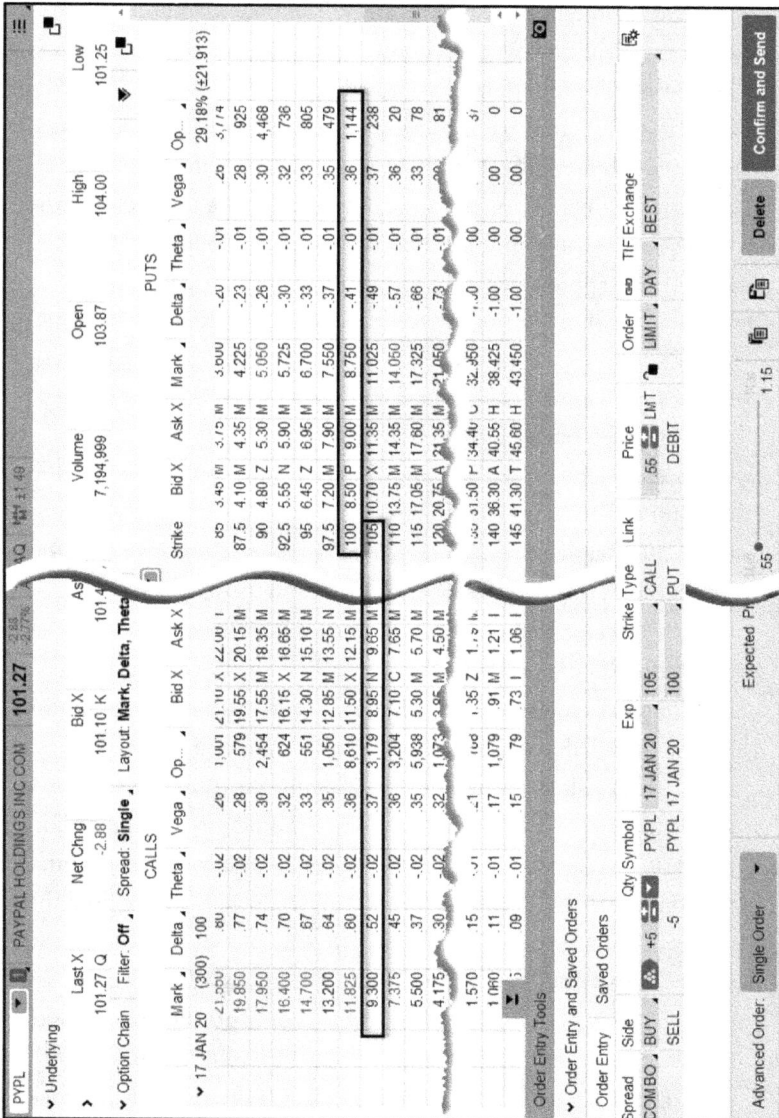

Figure 6.31 The Synthetic Long Stock on a Long-Term Option Chain

±Price Movement: The current price movement value of ±$21.983 places the five short puts well within the price movement. Of course, this is necessary when the ATM or slightly OTM short put is used with the synthetic long stock strategy. The trader has an exceptionally strong bullish bias and chooses an option chain with 300 days remaining till expiration. This provides plenty of time to adjust the trade if it becomes necessary. However, if the trader's bullish bias is unfounded, the trader would become concerned about the vulnerable short put if it begins to move several strikes up and into the money. This would prompt the trader to open a buy-to-close order if this trade approaches a few months until expiration.

Delta: The ATM, or very close to the ATM strike, have Delta values very close to .50. This will almost always be the case for the synthetic long stock strategy. And the trader's bullish bias must be rational based on his or her chart analysis.

Open Interest: The Open Interest values are both well above the 300 rule value. The call's Open Interest value is at an extremely impressive 9,300, while the put's Open Interest value is at a strong 1,144. These values should promote fast order fills as long as the price is reasonably close to the net Mark value.

Theta: With 300 days till expiration, the Theta values are quite small. The long calls have a Theta value of 2 cents, while the short puts have a Theta value of 1 cent. If PayPal's stock price increases, these small Theta values are reasonably insignificant. Of course, Theta values increase with each passing day, especially when the option expiration draws within a matter of a few weeks to contract expiration. However, it's likely that the trader will have already closed the synthetic long stock for profit.

Vega: The Vega values are both positive. Changes in volatility increases or decreases both the long calls and the short puts. Hence, changes in volatility either increase or decrease the premium values of both the call and put sides of this trade. A rally in the price of the stock rewards both the long call and the short put; a drop in price punishes both the long call and the short put.

Bid-to-Ask Spread: The Bid-to-Ask spreads are all quite narrow for this $100 per share stock. This is the result of high trading volume and Open Interest values. With this much volume and corresponding narrow Bid-to-Ask spread values, fairly priced orders should fill rapidly, especially when only two different options are included in this option strategy.

Mark Value: The synthetic long stock strategy is usually a small debit trade, although the example returns a small credit due to the higher premium values of the puts. Both Mark values will decline with the passage of time. However, if the trader's bullish bias results in a price rally in PayPal stock, the long calls move deeper ITM, while the short puts drop farther OTM toward safety.

Checking the Risk Profile

The risk profile in Figure 6.32 shows a short horizontal plot section between the price of the long calls and the short puts of this synthetic long stock, i.e., the $100 and $105 strikes. Had both options been placed at either $100 or $105, the plotline would be a smooth upward trend line. And if the risk profile were widened to display higher prices, you would be able to see how a strong rally would return even more profit. If you examine the dashed line above $111.40, this small price increase in PayPal stock would return approximately $3,000 for a small debit of $275—an 11× return on investment.

Checking the Order Bar

The order bar in Figure 6.33 shows the structure of this synthetic long stock trade. Notice how it includes the five long calls and five short puts. Also check the strikes at $100 and $105. The $0.55 per share net debit (the cost of this trade if filled) is shown in the Price column. Also notice that it is a limit day order. If not filled, the order will expire when the market closes at the end of the day.

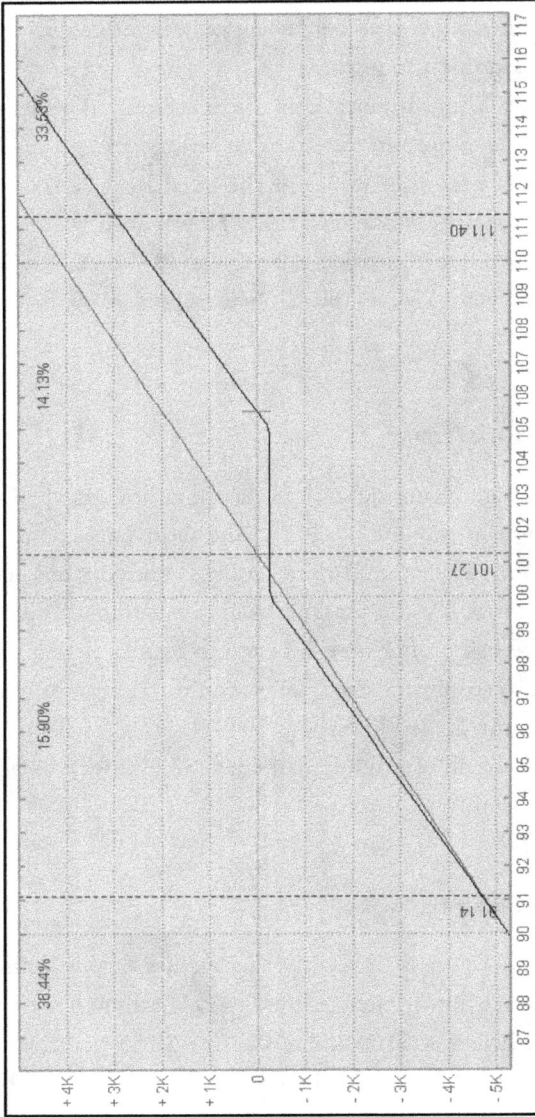

Figure 6.32 The synthetic long stock risk profile

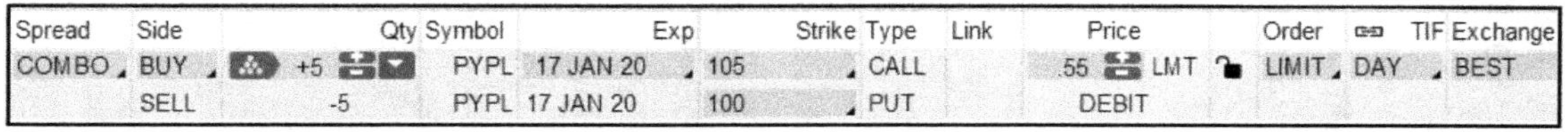

Spread	Side	Qty	Symbol	Exp	Strike	Type	Link	Price		Order	⊡	TIF	Exchange
COMBO ▾	BUY ▾	⚙ +5 ⚙ ▶	PYPL	17 JAN 20	105	CALL ▾		.55 ⚙ LMT ▾		LIMIT ▾		DAY ▾	BEST ▾
	SELL ▾	-5	PYPL	17 JAN 20	100	PUT ▾		DEBIT					

Figure 6.33 The synthetic long stock order bar

©2019 TD Ameritrade IP Company, Inc. For illustrative purposes only.

Reviewing the Order Confirmation Dialog

The order confirmation dialog shown in Figure 6.34 describes the order with its cost, including commissions and exchange fees. Notice the trade would break even if the price of PayPal stock is $105. This rewards the short $100 puts, which would be $5.00 OTM. More importantly, notice the Infinite Max Profit value, which is one reason traders use this strategy when they are confident in their bullish bias. Finally, notice the $7,124.26 Buying Power Effect. This represents a reduction in available trading margin, which shows the trader how much equity is available for use in additional trades.

Trade Management

1. If the trader's bullish bias is confirmed by a sustained, long-term price rally, the trader would let the trade continue to work until satisfied with the return in profit, which will likely be in the tens of thousands of dollars.

2. If the PayPal stock value hits a resistance level, stops its upward price trend, and begins to drop from new selling momentum, the trade should be closed in order to keep any profit that may exist.

3. This trade must be carefully monitored by the trader. A price drop could move the short put ITM. However, with 7 or 8 months remaining, if a minor, temporary pullback in the price of PayPal stock occurs, the Extrinsic value added to the current Intrinsic value would make the short put too expensive to exercise. This condition should last for a period of several months, but if only a few weeks to 30 days remain, the short put could become vulnerable. In addition, the long call will also begin losing value from the effect of Theta's daily erosion in time value. This is why the trader's bullish bias *must be* right!

4. If the price of PayPal's stock continues to move against the trade, consider closing it unless you believe a price pullback is simply a bull flag that will recover within the next few days.

5. As the synthetic short stock continues to work and the passage of time begins to increase the value of Theta, the profit of the long calls begins to decline as Delta loses its incremental value as the call

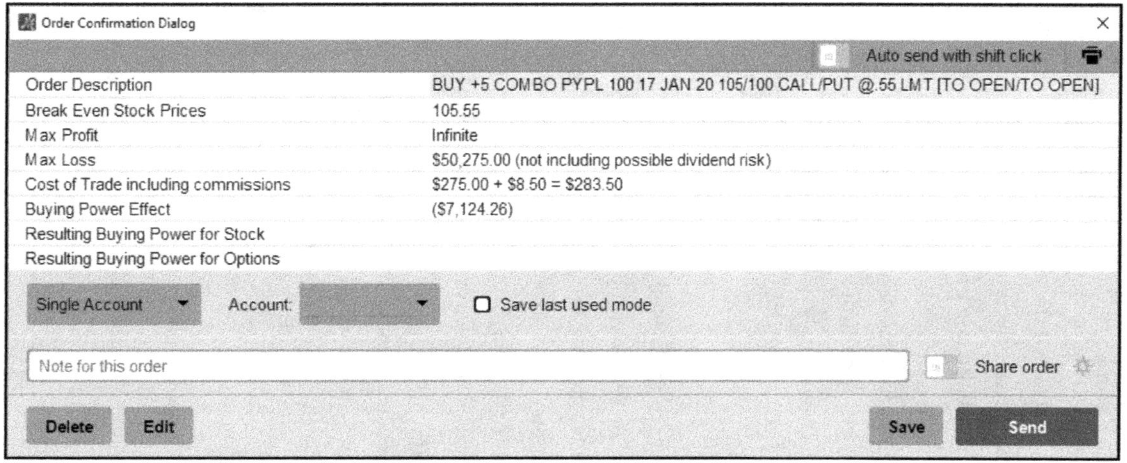

Figure 6.34 *The synthetic long stock order confirmation dialog*

©2019 TD Ameritrade IP Company, Inc. For illustrative purposes only.

options move deeper ITM and the puts move farther OTM. The trader will likely close the long calls for profit. If several months remain, the trader can either close the short puts with a buy-to-close order to recover the margin used to finance the short puts or simply keep them as cash-secured short puts until they expire worthless, especially if the strike of the short puts has a Delta value at or outside .32, i.e., one standard deviation.

6. The trader could also use protective stop orders on this trade's five long calls and five short puts. This protects both the long and the short options from excessive loss. These could be triggered if and when the stock price drops below a specified dollar value or the call option breaches a specified Delta value, such as a Delta .40, rather than increasing in value beyond .50 as Delta values move deeper ITM.

NOTE: Remember to trade small, trade often. Never risk more than you can afford to lose. A close friend of the author, who is also a very talented option trader, made extensive use of the synthetic short stock strategy. He made several million dollars in a matter of months. One trade included several dozen synthetic long stock options on AMZN just before the stock price dropped by $80 per share in a single day. That trade lost nearly one million dollars in one day. The loss sidelined his trading for several weeks. Fortunately, he's back in the market and is again succeeding. But even the best traders in the world can make mistakes. And overtrading is a common one. Books have been written about some of the bad trades made by great traders.

Synthetic Long Stock Combination

This trade adds an OTM short call and an OTM long put to the synthetic long stock described previously. The addition of one or more short calls results in a bull call vertical spread, while the addition of the long puts results in a bull put vertical spread. These additional options convert the unlimited risk strategy to a risk-defined strategy, although the amount put at risk can be substantial. This conversion permits low-level option traders to use this strategy. It can also be used in rollover IRA accounts.

Structure (Applying Your Trading Rules)

> Trader Bias: Bullish
>
> +*n* ATM CALL OPTIONS
>
> -*n* ATM PUT OPTION
>
> -*n* OTM CALL OPTIONS (This adds a bull call vertical spread when added to the ATM long calls.)
>
> +*n* OTM PUT OPTIONS (This adds a bull put vertical spread when added to the ATM short puts.)
>
> Option Expiration < 90 days (More time is better; LEAPS options are often used.)
>
> IV% ≤ 30% (A lower IV% is better to reduce premium debit paid when traded.)
>
> ±Price Movement: (> than the difference between the ATM strike and the short call options strike)
>
> Long Call Delta ≈ .50
>
> Short Put Delta ≈.50
>
> Long Put Delta ≤ .25
>
> Short Call Delta ≈ .25
>
> Open Interest: ≥ 300 at all four call and put strikes

Goals

This bullish trading strategy relies on a long-term price rally in the underlying security. If the price rallies according to the trader's analysis, it can return a substantial profit, although not as much as the synthetic short stock, primarily owing to the cost of the long OTM protective put and its loss in value due to the passage of time.

Description

This trade almost always requires a debit when filled, as the long ATM calls and OTM long puts are more expensive than the credit received from the OTM short calls and ATM short puts. However, the addition of the long puts reduces the risk created by the ATM short put, especially if the trader's bullish bias is wrong and the price of the underlying begins to drop.

Chart Analysis

The chart illustration in Figure 6.30 that is used with the synthetic long stock is typical of what a trader would use for this combination trade. Both require the trader to have a bullish bias to consider these two strategies. The primary motive for adding the short call and the long put is to limit risk.

Using the Option Chain

Notice the PayPal option chain in Figure 6.35 was also used with the synthetic long stock. It now includes the OTM short calls and long puts. Notice how the long call and short put are now both at the 100 strike, which is common for both this strategy and the more conventional synthetic long stock. The debit paid when this trade fills is $3.52, compared with the $0.55 to enter the long synthetic stock. As shown on the order confirmation dialogs, the total costs are $275 for the conventional synthetic long stock compared with $1,760 for this combination. But much of the added cost was caused by moving the long call from the $105 strike to the $100 ITM strike. As you can see in Figure 6.35, the 100 Mark value is $11.825, compared with the 105 Mark value of $9.30, a $2.52 difference, which is the primary reason for the increase in cost between the two strategies.

Applying the Order Rules

Time to Expiration: The synthetic long stock combination example shows 300 days until these four options expire. Even longer times till expiration are common for this option strategy. As mentioned earlier and in the synthetic long stock strategy, LEAPS options are often used with this synthetic long stock combination strategy.

IV%: Because the synthetic long stock combination includes both long and short calls and puts, the impact of the IV% is neutralized. The 29.18 IV% is not a major factor in the cost of the trade when it is filled. In fact, a swing in volatility always affects the premium of ITM options more than OTM options. This is evident by comparing the Vega values of ITM options with OTM

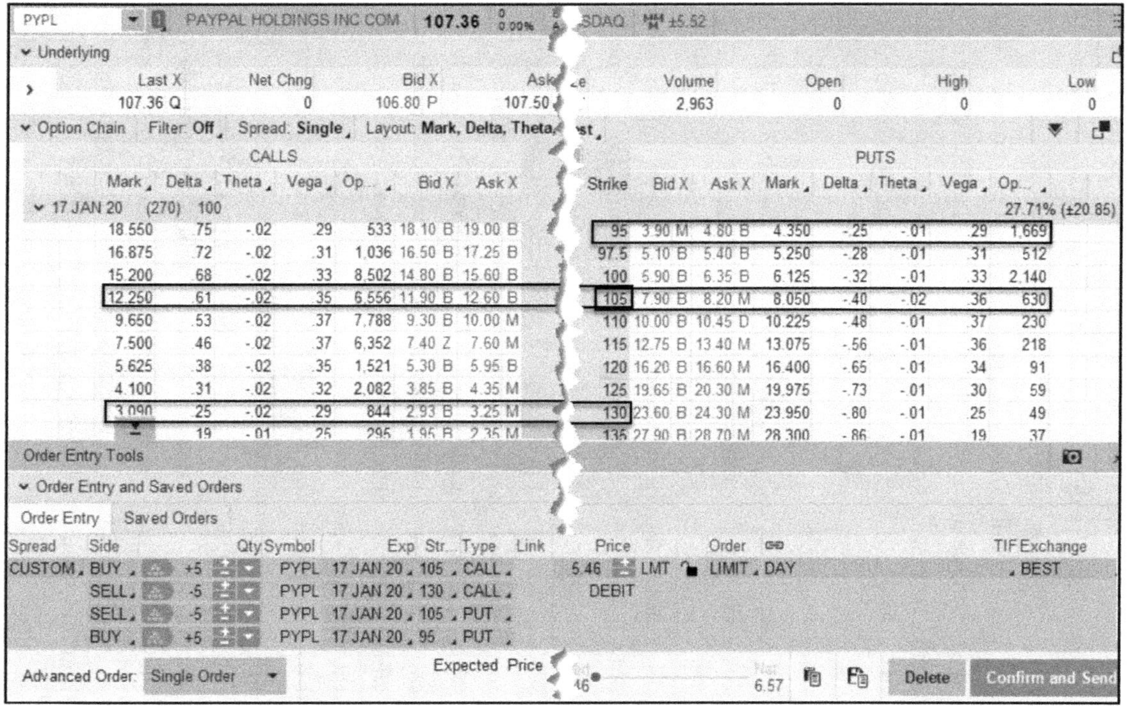

Figure 6.35 Placing a synthetic long stock combination on an option chain

©2019 TD Ameritrade IP Company, Inc. For illustrative purposes only.

options. And because the Vega values of the OTM options are within 3 cents of each other, they are also reasonably neutral.

±Price Movement: The current price movement value of ±$21.911 puts the five short calls $8.89 beyond the price movement's value. But, as with the traditional synthetic long stock strategy, this strategy includes the highly vulnerable short ATM put that's well within the range of the price movement.

Delta: The long call's Delta value is at .60, which indicates it is slightly ITM. And the short put is slightly OTM with a Delta value of .41. Again, because this strategy buys and sells ATM calls and puts and OTM calls and puts, the sum of the Delta values is close to neutral. As with the synthetic short stock, the trader's bullish bias *must* be correct to succeed.

Open Interest: The Open Interest values are all above 1,000, well above the 300-rule value.

Theta: With 300 days till expiration, the Theta values are quite small. Three out of four Theta values of the strikes used in this trade are only 1 cent, while the fourth is only 2 cents. These values will increase with the passage of time, but if the price of the PayPal stock increases, and in spite of Theta's increase in values, the stock's increase in value can begin to return thousands of dollars in profit.

Vega: As mentioned earlier, the net Vega values are reasonably small owing to the way the long calls and short puts offset each other, which essentially neutralizes the effect of increases and decreases in the values of Vega.

Bid-to-Ask Spread: The Bid-to-Ask spreads are all quite narrow for this $100 per share stock. This is the result of high trading volume and Open Interest values. With this much volume and corresponding narrow Bid-to-Ask spread values, fairly priced orders should fill rapidly. As mentioned earlier, traders often separate four-strike trades to expedite order fills. Although the strong liquidity should accelerate order fulfillment for all four strikes within this strategy, it could be submitted as two vertical spread orders using five bull calls and five bull puts, both described earlier in this chapter.

Mark Value: The synthetic long stock combination strategy is always a debit trade owing to the higher cost of the long calls and long puts compared with the credit of the short puts and short calls. The Mark values will all decline in value with the passage of time. But when the trader's bullish bias is correct, the long ATM calls and short ATM puts will both begin to reward this trade. At some point, the trade can be closed for a substantial profit.

Checking the Risk Profile

This risk profile is quite similar to the synthetic long stock risk profile shown in Figure 6.32. However, the slope of the profit plot is shallower. In this graph, notice how the return in profit is approximately $3,150, while the plot in Figure 6.32 for the synthetic long stock is more than $4,000 (Figure 6.36).

Checking the Order Bar

The above Synthetic Long Stock Combination Order Bar shows how each option is bought and sold, the number of contracts, the expiration dates, the strike prices, and the debit paid when filled. Notice this is a limit day order (Figure 6.37). If not filled, the price can be increased, although this may not be necessary given the strong Open Interest values (liquidity). If the trade does not fill during the current day, it will expire when the market closes at the end of the day.

Reviewing the Order Confirmation Dialog

As you can see in the order confirmation dialog shown in Figure 6.38 above, this trade needs only rally to $103.52 to achieve breakeven. Once PayPal's stock price increases above $103.52, the trader begins to realize a profit. Notice the maximum loss. Although this is substantial, it is limited to $11,760 if the trader does nothing. However, experienced option traders have several techniques, including closing the losing legs and keeping the profitable ones, to substantially reduce the maximum loss.

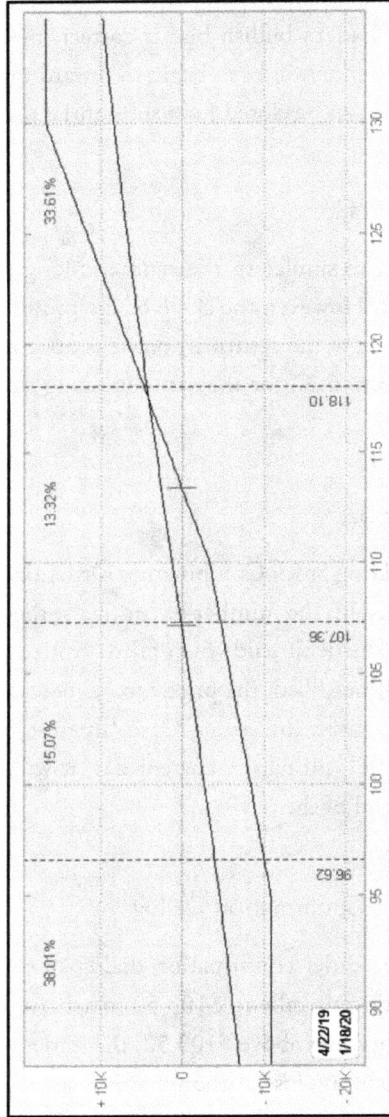

Figure 6.36 A synthetic long stock combination risk profile

©2019 TD Ameritrade IP Company, Inc. For illustrative purposes only.

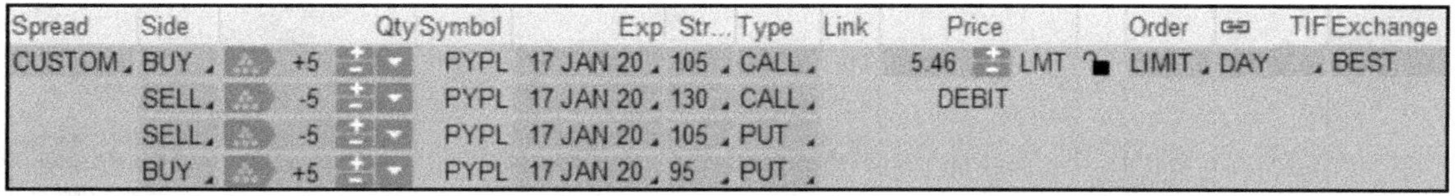

Spread	Side	Qty/Symbol	Exp	Str...	Type	Link	Price	Order	TIF Exchange
CUSTOM ,	BUY ,	+5 PYPL	17 JAN 20 ,	105 ,	CALL ,		5.46 LMT	LIMIT , DAY	, BEST
	SELL ,	-5 PYPL	17 JAN 20 ,	130 ,	CALL ,		DEBIT		
	SELL ,	-5 PYPL	17 JAN 20 ,	105 ,	PUT ,				
	BUY ,	+5 PYPL	17 JAN 20 ,	95 ,	PUT ,				

Figure 6.37 A synthetic long stock combination order bar

©2019 TD Ameritrade IP Company, Inc. For illustrative purposes only.

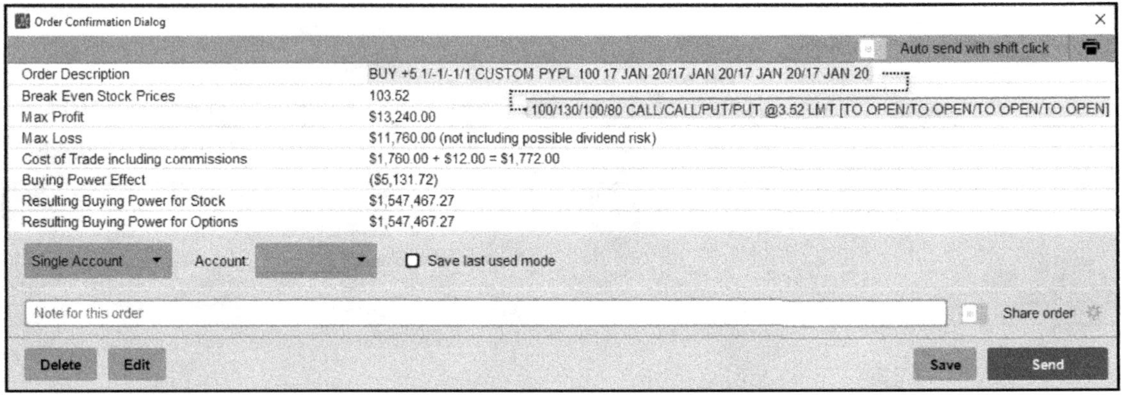

Order Confirmation Dialog ☐ Auto send with shift click ✕

Order Description	BUY +5 1/-1/-1/1 CUSTOM PYPL 100 17 JAN 20/17 JAN 20/17 JAN 20 ┄┄┄
	┄┄→ 100/130/100/80 CALL/CALL/PUT/PUT @3.52 LMT [TO OPEN/TO OPEN/TO OPEN/TO OPEN]
Break Even Stock Prices	103.52
Max Profit	$13,240.00
Max Loss	$11,760.00 (not including possible dividend risk)
Cost of Trade including commissions	$1,760.00 + $12.00 = $1,772.00
Buying Power Effect	($6,131.72)
Resulting Buying Power for Stock	$1,547,467.27
Resulting Buying Power for Options	$1,547,467.27

Single Account ▸ Account: ▸   ☐ Save last used mode

Note for this order   ☐ Share order ⚙

Delete Edit   Save   Send

Figure 6.38 A synthetic long stock combination order confirmation dialog

©2019 TD Ameritrade IP Company, Inc. For illustrative purposes only.

Trade Management

1. If the trader's bullish bias is confirmed by a sustained, long-term price rally, the trader would let the trade continue to work until satisfied with the return in profit, which, given enough time for the PayPal stock price to rally, could be several thousand dollars.

2. The long OTM puts and short OTM calls can be rolled when their strikes and premium values present an opportunity to increase profits. In particular, the short calls might be closed and then five new short calls sold at a farther OTM strike.

3. If the PayPal stock value hits a resistance level, stops its upward price trend, and begins to drop from new selling momentum, the long calls and short puts should be closed in order to keep any profit that may exist. If the premium value of the long puts and short calls are increasing, check to determine whether buying an inexpensive long call would result in a profitable bear call. As long as the price of PayPal stock continues to drop, the remaining options could increase in value. However, be prepared to close the entire trade immediately if (and when) the stock price bounces off support and begins to rally.

4. This trade must be carefully monitored by the trader. If a price drop occurs within a few days or weeks after it is opened, consider closing the vulnerable legs if the stock price appears to be making a sustained directional downward move. However, if several months still remain, and even if the short puts are a few dollars ITM, the Extrinsic value may prevent buyers from exercising the short calls. (Consider adding the Extrinsic column to your option chain to ensure the short puts would cost more in premium than they're worth. This will prevent being exercised.) However, if only a few weeks to perhaps 30 days remain, the short put is likely vulnerable. In addition, the long call will also begin losing value from Theta's daily increase in value. Close the trade.

5. If the price of PayPal's stock continues to move against the trade, consider closing it. But if your analysis indicates that the current price pullback is temporary with several months till expiration and simply a bull flag that will recover within the next few days, keep the trade for a while longer.

6. As the synthetic short stock combination continues to work and the passage of time begins to increase the value of Theta, the profit of both the long calls and puts begins to decline as Delta loses its incremental value, the call options move deeper ITM, and the puts move farther OTM. The trader would likely close the long calls for profit. If several months remain, the trader can either close the short puts with a buy-to-close order to recover the margin used to finance the short puts or simply keep them as cash-secured short puts and let them expire worthless. Ensure that the strike of the short puts have a Delta value at or outside .32, i.e., one standard deviation.

7. As in the synthetic long stock strategy, the trader might use protective stop orders on this trade's five long calls and five short puts. This protects both the long and the short options from excessive loss. These could be triggered if and when the stock price drops below a specified dollar value or the call option breaches a specified Delta value, such as a Delta .40, rather than increasing in value beyond .50 as Delta values move deeper ITM.

Unbalanced Broken Wing Long Call Butterfly

This version of the butterfly spread can return a profit regardless of the direction of a price move in the underlying security. It is constructed by the option trader to return a credit when filled by ensuring that the central short calls comprising the butterfly's body return more premium when sold than the debit spent buying the long call wings above and below.

Structure (Applying Your Trading Rules)

Trader Bias: Neutral, Bearish, or mildly bullish
$+n - x$ OTM CALL OPTIONS
$-2n$ OTM CALL OPTIONS, typically one strike higher
$+n + x$ OTM CALL OPTIONS, typically two or more strikes higher
Option Expiration ≈ 1 to 3 weeks
IV% ≥ 30 percent
±Price Movement: < Short Call Strike − ATM Strike
Short Call Delta ≤ .30
Open Interest at all three strikes: ≥ 300 (Higher is always better.)

Goals

This unbalanced, broken wing butterfly returns a small profit in credit when filled. One goal is for the short calls that comprise the butterfly's short option body to remain OTM throughout the life of the trade. However, if the price of the underlying security does rally and approaches the strike of the short calls, the trader will close the trade when the price begins to return a profit that exceeds the initial credit received when the trade was originally filled.

Description

This long call butterfly version might be constructed as follows:

Using options having $1.00 between each strike, i.e., the *strike widths*:

Buy 2 $50 calls (cost = 2 × $1.510 × 100 shares/option = $302 debit)

Sell 8 $51 calls one strike above (8 × $.955 × 100 shares/option = $764 credit)

Buy 6 $53 calls two strikes above (6 × $.245 × 100 shares/option = $147 debit)

Returns a $315 credit when filled from $764 − ($302 + $147) = $315

The trader can see the net credit of $1.57 on the order bar, while the total calculated credit or debit is displayed on the order confirmation dialog. Of course, traders can also calculate total credits and debits of complex trades as is done above by multiplying the number of contracts by the corresponding Mark values. These are multiplied by 100 shares per option contract. Once each strike is known, the total credit or debit is found by summing the totals.

Chart Analysis

Notice how the Mastercard price chart is moving sideways, making the trader's bias reasonably neutral, although the chart reveals a slight upward trend (Figure 6.39). This is ideal for a short-term unbalanced broken wing butterfly option strategy. This encourages the trader to begin examining Mastercard option chains to see if the premiums

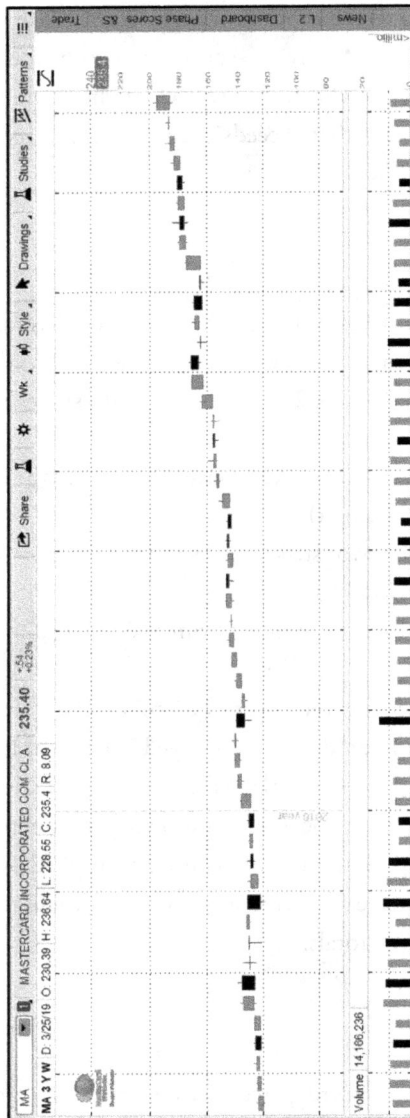

Figure 6.39 The Mastercard Incorporated price chart

and Greek values will support an option trade before settling on a trading strategy. There are other strategies, such as the iron condor described earlier in this chapter, that work nicely. The final strategy decision is made only after a trader considers a handful of reasonably safe and profitable trading possibilities. In this case, our trader considers Mastercard Incorporated's option chain, ticker symbol MA, shown in Figure 6.40.

Using the Option Chain

The Mastercard option chain includes many of the elements required for a successful option trade. For example, the option chain reveals reasonably good premiums at strikes having acceptable OTM Delta values. The strikes of interest also have ample Open Interest values. Although there are several option strategies that could work, the trader favors the unbalanced broken wing long call butterfly because it is a limited risk strategy, familiar, and it has usually succeeded when used in the past.

The trader will try a few different setups until the one shown in Figure 6.40 is settled on. The credit of $1.57 is certainly acceptable. If Mastercard's price drops unexpectedly, the trader still earns more than $300 in net premium. If Mastercard's stock price rallies, and the trade is managed properly, the trader could earn as much as $800, although a profit of between $300 and $500 would certainly suffice.

Applying the Order Rules

Time to Expiration: When traded, the option contracts used in this butterfly all expire in 13 days. This short period limits the amount of time Mastercard stock has to work against the trader. As you've learned, option traders always prefer using short-term credit spreads.

IV%: Because the long call butterfly includes both long and short calls, the impact of the IV% is somewhat neutral. The 26.01 IV% is not a major factor in the cost of the trade when it is filled, although premium values collected and paid are both higher when the IV% is higher.

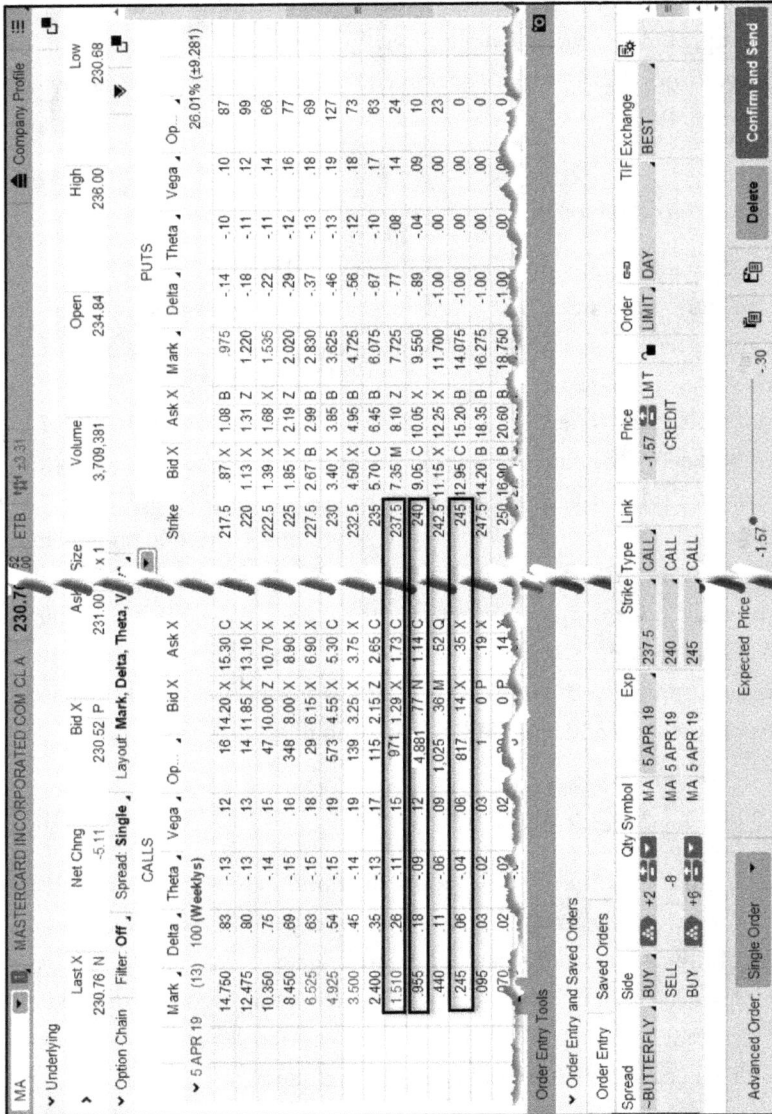

Figure 6.40 The unbalanced broken wing long call butterfly option chain

±Price Movement: The current price movement value of ±$9.28 puts the eight short calls at the $240 strike slightly out of the range by several cents. Being farther above the price movement calculation is always desirable, but since this is a limited risk strategy that the trader knows how to manage, the trader will close the trade as soon as the stock price moves within the "tent" that's plotted on the risk profile in Figure 6.41.

Delta: The long call's Delta value is at .26, which tells the trader the two long calls used in the bottom wing will most likely remain OTM for the duration of this trade. The Delta value of the eight short calls located at the 240 strike are even more unlikely to become ITM for this trade's duration. Finally, the six long calls are nearly two standard deviations OTM at a strike that is extremely unlikely to become ITM.

Open Interest: The Open Interest values are all above the 300-rule value. These values should help this butterfly trade fill prior to the end of the trading day.

Theta: With only 13 days till expiration, the Theta values are beginning to reduce premium values. This benefits the short calls and punishes the values of the long calls. Regardless of the decline in premium value, if the price of the Mastercard stock remains within a fairly narrow price range and all three strikes within the butterfly remain OTM, the trader will likely let it expire OTM.

Vega: As mentioned earlier, the net Vega values are reasonably small owing to the way the long calls and short puts offset each other. This neutralizes the effect of increases and decreases in the values of Vega.

Bid-to-Ask Spread: The Bid-to-Ask spreads are marginal owing to the lower Open Interest values. This is sometimes typical of weekly options when compared with the liquidity available within monthly options that expire on the third Friday of the month. The overall liquidity is slightly lower than usual because the Open Interest at several strikes is quite low. As you scan your option chains, look for those with narrow Bid-to-Ask spreads and high Open Interest values because they fill much faster. Recall how narrow Bid-to-Ask

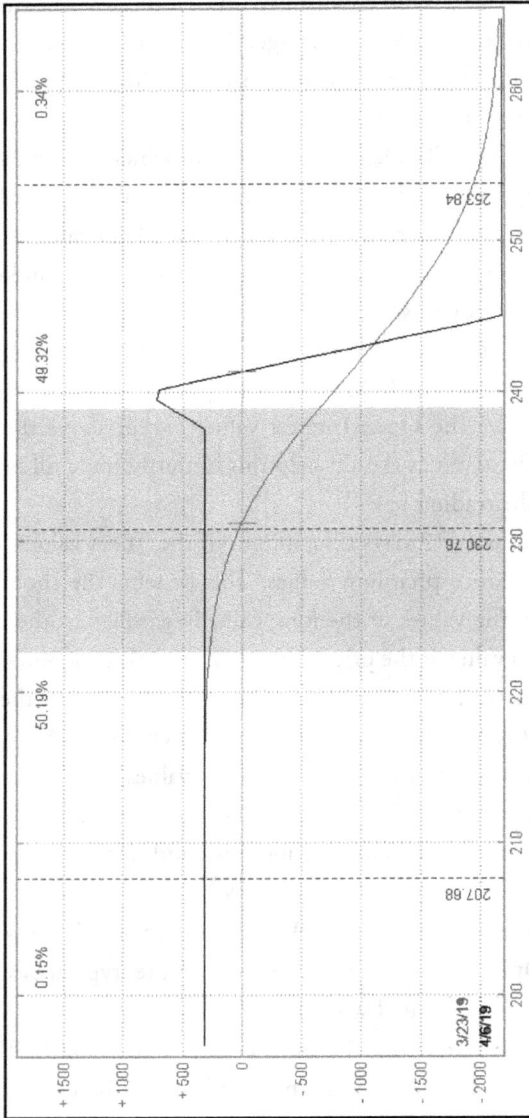

Figure 6.41 The unbalanced broken wing long call butterfly risk profile

spreads reduce premium slippage when either buying or selling options. When slippage becomes an issue, never force a trade by offering to buy at an excessively high premium or to sell at an unreasonably low premium. Move on by continuing to scan for a more reasonable trade setup on a different symbol. And always use your option trading rules.

Mark Value: The premium values of all three strikes are acceptable at all three legs of this long call butterfly. However, the slippage due to the wider than usual Bid-to-Ask spread could discourage conservative traders from negotiating for more than a few minutes to achieve a reasonable fill, i.e., the amount of credit offered to fill the trade.

Checking the Risk Profile

The risk profile in Figure 6.41 illustrates how the $314 credit exists when the price of the Mastercard stock remains within one standard deviation of the current $230.78 price. However, there is an uptick in credit if the stock price becomes within a few dollars below $240.

Also notice how the trader retains the $300 credit as long as the stock price stays at or below the upper $247. The trader must be prepared to close this trade if the price of MA stock experiences a strong rally. However, the above price chart analysis indicates a predominantly sideways-price movement with a very minor upward trajectory.

Checking the Order Bar

Figure 6.42 shows the buying and selling quantities for MA in addition to the expiration dates, strike prices, option types, and the price, which is a credit. And as you saw, the credit was created by the trader's choice of strikes (broken wing) and the number of contracts in each (unbalanced).

The trader will definitely check the risk profile and order confirmation dialog before submitting this order to see how this trade reacts to price movement. In contrast, a traditional balanced butterfly with the same number of option contracts would include four long calls in each of the wings and eight short calls in the body. But this would change the

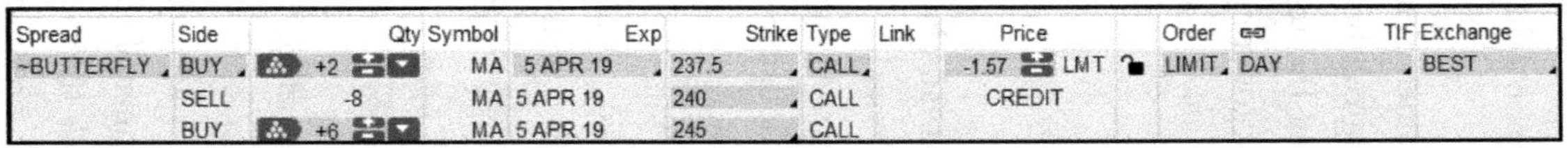

Spread	Side		Qty	Symbol		Exp	Strike	Type	Link	Price		Order		TIF	Exchange
~BUTTERFLY	BUY	+2		MA	5 APR 19		237.5	CALL		-1.57 LMT		LIMIT	DAY		BEST
	SELL	-8		MA	5 APR 19		240	CALL		CREDIT					
	BUY	+6		MA	5 APR 19		245	CALL							

Figure 6.42 The unbalanced broken wing long call butterfly order bar

©2019 TD Ameritrade IP Company, Inc. For illustrative purposes only.

butterfly from a credit spread to a debit spread. This modification also requires the trader to move the strikes closer to the ATM price of the MA stock. Although a debit spread, the risk graph would change to resemble the one shown in Figure 5.10. As shown in that risk profile, the price must move into the tent and be closed for the trade to return a profit. Otherwise, the trader will lose the initial debit in premium when the traditional long call butterfly order is filled.

Reviewing the Order Confirmation Dialog

The order confirmation dialog in Figure 6.43 describes this trade in addition to presenting a substantial amount of information about this broken wing long call butterfly. Notice the maximum profit and loss values. If the trader does not intervene and the price of the Mastercard stock rallies to $245, the trader can lose a total of $2,186. This is why we check our order confirmation dialogs before submitting our trades to the market.

Trade Management

1. By now you probably know that this trade must be managed by checking it on your smartphone or computer's trading applications. Consider setting a trade alert if the price moves into the tent of the risk profile.
2. You could also send a Mark-based alert or set a Mark-triggered stop order. These would be triggered if the MA stock price breached approximately $239.
3. If the stock price remains within a narrow range or drops, the trader will let all three calls expire OTM and keep the $300 credit that was received when this trade was filled. As you can see, once set up properly, this is a simple and fairly reliable trade. But be sure to try it in paper simulation before you begin risking money. Once you are comfortable in both the setup and several profitable results, you may be confident enough to begin using this strategy in the live market.

Iron Butterfly

The iron butterfly has the same structure as an iron condor except for its placement on the option chain. The iron butterfly used in this example

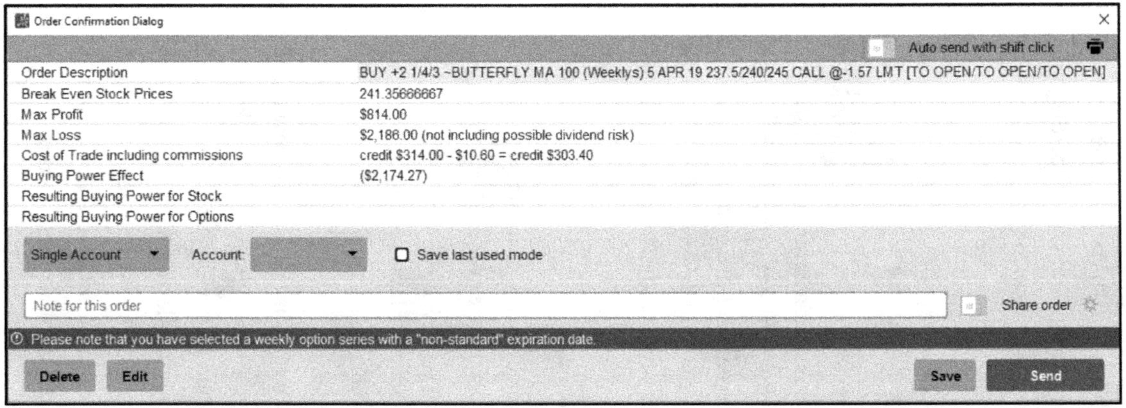

Order Confirmation Dialog

☐ Auto send with shift click

Order Description	BUY +2 1/4/3 - BUTTERFLY MA 100 (Weeklys) 5 APR 19 237.5/240/245 CALL @-1.57 LMT [TO OPEN:TO OPEN:TO OPEN]
Break Even Stock Prices	241.35666667
Max Profit	$814.00
Max Loss	$2,188.00 (not including possible dividend risk)
Cost of Trade including commissions	credit $314.00 - $10.60 = credit $303.40
Buying Power Effect	($2,174.27)
Resulting Buying Power for Stock	
Resulting Buying Power for Options	

Single Account ▼   Account: ▶

☐ Save last used mode

Note for this order

Share order ☼

ⓘ Please note that you have selected a weekly option series with a "non-standard" expiration date.

Delete   Edit

Save   Send

Figure 6.43   The unbalanced broken wing long call butterfly order confirmation dialog

includes an equal number of options at each of four strikes on the S&P 500 index, symbol SPX. Short calls and short puts are placed ATM. An equal number of long calls and long puts are placed two strikes OTM, i.e., the calls above and the puts below.

The iron butterfly contains two vertical spreads and can be traded on any security that expires within a matter of a few days to several weeks. And it must be monitored, because when the price of the underlying begins to make a directional move, either up or down, the trader must close the losing options, keep the winners, and ultimately close them for profit. The strategy includes a short straddle (an equal number of short ATM calls and puts) with the benefit of protective long calls and puts, which creates two vertical spreads that limit the trader's risk. Because the short ATM options return more premium than is spent for the OTM options, the iron butterfly is a credit spread.

According to a Chicago Board Options Exchange (CBOE) presentation conducted by an option trader and instructor named Dan Sheridan, the iron butterfly described in this section usually returns a profit of about 10 to 15 percent and is often closed within a few hours. This is a high-frequency, short-term trade that is opened 1 hour after the market opens on Monday and Wednesday mornings. The trade uses options that expire in just two days. The author has tested this trade with good results.

Structure (Applying Your Trading Rules)

−n ATM CALL OPTION

−n ATM PUT OPTION

+n OTM CALL OPTIONS, 2 strikes above

+n OTM PUT OPTIONS, 2 strikes below

Option Expiration < 2 days

IV% (Not relevant)

±Price Movement: (Not relevant)

Short ATM Call and Put Deltas ≈ .50

Long OTM Call and Put Deltas ≥ .30

Open Interest: ≥ 300 at all four strikes

Goals

According to Mr. Sheridan, each semiweekly two-day iron butterfly traded on the SPX returns a profit of approximately 10 to 15 percent eight out of each 10 trades. Entering this trade twice each week totals approximately 100 trades each year. The earnings mount up rapidly. And because it is a defined-risk trade, the structure of the trade limits the potential loss.

The key is learning how to manage the trade. This requires the trader to close the losing legs and to keep the profitable legs until a satisfactory profit level is achieved. However, this trade is reasonably easy to monitor on practically any trading platform to see which legs are returning a profit and which legs must be closed.

Description

This trade is entered twice each week, on Mondays and Wednesdays. The Monday trades select SPX options that expire on Wednesday, while the Wednesday trades select SPX options that expire on Friday. Because this strategy always trades ATM short options, it becomes a credit spread as soon as it fills.

This is when the work begins. The trade must be closely watched until the trader detects a directional movement in the SPX index. Once a sustained directional move is detected, the trader closes the losing position and retains the winning ones. Once an upward price move is validated, the losing short calls and long puts are closed, and the profitable long calls and short puts are retained. When the price of the SPX begins to drop, the vulnerable short puts and the long calls are closed. Once the profit reaches 10 to 15 percent, the trader should consider closing the trade for the accrued profit. Staying in longer could see a price reversal, which could result in a loss. So the trader would settle for a small profit rather than waiting for a loss.

Chart Analysis

As you can see on the price chart in Figure 6.44, the SPX has been experiencing a substantial number of price moves. The price trend was slightly downward on the first Monday, rallied on the first Wednesday,

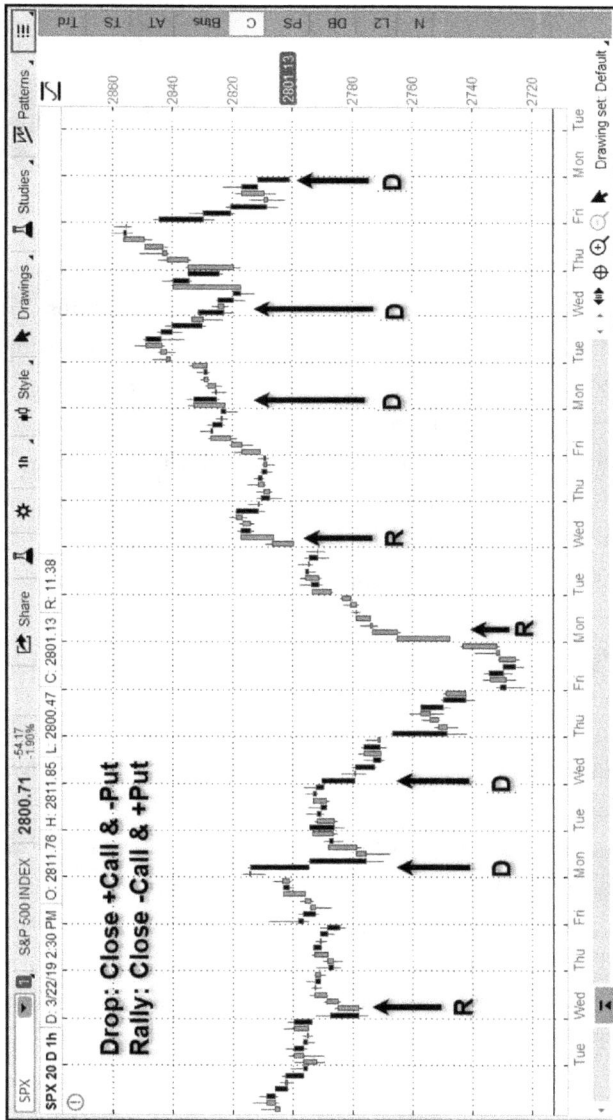

Figure 6.44 An S&P 500 (SPX) price chart

and dropped again on the following Monday (the first "D"). Most of these moves will return a reasonable profit of at least 10 percent if the trader is patient enough to wait for a sustained move. Of course, there are a number of variables, and the market can reverse direction before the trader can intervene. But as you can see, watching the rallies and drops and settling for 10 to 15 percent returns a profit in almost every case. Becoming greedy and waiting too long is not recommended when trading an iron butterfly.

Using the Option Chain

The option chain in Figure 6.45 outlines the short calls and puts in the Bid columns and the long calls and puts in the Ask columns. These are the cells that are clicked by the trader to create this trade on the order bar. Notice that a credit of $8.80 is received when this trade fills—a total of $4,400 less commissions and 20 exchange fees, as you can see on the order confirmation dialog. This order should fill with the current levels of Open Interest shown in the option chain. And, as you can see on the risk profile and in the order confirmation dialog, the trade has a maximum loss of $800—an exceptional reward to risk ratio.

Applying the Order Rules

Time to Expiration: This particular iron butterfly strategy is designed to expire in 2 days. However, the iron butterfly can be used with securities other than the SPX and for longer periods of time but typically inside 56 days (8 weeks). Using a stock or ETF with the iron butterfly will also provide a credit, although smaller, when entered. But it would be managed identically by closing the losing trades and keeping the winning ones. But before trading a stock or ETF, perform your price analysis and develop a trading bias.

IV%: Because the iron butterfly includes both long and short calls, the impact of the 12.83 IV% is neutral. In fact, the initial $8.80 in premium credit and the $4,400 credit received when this trade was opened is excellent. Of course, a $2,800 index price contributes to these values. But, as explained, this is not the end of the story, as more work is required.

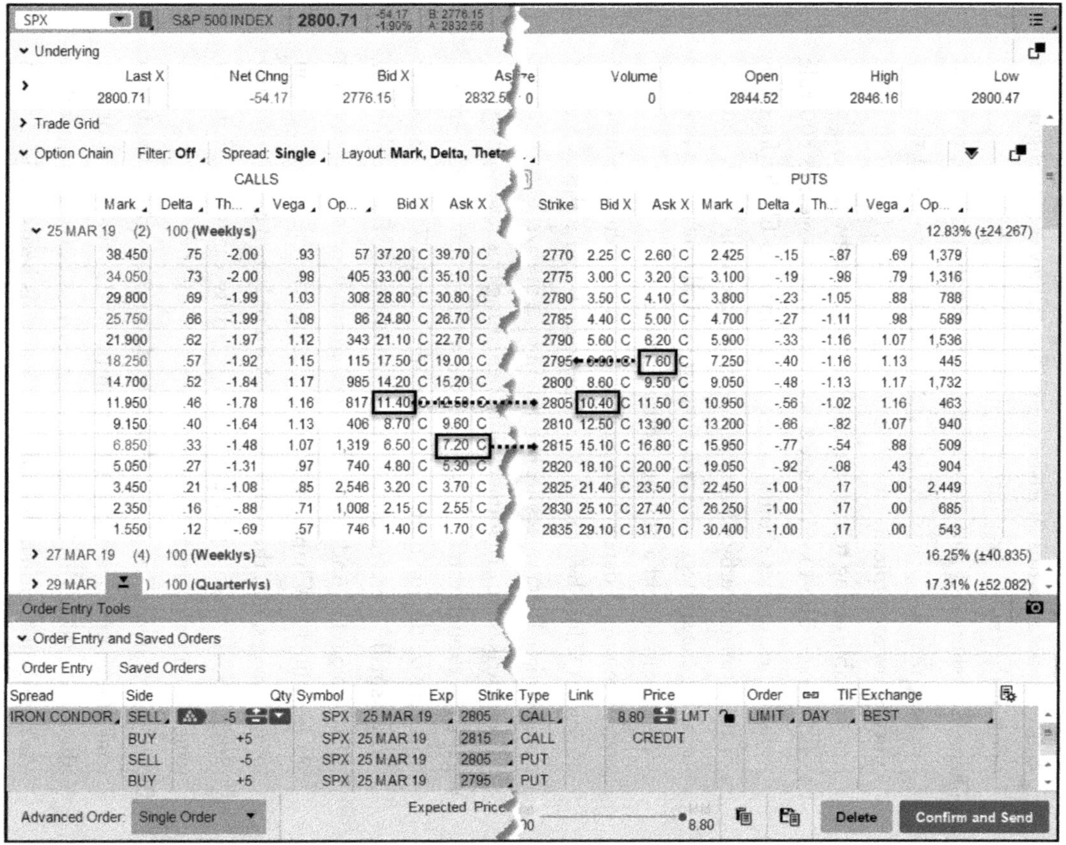

Figure 6.45 *An SPX option chain*

©2019 TD Ameritrade IP Company, Inc. For illustrative purposes only.

±Price Movement: The current price movement value of ±$24.267 cannot be a factor in the iron butterfly strategy because all call and put options are well within this price. The short calls and puts are ATM, which would be an unwanted situation in most credit collection strategies. But this is not a factor when entering an iron butterfly because this short-term option strategy is reconfigured as soon as the trader has a directional bias.

Delta: The short call and put Delta values are always close to ±.50 because they are placed ATM. The long calls above and the long puts below are typically inside ±.30. Again, these Delta values are unavoidable owing to the structure of this strategy.

Open Interest: The Open Interest values are all above the 300-rule value. These values should be ample in order to fill the four legs of this iron butterfly. If unable to fill a reasonable offer, consider breaking the strategy into two separate vertical spreads—a bear call vertical spread and a bull put vertical spread.

Theta: With only 2 days till expiration, the Theta values are reducing premium values by around $1.00 per day. Because this is a credit spread, high Theta values are helpful. In fact, the overall premium of all four strikes are dropping rapidly, benefiting this strategy as profit.

Vega: Even though the IV% is at an exceptionally low 12.83 percent, the Vega values are quite high, ranging from 1.07 to 1.16. Recall how a small 1 percent change in IV% will change the premium by $1.07 to $1.16. And this will change throughout the current day. As explained in Chapter 4, Vega's value has the most influence on option prices, i.e., the Mark values. With only two days remaining until expiration, a small change in volatility can result in major changes in premium values.

Bid-to-Ask Spread: The Bid-to-Ask spreads on the high-priced financial indices are reasonably narrow on the strikes that are at or near the ATM strike. This is especially true for a $2,800 per share index. As mentioned earlier, the Bid-to-Ask spreads become wider when Open Interest values decline.

Mark Value: The premium values of all four strikes are quite good, which is typical of index option strikes that reside at strikes with Delta values of .30 or higher.

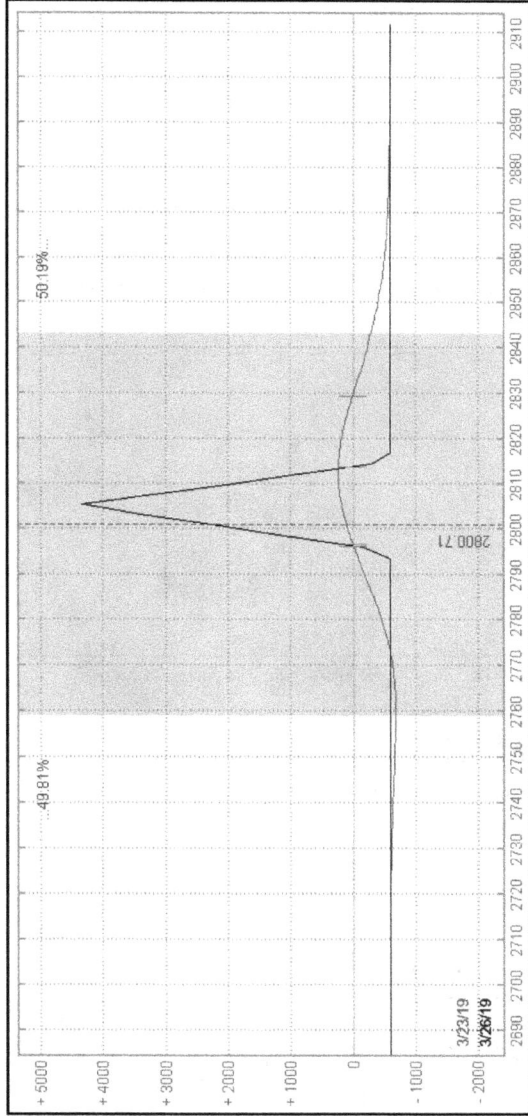

Figure 6.46 An SPX iron butterfly risk profile

©2019 TD Ameritrade IP Company, Inc. For illustrative purposes only.

Checking the Risk Profile

Notice the risk profile is almost identical to the long call butterfly risk profile shown in Figure 5.10 of Chapter 5. Also notice the peak of the tent is substantially higher than in the long call butterfly's risk graph.

The preceding risk graph will change into a diagonal line when the two losing options are closed and the profitable ones retained. It will resemble the risk profile of the synthetic long stock in Figure 6.32, except the horizontal flat line at the center is longer owing to the $10 strike width between the short puts and long calls. The following risk profile plots five short ATM puts and five calls ten strikes above.

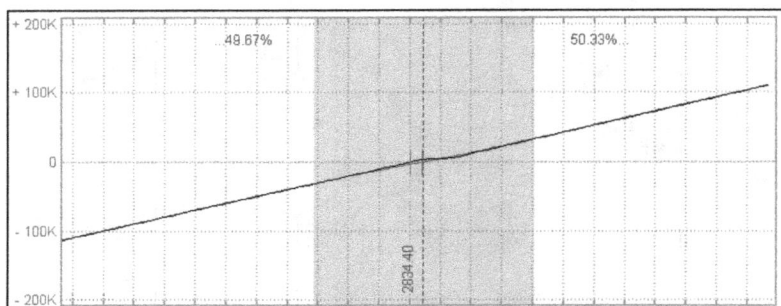

©2019 TD Ameritrade IP Company, Inc. For illustrative purposes only.

Because the SPX is presently above $2,800, the potential profit is in the tens of thousands of dollars. However, do not become greedy. Take your usual 10 to 15 percent profit and survive to trade again on the usual Monday or Wednesday morning.

Checking the Order Bar

The above order bar is also included at the bottom of the preceding option chain figure. All information is available, including the buying and selling actions, the number of contracts, symbol, expiration date, option types (CALL or PUT), the price (a credit), and the order type: a limit day order. Also, the SPX is used because it is an European-style option and cannot be exercised prior to expiration.

Reviewing the Order Confirmation Dialog

The order confirmation dialog shown in Figure 6.48 describes the iron butterfly trade as an iron condor, as does the order bar in Figure 6.47. And the structures are indeed identical. But the goals of the iron butterfly and the iron condor are not the same. The iron butterfly is a mixture of a short straddle with OTM calls and puts, which create two vertical spreads—a bear call and a bull put. But the ATM options perform double duty. The short straddle is nothing more than an ATM put and an ATM call. Once the trader confirms a directional price move, the losing short options are closed as the winning side begins to move deeper ITM and is held for profit. If the price of the underlying security rallies, the long calls are kept and the long puts are closed.

Figure 6.48 describes the Iron Butterfly as an Iron Condor. Both have the same construction, except iron condors are placed considerably farther OTM. Recall from the iron condor description how the short options are placed at strikes having Delta values of .25 or less. Also recall how the iron condor is a credit collection strategy that is often held through option expiration. Although nearly identical, the iron butterfly's short calls and puts are placed ATM rather than OTM. But because these two option strategies use identical spreads, the trading platform uses the iron condor name.

Trade Management

1. The initial credit should be impressive. But closing the trade within minutes after it is opened will be expensive. Let the market work until you develop a directional bias. Close the losers and keep the winners. Then close the trade for a few hundred dollars in profit, and do it again in a few days.

2. The SPX price changes must be closely watched. The iron butterfly trader always anticipates a directional move. The losing options are closed and the profiting options are retained, although the entire iron butterfly is typically closed within a matter of minutes to a few hours.

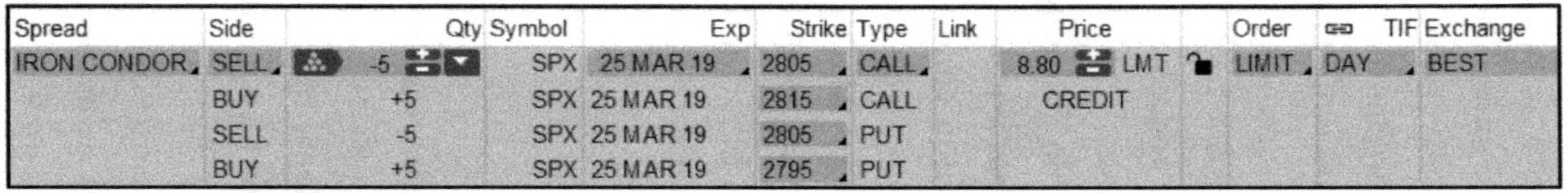

Spread	Side	Qty	Symbol	Exp	Strike	Type	Link	Price		Order		TIF	Exchange
IRON CONDOR ▾	SELL ▾	-5	SPX	25 MAR 19 ▾	2805 ▾	CALL ▾		8.80 LMT	▪	LIMIT ▾	DAY ▾	BEST
	BUY	+5	SPX	25 MAR 19	2815 ▾	CALL		CREDIT				
	SELL	-5	SPX	25 MAR 19	2805 ▾	PUT						
	BUY	+5	SPX	25 MAR 19	2795 ▾	PUT						

Figure 6.47 The SPX iron butterfly order bar

©2019 TD Ameritrade IP Company, Inc. For illustrative purposes only.

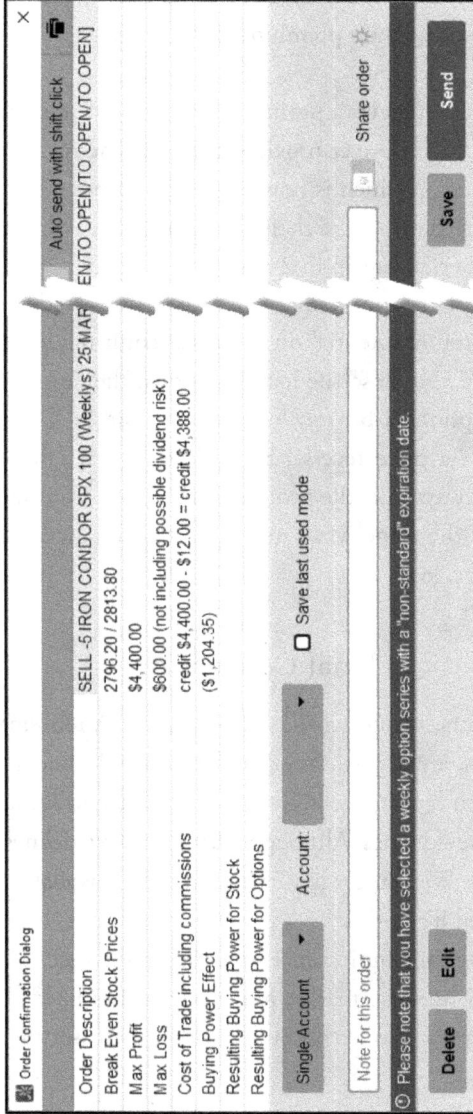

Figure 6.48 The SPX iron butterfly order confirmation dialog

©2019 TD Ameritrade IP Company, Inc. For illustrative purposes only.

3. If the price of the SPX begins to rally, the short call and the long put are closed because their premium values are dropping rapidly owing to Theta's high value.

4. If the price of the SPX begins to drop, the short put and the long call are closed because their premium values are dropping rapidly owing to Theta's high value.

5. Once the trade achieves a profit of 10 to 15 percent in premium, it is closed. Keeping it longer provides enough time for a reversal in the price of the SPX, which is how this trade becomes a losing one. So iron butterfly traders take their profit and run, only to use another iron butterfly trade again in 2 days.

6. Becoming greedy can result in a major loss. Traders can see the trade's maximum potential on the order confirmation dialog. Once they identify and close the losing options, they can hang onto the profitable options a bit too long. Giving the SPX too much time can result in a price reversal and a loss, which can be punishing. Therefore, always take the profit offered by the iron butterfly before the price of the underlying stock, ETF, or financial index reverses direction for a loss.

Final Comments

Almost all investors, including those who have IRA retirement accounts and mutual funds, are frequently punished from a decline in the national economy, poor job reports, Fed interest rate hikes, and similar issues that send traders to the sidelines. Although sitting on the sidelines is a strategy, it costs investors. We trade when the market is reasonably predictable. Stop trading when it's not.

Favorable economic indicators encourage an increase in buying activity. The economy and the market are inextricably linked. Like the tide that raises all ships, a good economic outlook increases the value of the financial markets.

In 1900, Charles Dow wrote several articles about how the market works. One of them described how the economy and the market are tightly coupled. He even picked eleven of the largest company stocks as part of the early Dow Jones Industrial Index. The stock prices of these companies were used as a measure of the health of the US economy. Today, the Dow Jones Industrial Index includes thirty of the largest US companies.

While the Dow Jones Industrial Index remains important, the brokerages use the S&P 500 index to evaluate volatility and current risk. And because technology has become a dominant factor, the NASDAQ index is also important. Watch them all, and remember to keep an eye on the value of the VIX volatility index. You may even want to consider trading VIX options.

Glossary

There are many common terms that option traders use. A good many have already been used within the pages of this book. If you ran across an unfamiliar, option-specific term, perhaps the definition within this glossary would be useful.

Alert. A trader-established notification based on a preset value sent to inform the trader by e-mail and/or text messaging when a specified condition occurs. For example, if the price of the underlying security pierces an established price, the trader receives an alert either for information or in order to take action.

Ask Price. The buying price, or option premium, in dollars and cents, to be paid for each share of the underlying optionable security within an option contract (most often 100 shares per option contract). When trading shares of stock, Ask is used to sell, and Bid is used to buy.

At the money (ATM). An option strike price (or *exercise* price) that is closest to the current price of the underlying optionable security.

Backwardation (or Normal Backwardation). See *Contango*.

Base or Basing. A term used to describe a sideways movement on a price chart. Rally, base, and drop describe a sequence of upward, sideways, and downward price moves.

Bearish. A negative bias held by a trader who expects a security or market to decline in value.

Bearish Spread. An option spread designed to be profitable if the underlying security declines in price. A common bearish spread consists of buying an in the money put and selling an out of the money put. This is called a *bear put spread*.

Beta. A measure of how closely the movement of the market price of a stock corresponds to the movement of the financial index to which it belongs. For example, the beta value of AAPL stock is a comparison of its market price volatility with that of the S&P 500 financial index.

Bid Price. Option sell orders are initiated using the Bid cell on the selected strike price row of an option chain. The default price is the Mark, which is midway between the Bid and Ask prices.

Bid-to-Ask Spread. The difference in price between the Bid and Ask values on an option chain. An option chain's Mark value is midway between the Bid and Ask values. Narrow Bid-to-Ask spreads reflect brisk trading activity and minimize *slippage* in the premium paid or received for a trade.

Bracketed Trade. A trade that includes a limit entry, a protective stop, and a profit target. It is typically used when buying shares of stock or exchange traded funds (ETFs).

Breakout. As applied to market price, a breakout refers to a strong price rally or drop. Traders look for entry opportunities when their analysis signals a possible price breakout.

Brokerage Account. An account held by the client of a brokerage firm that includes securities and cash. The value of the account may be used as collateral (or *margin*) to finance the purchase of stocks, options, futures contracts, and other marketable securities.

Bullish. A positive bias held by a trader who expects a security or market to increase in value.

Bullish Spread. An option spread designed to be profitable if the underlying security rises in price. A common bullish spread consists of buying an ATM call and selling an out of the money call. This spread is called a *bull call spread.*

Buy to Close Order. A buy order placed by an option trader who originally sold one or more option contracts. The buy to close order requires the option trader to pay premium to close an active position.

Calendar (or Time Spread). An option spread created by selling one option and buying another on the same security. The option sold expires sooner than the option bought. This spread is named *calendar spread* because the two contracts have different expiration dates. The goal of a calendar spread is to receive more income from the sold option compared with the option that is purchased. If sufficient time remains in the option bought, another option may be sold for additional premium income.

Call. A call option contract entitles the buyer to acquire (or "call away") 100 shares per contract of the underlying security from the seller, who is contractually obligated to deliver the stock to the buyer if the call's strike price becomes in the money and is exercised. This transaction must occur prior to contract expiration.

Called Away. The buyer of a call option may call the optioned security away from the seller if the option becomes in the money (ITM) by one cent. (See *in the money.*) The seller must deliver the stock to the buyer, who must pay the seller the option price. If the seller does not own the called stock, he or she must purchase and deliver the stock to the buyer for a loss. If the sold options expire ITM by one penny, they are auto-exercised by The Options Clearing Corporation.

Candlestick Chart. A price chart that uses red and green rectangles that resemble the bodies of candles. The candles have lines above and below, called *shadows* or *wicks.* The bottom and top of each candle body represents the opening and closing price for the selected time interval, i.e., week, day, hour, and so on. A green candle body represents a rally (a higher closing price than that of the opening price). Red candle bodies represent a drop candle, i.e., a lower closing price than the opening price.

Cash Settlement Option. Option contracts on financial indexes are cash settled rather than stock settled. In the case of either a call or a put, the seller must pay the buyer the difference between the option price and the current ITM price.

Chart Interval. Any of several chart time intervals used on price charts. Examples are weekly, daily, hourly, and minute charts. Most traders look across several time intervals to determine the characteristics of price movements across time. Experienced chart analysts use candlestick charts beginning with weekly intervals and working their way to shorter time intervals to develop an understanding of price characteristics. Chart studies are often applied to enhance a trader's expectation relative to future price movements.

Chart Study. A mathematical indicator used on security price charts to show price averages, overbought/oversold conditions, trading volume, average price movements, and much more.

Chicago Board of Exchange (CBOE). The company responsible for providing live options data used by client brokerages throughout the world.

Closeout Date. A predetermined date on which a contract should be closed to preserve the value that remains within an option position.

Closing Price. The final price at which a security traded at the end of the trading day. When applied to an option contract, this is the premium paid or received when a buy to close or sell to close transaction is processed.

Closing Purchase. A buy to close transaction conducted by the holder of a short option (the option writer) to liquidate an option position.

Closing Sale. A sell to close transaction conducted by the holder of a long option (the option buyer) to liquidate an option position.

Contango. This is a term related to a comparison between the spot price of a future and the current contract price. Some option traders borrow and misapply the term, in spite of the fact that options do not have *spot prices*. When the price of an option or futures contract is either rising or falling in value, it is said to be either contango or in normal backwardation. Contango is when the contract price exceeds the expected future spot price. In options, contango implies the current premium at the strike price of a short position has lost value, profiting the holder of a short option. Normal backwardation relates to the loss in the premium value of a long option.

Contract (or Option Contract). An agreement to relinquish an underlying security if the agreed upon option price either exceeds the contracted call price by one cent or falls below the contracted put price by one cent. Contracts are managed by The Options Clearing Corporation.

Covered Option. A call option position that is collateralized by a security, such as shares of stock or a put option contract that is collateralized by cash. When a covered call option contract is exercised by the option buyer, the seller must deliver the optioned securities to the buyer at the option price agreed upon.

Crossovers. On price charts, a crossover is the point at which one element or line crosses another. This can be the crossover of two moving average plots, a crossover of two study envelope lines, as when a Bollinger band envelope crosses inside the Keltner channel envelope, or when one or more price plots cross a standard moving average plotline.

Day Order. A limit or protective stop order that automatically expires at the end of the trading day. (See *good till canceled* order).

Delta. A mathematical value that determines the change in option premium value resulting from a $1.00 change in the market price of the underlying option security, such as a stock or ETF. Call Delta values are positive and increase from 0.0 to 1.0 as calls drop deeper ITM. Put Deltas are negative and range from 0.0 to –1.0. Put Deltas move closer to –1.0 as the put strike prices increase.

Discount Brokerage. A brokerage that offers unusually low commission and exchange fees.

Distal. A line drawn on a price chart at the bottom of a demand zone near support or the top of a supply zone near resistance to represent the location of a protective stop. Distal lines are the most distant from the current price.

Diversification. An investing strategy that spreads risk across a variety of companies, industry sectors, or both to reduce exposure to a single industry.

Drawing Tools. A toolset contained on most trading platforms that permits the user to draw trend lines, price lines, symbols, text, and other marks on the price chart.

Drop. A term used to describe a downward price movement.

E-mini Future. A futures derivative of a financial index such as the S&P 500 index. The e-mini futures are traded directly in the futures market or indirectly through options on futures. The e-mini financial index symbols are: S&P 500 = ES, NASDAQ = NQ, DJIA = YM, Russell 2000 = TF, and S&P 400 = EMD.

Electronic Communication Exchange Networks (ECNs). ECNs are also called alternative trading networks. The ECNs support stock and currency trading outside the traditional stock exchanges. They are computer-driven networks designed to match limit orders.

Exchange Fees. An options exchange originated fee charged by an option exchange for each option contract bought or sold.

Exchange Traded Fund (ETF). A security comprised of several stocks or a market index. ETFs are frequently made up of stocks belonging to the same market sector or geographical region. For example, an ETF may bundle several Asia-Pacific or European stocks.

Execution. The completion of a buy or sell order. This is transacted by market makers or, to a lesser extent, on the floor of a stock exchange.

Exercise. Option buyers may execute (or "exercise") their contractual rights when the price of the underlying pierces an option price prior to contract expiration. Call buyers pay the option price for receipt of the optioned security (call stock away from the seller). Put buyers put stock to the option seller. The underlying optioned securities and cash are transferred between buyer and seller accounts.

Exercise (or Strike) Price. The agreed upon option price (or strike price) per share of the underlying security. The call buyer pays the call seller, and the put seller pays the put buyer. The underlying optionable security and cash are transferred between buyer and seller accounts.

Expiration Day (or Maturity Date). The final day of an option contract. Once an option contract expires, the option contract is null and void. The goal of an option seller is to have the option contract expire worthless, at which time the option can no longer be exercised.

Extrinsic Value. An ITM option's current premium value. When a long option is exercised, its value consists of an option's intrinsic value (the distance from the current price of the underlying security) less the extrinsic value (the option's remaining time value).

Foreign Currency Exchange (Forex). The forex market is the largest security market in the world, trading in trillions of dollars each day. Traders speculate on the increase and decrease in one currency, such as the dollar, against another currency, such as the British pound or Euro. They buy currency pairs comprised of a base and a quote currency. Forex buyers buy a base currency against the quote currency if the buyer expects the base currency to increase against the quote currency. If correct, the buyer sells the pair for a profit once the base currency has rallied to his or her satisfaction.

Full-Service Broker. A brokerage firm that provides a full array of products and services. This may include banking, market research, investment counseling, and a variety of investment quality securities. Full-service brokerages usually charge higher transaction fees to cover the higher cost of their services.

Futures Contracts. A contract between a producer and a processor for the production and delivery of a product by the producer to the processor at a contract price agreed upon. The processor pays the processor in advance of delivery. Each futures contract has an expiration date and must be fulfilled prior to expiration. Futures speculators buy and sell futures contracts with an expectation of making profit margins from the difference between the buying and selling prices.

Gamma. Gamma is an option *Greek*. The value of Gamma controls the sensitivity of Delta to a change in the market price of the underlying optionable security. A 0.15 change in Gamma causes the value of Delta to change by 0.15 with a $1.00 change in the underlying. Experienced option traders are sensitive to the effect of Gamma, particularly near option expiration, where option premiums are most sensitive to changes in the values of Gamma.

Gamma Risk. Since Gamma has a strong influence on option premium values, option traders are sensitive to *gamma risk*. This phenomenon occurs when an option contract approaches expiration at strikes that are at or close to the ATM strike.

Good Till Canceled (GTC) Order. A limit or a stop order that remains in force for a sustained period. The amount of time a GTC order continues to work depends on the brokerage. Some limit GTC order to 60 or 90 days. Others allow their clients to specify GTC expiration dates.

Greeks. Greek letters used on several of the option chain column headings. The Greeks are found in the formulas used to compute option premium values. Some represent English words such as Delta (difference), Rho (rate of interest), Theta (time value), Vega (volatility). The Greek letter Gamma is used to determine the rate of change in Delta. (Although Vega is not a Greek letter, it was adopted to represent volatility.)

Hedge. A financial position designed to offset losses suffered by the failure of a secondary investment. It can be thought of as insurance against an unlimited loss. A perfect hedge returns 100 percent of the value of a secondary investment in the event it fails to produce the intended results.

Index Option. An option whose underlying security is a stock index. Three popular index option symbols are the SPX (S&P 500), NDX (NASDAQ), the RUT (Russell 2000), all of which are heavily traded.

In the Money (ITM). A call option is ITM when the market price of the underlying security is greater than the option's strike (exercise) price. A put option is

ITM when the market price of the underlying security is less than the put option's strike (exercise) price.

Intrinsic Value. The difference between the current market value of the underlying security that is ITM and an option's strike price. A call that is $5 ITM has an intrinsic value of $5. Intrinsic value applies to the value of the underlying security. *Extrinsic* value applies to an ITM option's current premium value.

Inverted. Used as a maintenance technique to either offset a loss or receive a limited profit when one leg of a short strangle is jeopardized by becoming in the money. Becoming inverted occurs when a trader either buys a put above a short call or buys a call below a short put. The trader's goal is to minimize loss, and in some cases the inversion may return a small profit. (A short strangle is constructed by selling the same number of option contracts of out of the money calls and out of the money puts that both expire on the same date.)

IV Rank. Used in place of IV% by many long-term option traders, IV Rank compares current IV% with its yearly high and low values. IV Rank values range from 0% to 100%.

Kappa. An option *Greek* constant used to compare a change in option premium value with a 1% change in current option volatility.

Lambda. An option *Greek* used to compare the change in option premium value with a 1% change in current option volatility.

Last Sale Price. The final price of an equity security (stock, ETF, option, etc.) when last sold or purchased. (Last is available on option chains to show the last premium amount paid at the strike prices of all call and put options.)

LEAPS. The acronym used for **L**ong-term **E**quity **A**ntici**P**ation **S**ecurities. LEAPS are typically used with call option contracts in anticipation of a strong price rally over one to three years. Many option contracts have expiration dates as far out as three years.

Legging In. Converting an existing option strategy to another as a maintenance action. Creating ("legging into") a butterfly from a working long call debit spread or a bull put credit spread to either limit risk exposure or to achieve profit are two examples.

Leverage, Financial. An investment instrument that provides a higher rate of return using a smaller amount of money.

Limit Order. An order to purchase or sell at a specified price. When buying, the limit order requires the price of the underlying security to be at or below the limit price. When selling, the price of the underlying security must be at or above the specified price. Limit orders are transacted as either DAY or GTC orders.

Limited Risk. A risk management strategy. An example is buying an option contract in which the maximum risk is the premium paid at entry.

Liquid (or Liquidity). The speed at which a security can be traded. In options, a high level of Open Interest signifies an acceptable level of liquidity.

Liquidity and Liquidity Risk. Market liquidity is required for trades to execute in a reasonable amount of time. A low-liquidity level indicates a lack of interest on the part of market traders. An illiquid security can languish unbought and unsold for months and years. Traders arev advised to avoid entry into low-liquidity securities. Funding liquidity is a concern of corporate treasurers who must find sufficient funds to keep the company afloat, i.e., pay bills and make payroll to sustain normal business operations.

Listed Options. Actively traded options that are listed on an options exchange, such as the CBOE.

Long Order. Buying a security is said to be taking a long position in that security.

Longer-Term Options. Option contracts with long-term expiration dates, typically those contracts that expire in more than 90 days. Some longer-term options are classified as LEAPS. These expire in one year or more. Some option contracts remain active for up to three years.

Market Depth. The resistance to price change based on trading volume. Market depth is a measure of the trading volume required to move the price of the underlying security. A 100-share trade is not sufficient to impact the price when market depth is high. A trade of one million shares typically exceeds the market depth and moves the market price of the underlying security.

Market Order. An order to purchase or sell a security at the current listed market price. The price is established by an authorized *market maker,* who represents the security exchange responsible for the selected security. Market orders are executed immediately and have priority over limit orders. Market orders are used with protective stops.

Market Sector. A market category that includes a specific type of business. Categories include basic materials, capital goods, consumer discretionary, consumer staples, energy, financial, health care, technology, telecommunications, transportation, and utilities.

Maturity Date. Also called *contract expiration date*, the maturity date is the final trading day of an option contract. Upon contract expiration, all open positions cease to exist.

Moving Average. A mathematical average of data points over a specified period. Moving averages are used on financial price charts to show the average price over a selected interval of time. Examples are the SMA(9), SMA(20), SMA(50), or SMA(200), referring, respectively, to 9-, 20-, 50-, or 200-period simple moving averages. Other types of moving averages also exist, such as exponential moving average (EMA) and triangular moving averages (TMA). The EMA places more emphasis on the most recent data points. The TMA places more emphasis on the center data points of the specified range, i.e., 9, 20, 50, 200, and so on.

Naked Writing (or *Uncovered Short Puts or Calls*). Selling an uncollateralized call option or a *cash covered* put option. The naked call or put seller does not have a position in the underlying security, nor is it *covered* by a long option position as in a bull put spread strategy, which "covers" a farther out of the money (OTM) short call.

Neutral Option Strategy. An option strategy, such as the Gamma-Delta-Neutral spread, used to profit from a small fluctuation in the market price of the underlying stock. Neutral spreads are typically *ratio spreads*. An example is the purchase of a number of call option contracts at one strike price and the sale of a greater number of call contracts at a higher strike price to achieve Gamma neutrality. The sum of Deltas is used to determine how many shares of the underlying stock must be shorted, where each share of stock has a Delta value of 1.0.

Neutral Spread. An option spread in which the trader believes the price of the underlying security will move sideways, without either a strong price rally or drop. A common neutral spread consists of simultaneously selling an OTM call and an OTM put to collect premium. This spread is called a *short strangle*. The trader believes the market price of the underlying security will remain between the strike prices of the call and put through contract expiration.

Novice Trader. An amateur trader who is both uneducated and inexperienced in the dynamics of financial markets. Novice traders typically buy high and sell low and are rarely familiar with account management or risk management strategies.

Odds Enhancer. Any one of hundreds of mathematical studies used by traders to enhance the statistical probability of their trading success. Odds enhancers are used on charts and tables to indicate such metrics as trader sentiment, trading volume, price breakouts or reductions, and so on.

Open Interest. The number of working option contracts at each *strike price* listed on an option chain.

Opening Price. The first price at which a security or option is traded when the market initially opens.

Option. A derivative of a security that conveys a term-limited contract between a buyer and a seller. The buyer of a call option pays a contract premium for the right to buy call shares of the underlying security from a call seller, i.e., to call away shares at the option price. The buyer of a put option pays a contract premium for the right to put shares of the underlying security to the put seller, i.e., to put shares to the seller at the option price. However, the option contract can be exercised by the option buyer only if the market price of the underlying security exceeds the option price by at least one cent. This is called being in the money (ITM). If the option contract expires before the price of the underlying security becomes ITM, the option contract *expires worthless* and all contract obligations terminate.

Option Chain. A financial table used by option traders to buy and sell call and/or put option contracts at *strike prices* above, at, and below the current market price of the underlying security. Each option chain has a specific contract expiration date. Columns include essential information such as the Bid (sell) and Ask (buy) prices, current Open Interest, mathematical probabilities, time values, implied volatility, and so on.

Options Clearing. An issuer of tradable option contracts. Examples include the Chicago Board of Exchange, American Stock Exchange, Pacific Stock Exchange, Philadelphia Stock Exchange, International Securities Exchange, and so on.

Options Exchange. A for-profit company that transacts options trades. Examples include the Chicago Board Options Exchange, American Stock Exchange, and International Securities Exchange.

Option Selling (or Option Writing). Clicking the Bid cell of a selected strike price row within an option chain is used to sell (or *write*) one or more option contracts. Most option contracts represent 100 of an underlying security. (See *covered writing, naked writing*).

Option Spread. An option trading strategy that includes two or more *legs* on the same security at different strike prices. A spread may simultaneously buy a call and sell a farther OTM call (a *bull call spread*). Some option strategies, such as *butterfly* and *iron condor* spreads, include two puts and two calls at different strike prices.

Option Strategy. Any one of many option strategies for buying, selling, or buying and selling option call and/or put contracts.

Order. An offer to buy or sell a financial security, including equities, option or future contracts, or foreign exchange currency pairs. Orders are transmitted by traders to brokerage companies who submit orders to one or more governing securities exchanges. Once received, buy and sell orders are matched by a market maker. Option market makers are contracted by exchanges to fulfill option buy and sell orders. Once orders are matched, electronic records of the order fulfillment are returned to the originating brokerages, who in turn notify the trader. Option orders include call and/or put option contracts at one or more strike prices. Some option spreads may also include the purchase of underlying shares of stock.

Order Bar. A horizontal row containing order information, including buy and/or sell instructions, number of contracts, option price(s), option expiration date(s), order duration, order type (limit, market, stop, etc.).

One Cancels Other (OCO). A bracketed order that includes one or more stops. When one stop triggers, all orders that may remain are automatically canceled. For example, when a protective stop is executed, the companion profit target order is simultaneously canceled.

Order Confirmation Dialog. A dialog containing an order description and pricing information on a queued order ready for submission.

Order Duration. Order durations vary with the type of trade required to accomplish the trader's goal. There are DAY (expires at the close of normal trading hours), GTC (good till canceled orders), EXT (remains open during the day's extended trading hours), and GTC_EXT (an extended hours order that is good till canceled).

Order Rules Dialog. A dialog used to establish automated order triggers based on a price, an *option chain* value, or a chart study.

Out of the Money (OTM). A call option strike price that is higher than the market price of the underlying optionable security. A put option strike price is lower than the market price of the underlying optionable security. The value of an OTM option contract is the available premium at the option strike price(s). The premium value, i.e., the Mark, is typically midway between an option's Bid and Ask price.

Portfolio Margin. A margin account originally promulgated by the Securities and Exchange Commission (SEC). A portfolio margin account grants additional credit to brokerage clients on the basis of a minimum account balance (typically between $100,000 and $125,000) and the client's trading experience. While standard margin accounts are typically granted the use of 50% of their account equity, portfolio margin account holders may collateralize up to 85% of their account equity. This expands the ability of portfolio margin account holders to extend their trading activity.

Position. The position of a working trade is the number of shares, or option contracts, that are either bought or sold in anticipation of a profit. Option contracts often include two or more *legs* (or *spreads*) comprised of simultaneous buy (long) and sell (short) orders.

Premium. The value of each optioned share of an underlying security at the specified strike price. The premium value is typically midway between the Bid (sell) and Ask (buy) price and is called the Mark (market price). Premium is highest when an option is initially traded. Premium values erode as the underlying option contract approaches the contract expiration date.

Professional Trader. A knowledgeable, experienced trader who makes a full-time living buying and selling securities listed on one or more financial markets is considered a professional trader.

Proximal. A line drawn on a price chart at the top of a demand zone near support or the bottom of a supply zone near resistance to represent a location near the entry point of a trade. Proximal lines are the closest to the current price.

Put. A put option entitles the buyer to *put* the optioned shares of the underlying security to the seller of the *put* option contract if the option price falls below the contract's strike price and becomes ITM. Each option contract typically includes 100 shares of stock.

Rally. A term used to describe an upward move in price.

Return if Called. The amount of income received by a covered call writer, expressed as a percentage. The return includes the original premium received when traded, the appreciation in the value of the underlying stock, and any dividends paid prior to exercise.

Rho. Rho measures the sensitivity to option premium caused by changes in the prevailing rate of interest. A Rho value of .050 causes a decrease in the value of option premiums by .050 if interest rates rise by 1.0.

Risk/Reward Management (also Trade Management). The management of a working trade. May be closed for profit or rolled into another option position. The goal of trade management is to either avoid or minimize a financial loss.

Rolling Down. Closing an option and opening another that expires on the same date but at a lower strike price when rolling down puts farther OTM; can also be used to move short calls closer to the money for more premium when the price of the underlying is dropping.

Rolling Out. Simultaneously closing a working option position and opening a new position expiring at a later date.

Rolling Up. Closing an option and opening another that expires on the same date but at a higher strike price when rolling up calls, or at a lower strike price when rolling up puts.

Rolling Out and Up or Down. Simultaneously closing a working option position and opening a new position at a new strike above or below and expiring at a later date.

Scalp or Scalping. The action of taking small profits from a small price increase in a long trade or a small decrease in a short trade. For example, a pattern day trader may buy 100 shares of a stock for $25/share and then sell it several minutes later for $25.20/share for a small $20 profit. This requires day traders who scalp throughout each day to use low-commission discount brokerages.

Sell to Close Order. A sell order placed by an option trader who originally bought one or more option contracts. If the sell to close order is filled, the option trader will receive option premium.

Sentiment (or Market Sentiment). The current prevailing aggressiveness or timidity of buyers and/or sellers toward one or more securities or the financial market as a whole.

Simulated (Paper) Trading. A feature provided on many trading platforms that permits traders to practice their trading skills or to test new trading strategies.

Short Position. Selling a security, such as a stock, option, or future, is said to be shorting that position. Shorting a stock happens when a *bearish* trader sells a stock in anticipation of a drop in the market price of that stock. A *buy to cover* order is placed to close the position and take profit from the loss.

Short-Life Option. A short-life option contract expires within 60 days or less. Many weekly options that expire within days to a few weeks are traded.

Skew. Skew occurs when option premiums become inverted owing to a temporary inversion in implied volatility values. *Horizontal skew* causes shorter expiration options to have higher premium values than longer expiration options. *Vertical skew* causes farther OTM options to have higher premium values than strikes that exist closer to the money.

Slippage. A change in the premium midpoint that exists between the Bid and the Ask price of the underlying. Slippage is greatest on illiquid securities that typically have large Bid-to-Ask spread widths. Slippage is small on actively traded securities having narrow Bid-to-Ask spreads that are often only a few cents.

Stock Capitalization Categories. Stock categories are divided by *market capitalization*. Large cap stocks are greater than ten billion dollars. Midcap stocks range from one to ten billion dollars. Small cap stocks are less than one billion dollars.

Stock Scanner. A computer-based tool used to establish specific parameters, such as price ranges, volumes, current volatilities, moving average crossovers, and so on. These parameters are used to find and list stocks meeting the established scan criteria.

Straddle. The straddle is an option strategy designed to profit from a strong price move in the underlying security in either direction. Strong trading volatility is desirable. A long straddle includes the simultaneous purchase of a put and a call on the same security having the same strike price and expiration date. A short straddle includes the simultaneous sale of a put and a call at the same strike price and expiration date. Many straddles are traded at the current ATM (at the money) strike price.

Strangle. The short strangle is a neutral trade strategy that profits from the sale of an equivalent number of put and call option contracts on the same underlying security and with the same expiration dates. The strike prices are far OTM to avoid exercise throughout the option contract life. The goal of the short strangle is to collect premium by selling one or more put and call contracts. The long strangle buys put and call contracts at different strike prices that expire on the same contract date. The buyer of a long strangle seeks a strong movement in the price of the underlying security.

With a substantial move in the underlying, the profitable position can be sold for more premium than originally spent on both legs of the strangle option.

Strike Price. Strike prices are in a column at the center of an option chain. An ATM strike price is closest to the market value of the underlying security. OTM call strike prices are greater than the ATM strike price; OTM put strike prices are lower than the ATM strike price. Option traders evaluate premium, Open Interest, and other values at different strike prices when constructing an option strategy. An option's strike price is also referred to as *the exercise price*.

Swing Trader. A market trader that trades securities in anticipation of a *price swing* that returns a profit.

Tau. The absolute change in option price in response to a 1.0% change in volatility. Tau is also used to capture the sensitivity of an option's premium to a change in implied volatility.

Target Exit Point. A predetermined price to close a working order. The trader 1) buys an option contract for less than paid at entry, or 2) sells an option contract for more than paid at entry. (Buy for a dime and sell to close for a dollar, or sell for a dollar and buy to close for a dime.)

Time Premium. The reduction of an option's premium value, measured by the Greek Theta, caused by the passage of time. The decay of time premium is also referred to as *extrinsic value*. Premium value declines more rapidly as an option contract approaches the contract expiration date.

Time Spread. An option spread consisting of the purchase of an option and the simultaneous sale of a *different* option on the *same* security with a *nearer* expiration date. The purpose of a time spread is to profit from the accelerated loss in time value of the option that is written, relative to the option that is purchased. Time spreading is often a *neutral* strategy, but it can also be bullish or bearish, depending on the options involved (more often referred to as a *calendar spread*).

Trading Days. There are 252 trading days in the year. (Also see *trading hours*.)

Trading Floor. The main floor of a stock or options exchange where market makers fill sell and buy orders. Most trading floor activity is being replaced by automated, computer-based trading.

Trading Hours. Normal trading hours begin at 9:30 a.m. and close at 4:00 p.m. EST. Morning extended trading hours are from 4:00 a.m. till 9:30 a.m. EST. Evening extended trading hours are from 4:00 p.m. through 8:00 p.m. EST.

Trading Ladder. A trading interface on a computer with vertical green and red bars that look like ladders. Each bar represents a price point of the underlying security. Clicking a green bar is used to buy a security at the selected price; clicking a red bar is used to sell a security at the selected price. Multiple OCO-style orders with a limit buy order, a protective stop, and a profit target (a *bracketed order*) are often structured and sent on trading ladders. Trading ladders are popular for use by pattern day traders and futures speculators.

Trading Platform. A trading platform is a computer-based trading application, either installed directly on a brokerage client's computer or accessible through the Internet. Trading platforms provide an interface between a brokerage client and the brokerage for round trip order entry, processing, and confirmation.

Transaction Fees (Commissions and Exchange Fees). The cost of buying or selling a security. Commissions and exchange fees are charged by brokerage firms. The commissions paid are typically governed by a brokerage schedule. They can be a fixed fee per equity trade, such as $6.99 or $9.99 per trade or a per-share fee, such as $0.005 per share. Exchange fees originate at the options exchange, such as the CBOE. An exchange fee is charged for each option contract traded and can range from $0.50 per contract to $1.50 per contract. Financial index option exchange fees are among the highest exchange fees charged to brokerages, which pass exchange fees through to their client transactions. Exchange fees are paid round trip, i.e., on both trade entry and exit.

Trend Line. Trend lines are used on price charts to show price direction. An upward trend line is called a *rally*, whereas a downward trend line is called a *drop*. A sideways trend line is said to be *basing*. If a price is making a series of higher highs and higher lows, it is said to be on an uptrend; if it is making a series of lower lows and lower highs, it is said to be in a downtrend.

Truncated Risk. Risk can be *truncated* (or hedged) by entering a stop-loss or buying/selling a position to limit possible losses of a working position. When an option contract is purchased, it has limited risk and unlimited reward. The risk is the money originally spent on option premium. Unlimited reward is based on a movement in the underlying in the trader's favor. For example, buying a call that moves ITM can produce a profit that is many times greater than the original premium paid when the trade was entered.

Underlying. A stock, ETF, financial index, or futures contract. Option contracts are financial derivatives of an *underlying* security. This term is commonly used by traders who buy and sell equities, futures, and forex pairs.

Vega. Vega reflects a change in an option's price resulting from a change in the underlying security's *implied volatility*. Vega causes a change in premium value for every 1% change in implied volatility. A Vega value of 0.10 causes a premium change of $0.10 for each 1% change in implied volatility.

Vertical Spread. An option strategy comprised of two call or two put positions, one above the other, i.e., arranged vertically. A *bull call spread* is an example that includes buying a call and selling a call above, i.e., at a higher strike price. A *bear put spread* includes buying a put and selling a put below, i.e., at a lower strike price.

Volatility. A measure of the frequency at which trading is occurring; also a measure of trader sentiment. High current volatility indicates higher than usual trading activity. Historical volatility for a specific security is the average number of daily trades conducted over the past twelve months. Implied volatility compares current trading volume with historical volatility. Option traders make extensive use of implied volatility data. Volatility can have the greatest impact on the time value of option premium. High volatility causes greater price fluctuation, increasing risk, and corresponding option premiums and is most noticeable for ATM options.

Volume. For options, the number of contracts that have been traded within a specific period, usually a day or a week. For equity securities, futures, and forex, the volume represents the number of trades, typically in the millions, that are traded during each trading day.

VWAP. VWAP stands for *volume-weighted average price.* It is a measure of the underlying's price based on the number of shares or contracts traded at different prices. It is the weighted average price at which most of the trading has occurred.

Watch List. A table that lists tradable securities of interest to a trader, usually stocks, ETFs, and futures. Many traders have multiple watch lists that fall into different categories or market sectors.

Zeta. A rarely used option *Greek* constant that measures the sensitivity of an option price to volatility.

About the Author

Russell A. Stultz has written 60 books on computer technology, management, and investing. Many are distributed in 18 languages. This is his fifth options book. The second edition of his highly successful *The Only Options Book You'll Ever Need* and his *The Option Strategy Desk Reference* from Business Expert Press were both released in early 2019.

Upon completion of his military service in the U.S. Navy Submarine Service, Stultz attended college and worked in the electronics industry, including Dallas-based Texas Instruments Incorporated, as a technical writer, instructional designer, and department manager. He later wrote several management and technology books for Prentice-Hall, Inc.'s college textbook and trade divisions and founded Wordware Publishing, Inc. where he served as Wordware's CEO for 27 years. After the sale of Wordware in 2009, he took a series of formal market trading courses and became a full-time market trader specializing in options and futures.

Index

OTHER TITLES FROM THE ECONOMICS AND PUBLIC POLICY COLLECTION

Philip Romero, The University of Oregon and
Jeffrey Edwards, North Carolina A&T State University, *Editors*

- *Macroeconomics, Second Edition, Volume I* by David G. Tuerck
- *Macroeconomics, Second Edition, Volume II* by David G. Tuerck
- *Economic Renaissance In the Age of Artificial Intelligence* by Apek Mulay
- *Disaster Risk Management: Case Studies in South Asian Countries* by Huong Ha, R. Lalitha S. Fernando, and Sanjeev Kumar Mahajan
- *The Option Strategy Desk Reference: An Essential Reference for Option Traders* by Russell A. Stultz
- *Disaster Risk Management in Agriculture: Case Studies in South Asian Countries* by Huong Ha, Lalitha S. Fernando and Sanjeev Kumar Mahajan
- *Understanding Demonetization in India: A Deft Stroke of Economic Policy* by Shrawan Kumar Singh
- *Urban Development 2120* by Peter Nelson
- *Foreign Direct Investment: The Indian Experience* by Leena Ajit Kaushal
- *A Guide to International Economics* by Shahruz Mohtadi

Announcing the Business Expert Press Digital Library

Concise e-books business students need for classroom and research

This book can also be purchased in an e-book collection by your library as

- *a one-time purchase,*
- *that is owned forever,*
- *allows for simultaneous readers,*
- *has no restrictions on printing, and*
- *can be downloaded as PDFs from within the library community.*

Our digital library collections are a great solution to beat the rising cost of textbooks. E-books can be loaded into their course management systems or onto students' e-book readers.
The **Business Expert Press** digital libraries are very affordable, with no obligation to buy in future years. For more information, please visit **www.businessexpertpress.com/librarians**. To set up a trial in the United States, please email **sales@businessexpertpress.com**.

www.ingramcontent.com/pod-product-compliance
Lightning Source LLC
Chambersburg PA
CBHW061148220326
41599CB00025B/4396